GAINING
ON THE MARKET

Your Complete Guide to Investment Strategy

Stocks, Bonds, Options, Mutual Funds and Gold

CHARLES J. ROLO

An Atlantic Monthly Press Book
Little, Brown and Company — Boston–Toronto

First Edition

Chapters 14, 15, 17, 19, 20, 22, and 26 through 28 are based on
updated material from articles by the author that appeared in
MONEY Magazine © 1977, 1978, 1979, 1980, 1981, 1982 by Time,
Inc.

LIBRARY OF CONGRESS CATALOGING IN PUBLICATION DATA
Rolo, Charles James, 1916–
    Gaining on the market.
    "An Atlantic Monthly Press Book."
    Includes bibliographical references and index.
    1. Securities—United States—Handbooks, manuals,
etc. 2. Stock-exchange—United States—Handbooks,
manuals, etc. I. Title.
HG4921.R55   332.6'78   82–149
ISBN 0–316–75557–5   AACR2

ATLANTIC-LITTLE, BROWN BOOKS
ARE PUBLISHED BY
LITTLE, BROWN AND COMPANY
IN ASSOCIATION WITH
THE ATLANTIC MONTHLY PRESS

BP
Designed by Susan Windheim

*Published simultaneously in Canada
by Little, Brown & Company (Canada) Limited*

PRINTED IN THE UNITED STATES OF AMERICA

For Bess and Claude

Acknowledgments

My largest debt is to the former and present managing editors of *Money*—William S. Rukeyser (now managing editor of *Fortune*) and his successor, Marshall Loeb—who generously gave me time off to write this book and in other ways lent their support and encouragement. To Bill and Marshall I extend my warmest thanks. I must also thank Time Incorporated for permission to draw on articles of mine published in *Money*. None of the aforementioned, I must add, has edited or approved the manuscript; the responsibility for its opinions and shortcomings is entirely my own.

It is both a duty and a pleasure to thank the investment advisers and money managers whose ideas and writings are cited in the text. Those to whom I am especially indebted are Richard A. Crowell, David Dreman, Norman G. Fosback, George Lasry, and John Westergaard. I also wish to thank Edwin Caplin, an old friend and one of Wall Street's most conscientious stockbrokers, for answering a multitude of questions; Max G. Ansbacher, who helped me to unravel some of the complexities of options trading; and my colleagues at *Money*, Robert Klein and Michael Sivy, for patiently listening to my problems and coming up with valuable suggestions.

I am grateful to Arnold Ehrlich, my original editor at the Atlantic Monthly Press, for his enthusiastic backing of this project, and also to his successor, Peter Davison, who made perceptive suggestions and gave me the additional time needed to complete a book whose difficulties I had foolishly underestimated. My wife, Bess, endured with extraordinary grace the long-drawn-out rigors imposed on her by my immersion in this project. For the support she provided no words of appreciation would be adequate.

Contents

APPENDIXES

Foreword: What This Book Can Do for You

Many private investors feel that the cards are stacked against them in the stock market; they think they're doomed to be outgunned and outsmarted by the large financial institutions — banks, insurance companies, and the like. This discouraging belief, plausible though it may seem, is a myth that's been refuted by scholarly research. Studies cited in *The Changing Role of the Individual Investor*, a book by two distinguished professors of finance, Marshall E. Blume and Irwin Friend, show that there have been no long-range differences between the investment results obtained by individuals and by institutions. Moreover, since those studies were made in the early 1970s, far-reaching changes in the investment world have worked to the advantage of individual investors — for reasons that my opening chapter will explain. *Nowadays, private investors actually have far greater chances than giant institutions of beating the averages used to measure the performance of the market.*

But to exploit his or her* advantages, the individual needs some market savvy. And many of the nation's 32 million stockholders lack sufficient knowledge to handle their investments effectively. This forces them to rely more or less blindly on the advice of others, usually brokers — a disconcerting and potentially dangerous dependence. I'm not suggesting that a layman shouldn't seek the help of brokers and other professionals. But it takes some knowledge to choose such help wisely and to use it intelligently. So inescapably there's a do-it-yourself element in investing, and how well you cope with it could be of critical importance to your financial future. It follows that anyone seriously concerned with getting the best mileage out of his savings or inherited capital should master the fundamentals of investing. Any layman can do it. The main requirements are

---

*About 47 percent of adult American stockholders are women. But our language has yet to devise a singular pronoun that stands for both sexes. So for simplicity's sake, and with apologies to female readers, this text will henceforward use the traditional "he" and "his" rather than the unmanageable "he or she" and "his or her."

common sense, a command of simple arithmetic — and, above all, a willingness to recognize that managing your money deserves some time and effort. Many people who spend hours shopping for sporting goods, furniture, or bargains in kitchen equipment make investment decisions in minutes. They call up their broker and say, "Just tell me what to buy. Don't confuse me with the facts."

This book is written for people who wish to know the facts and understand them. As Robert Metz, a financial columnist of *The New York Times,* has said, "If more individuals would learn to think for themselves, there'd be fewer affluent brokers and more affluent customers." My text won't overtax your mental muscles, but it will invite you to stretch them. It seeks to fill the gap between the two major categories of books on investing — those addressed to professionals or experienced investors and simplistic primers that give you a useful introductory course but don't really equip you to operate on your own. Unlike the advanced texts, it doesn't take for granted any prior knowledge of investing or the jargon of Wall Street; investment terms, theories, and procedures are explained in simple English. It is therefore a book that can be read and assimilated by beginners. But it differs considerably from the typical primer. Here's precisely how it differs — and why.

1. *This book is action-oriented; it isn't a "what's what in the investment world," but rather a combined training course and combat manual.* I've shunned the conventional format — chapters that focus on the different types of investments: stocks, bonds, mutual funds, and so on. Understanding what they are is essential, but their anatomy really doesn't require lengthy explanation; *the bottom line is knowing how to use them.* Accordingly, the different types of investments are explained and discussed in the context of investment objectives — investing for growth or high income — and investment strategies.

2. *This book doesn't tell you what to do without telling you, wherever possible, precisely how to do it.* A common complaint about popular books on investment is that the advice they give is often too general. They say, for example: never fail to sell a stock that's risen so much in price you think it's overvalued. But they don't explain with sufficient depth or precision how to judge whether a stock is overvalued or undervalued. The precept I've tried to follow is: spare no effort to be specific. When I refer to information needed by investors, I tell you where to find it and, if it isn't

free, what it will cost you.* When I discuss risk, I explain specifically how
it can be measured and what are the methods for controlling it.

3. *This book goes far beyond the universe of popular guides to investing.* In
varying degrees, such books dodge complexities that can't be dodged
without slipping into glibness and dangerous oversimplification. Admittedly, simplification is desirable in any manual written for inexperienced
investors. But there are times when, to serve the reader honestly, a writer
must grapple with complexities and try to deal with them in language
that's intelligible even to a novice. This can be done; popularization does
not have to be pap. Accordingly, this book will not stop short at the
elementary level, except in certain highly specialized areas that I don't
consider vital for the average investor.

The approach taken here aims at showing the reader how to operate
like a pro to the extent that's possible without formal training and
professional experience. The text summarizes and discusses what
scholarly research claims to have discovered about the behavior of the
stock market. It takes a look at "modern portfolio theory"—an
investment doctrine that's become gospel to most high-level institutional money managers—and distills its usefulness for the individual
investor. It briefs the reader on the practical uses of "Contrary
Opinion Theory," which concerns itself with the role of human
emotions in the stock market and highlights the role that psychology
plays in successful investing. In sum, *my aim is to provide you with a
step-by-step grounding in the fundamentals of investing and money
management—how to judge the value of a stock; how to use tools that
have proved helpful in trying to anticipate major movements of the
market; how to choose and implement an overall investment strategy that
suits your goals and your temperament.*

Clearly, this isn't a "how-to-make-a-bundle" book; it charts no easy
shortcuts to fortune, because there are none. To my mind, the
"how-to-make-a-million" books are a menace to financial health; they
exploit gullibility and encourage greed, an investor's two deadliest
enemies. Their authors usually claim to have discovered an easy-to-
follow system that ensures smashing success in the stock market. But
anyone who's really devised such a system would keep it a fiercely

---

*Hundreds of addresses, telephone numbers, prices and other specifics are given in the
text. Inevitably, some will have changed by publication date and during the book's
lifetime. I'm sure readers will agree it was preferable to give them the data required than
to omit vital information because it's subject to change.

guarded secret. For if any easily followed formula for coining profits were in the public domain, it would inevitably cease to work. Every share of stock bought represents a share of stock sold. So if too many investors are using the same formula for picking stocks, there'll be too few investors willing to sell those stocks at acceptable prices.

There are, of course, many ways of making a killing in the stock market. But none of them is easy or safe; they call for an unusual combination of skill, dedication, and foresight, plus the guts to take and live with inordinately high risks. Mark Twain said, "October is one of the peculiarly dangerous months to speculate in stocks. Others are November, December, January, February, March, April, May, June, July, August and September." I see nothing "wrong" about speculation, provided you understand and can afford the risks you're taking. But never forget that, if you lose 90 percent of your capital, you have to make a 900 percent profit on the 10 percent left in order to wind up back where you started — and 900 percent is awfully hard to make. The basic ways of shooting for speculative gains in stocks will be discussed. But I do not cover trading in commodities futures, because I consider it a game best left to professionals. The chances are overwhelmingly large that an amateur who plays the commodities markets will lose most if not all of his stake, and sooner rather than later.

The main focus of this book will be on strategies that seek the best available returns compatible with prudence. *By prudence I do not mean conservatism, a doctrine that dictates avoidance of risk.* Paradoxically, total avoidance of risk entails, in an inflationary age, the certainty of loss — that is, loss of real purchasing power. Over the last decade, the returns of "riskless" investments have been substantially lower than the rate of inflation.

In contrast to conservatism, *prudence* is a way of handling yourself that involves taking justifiable risks for the sake of calculated returns based on reasonable expectations.* Prudence involves understanding value, staying alert to opportunities for profit, and recognizing that the future is truly uncertain. That means not assuming that things will turn out for the best or the worst, but choosing a course that takes

---

*For this and other valuable insights, I'm indebted to George Lasry, author of *Valuing Common Stocks* (AMACOM, 1979), an original and illuminating treatise on investing. "

into account a set of rational possibilities. Putting all one's investment eggs into the basket touted by the prophets of doom is not exercising prudence; for more than a decade they've screamed that catastrophe was around the corner, and though our troubles may be large, catastrophe is still a cloud on the horizon. Nor is one exercising prudence by shunning the stock market at all times simply because stock ownership entails risks. Depending upon the circumstances, the exercise of prudence can lead to a cautious policy, an aggressive one, or something in between. A strategy based on prudence can, when conditions are favorable, bring splendid profits, and it should, at all times, protect you against intolerable losses.

This book, though not a textbook, will tell you all (or nearly all) you've wanted to know about how to invest — the what, the why, the when, and the where. It starts out, so to speak, in the first grade and takes you all the way through college, throwing in an occasional idea for those who might want to go on to graduate school. My hope is that along the way an inexperienced investor, as he gains knowledge and understanding, will sense that learning to be his own investment manager is an exhilarating challenge. Managing money well is hard work — I won't kid you about that — but I also believe it can be fun. Nearly everybody enjoys a contest. And this one — as my opening chapter will show — isn't rigged. Its rewards are definitely within reach of all.

GAINING
ON THE MARKET

Introduction: The Individual Investor's New Edge

You, the individual investor, are better situated in the stock market than you think. Over the past decade, changes that this chapter will discuss have worked to your advantage; the strategic position of individuals has improved, whereas that of large financial institutions has worsened. If you have doubts about your ability to compete against the institutions, it's high time you got rid of them. They are probably based on myths and misconceptions that are still prevalent among investors who are leery of the market.

Myth Number One: Institutions control the market and can manipulate it to their advantage.

The Realities: If institutions could control the market, their results would be far better than those of private investors; yet scholarly studies have proved this isn't so. The notion that there's collusion between the institutions is a paranoid fantasy dreamed up by losers seeking a scapegoat for their misfortune. The truth is that institutional money managers are competing against each other in the market; what matters to them is how they perform in relation to their peers, not in relation to the John and Mary Does.

As for stock manipulation, it's a violation of federal securities laws and is punishable by fines and imprisonment. Over the years, the nation's major stock markets have greatly strengthened their self-policing procedures. They have set up elaborate electronic surveillance systems that instantly bring to light any suspicious or unusual activity in a stock—as, for example, when a stock that's been a sleeper has a sudden runup in price for no apparent reason. Exchange officials promptly contact the company and the brokers involved, and they may suspend trading in the stock until the situation has been investigated. The stock markets are also policed by the Securities and Exchange Commission, whose function is to enforce the securities laws and protect the public interest. Stock manipulation does, of course, occur, but nowadays it's increasingly difficult and dangerous. The people who engage in it are either professional criminals or dishonest speculators acting in concert with shady brokers. They are certainly not institutional investors.

Myth Number Two: Institutional investors profit from "inside" information. They are the first to learn about crucial company developments and private investors are usually the last.

The Realities: Over the past decades, a string of court decisions has widened the application of the law that prohibits corporate "insiders" (company officers and employees) from trading on the basis of inside information — that is, information not publicly disclosed that could have an appreciable influence on the price of the company's stock. Following two landmark cases (*SEC* v. *Texas Gulf Sulphur* and *SEC* v. *Merrill Lynch*), *the same prohibition now also applies to any investor who obtains, or even innocently receives, inside information.* And judges have imposed stiff penalties on so-called tippees, who profited from inside information relayed to them by an analyst or a broker handling their account. In a 1978 ruling, Judge David Markun, an administrative judge of the SEC, set forth this guiding principle: "One who knows himself to be a beneficiary of non-public, selectively disclosed inside information must fully disclose it or refrain from trading." From the beginning of 1978 to October 1981, the SEC pressed charges in forty cases involving the use of inside information — more cases than in all of the four previous decades — and it has intensified its surveillance in this area. Before the 1970s, institutions often profited from inside information; now, it's not legally usable. To be sure, the legal prohibition on insider trading is still widely flouted, but the culprits for the most part are individuals. Any institutional money manager who tries to take advantage of inside information would be risking his professional career.

Another development of recent years has lessened somewhat the difference between the quality of the research available to institutions and to individuals. The research-oriented brokerage houses that catered only to institutions were hard hit by the lower commissions they had to accept from institutions when fixed minimum commissions were abolished on May 1, 1975. Feeling shaky on their own, many of these research "boutiques" arranged to be taken over by nationwide brokerage houses that serve the public. Thus the earnings estimates and opinions of many top-flight institutional analysts became available — in digests of their reports and through brokers — to individual investors. According to surveys made by Greenwich Associates, nine of the fifteen brokerage firms most highly rated for their research by institutions are firms that have a large number of individual clients.

Myth Number Three: Institutional investors are bound to handle themselves in the market with far greater skill than individuals because they represent the top investment talent in the country.

The Realities: In spite of their professional know-how, their prodigious input of information, and their arsenal of sophisticated investment tools and techniques, institutional investors as a group have a dismal performance record. Hamilton Johnston & Co., a Princeton firm of investment consultants that monitors institutional performance, reported that in the ten-year period ending September 30, 1981, stock portfolios managed by banks achieved a total annual rate of return — price appreciation plus reinvested dividends — of only 4.2 percent; the return on Standard & Poor's 500-stock index was 6.1 percent, 45 percent higher. Other surveys tell the same story. For example, A. G. Becker's Fund Evaluation Service found that, in the decade ending 1979, 84 percent of the country's 3,000 largest pension-fund stock portfolios underperformed the S&P index.

An investor can underperform the market averages for two reasons: his timing is wrong — he buys when the market is high and sells when it is low — or he invests in stocks that do worse than those in the averages. The institutions as a group have often made both of these errors.

Evidence compiled by the SEC indicates that institutional investors did more buying than selling when the market was close to its highs in 1968, 1971, and 1972, and more selling than buying when the market was close to its bottom in 1974. In contrast, individuals sold heavily near the 1968 top and were buyers on balance at the market bottoms of 1970 and 1974. In the January 1981 issue of *Trusts & Estates*, Robert S. Waill, a New York investment counselor, wrote: "If one may generalize, at this moment the institutions represent the 'weak hands' and individuals the 'strong hands.' The impulsive old lady from Dubuque has steadied. . . . The institutions have become the nervous and irrational sellers."

Some of the horrendous mistakes in stock-picking made by institutional money managers are cited in two excellent books by David N. Dreman, *Psychology and the Stock Market* (AMACOM, 1977) and *The Contrarian Investment Strategy* (Random House, 1980). At the third annual Institutional Investor Conference, held in New York in early 1970, the professional money managers picked National Student Marketing as the stock that would do best that year; five months later, its price had dropped 95 percent and the company later went bankrupt. In the early 1970s, *Institutional Investor*, a magazine addressed to stock market professionals, conducted annual polls that asked some 150 institutional money managers across the country to name their favorite stocks for the year to come. The ten favorites for 1972 rose on average roughly 1 percent, whereas the S&P index rose 15 percent; and the ten choices for 1973 dropped on average 40 percent, more than double the decline of the S&P stocks. Mercifully, the following year the *Institutional Investor* poll was discontinued.

What accounts for this startling record of bad judgment on the part of the institutional superpros? My experience with institutions as a Wall Street analyst jibes with the explanation given by David Dreman: institutional money managers are led astray by groupthink, a herd psychology of their own. As members of the institutional herd, otherwise intelligent, rational professionals take leave of common sense and follow to extremes the investment fads and concepts currently in vogue among their peers. A flagrant example of this mindless conformism was the institutional craze of the early 1970s for the top-quality growth companies—nicknamed the "nifty fifty" —which included Avon, Walt Disney, Eastman Kodak, Johnson & Johnson, and IBM. Never before have so many money managers put so much money into so few stocks with such total disregard for the inevitable consequences of their folly. Their rationale was that the future earnings growth of these companies had "high visibility," meaning that their growth could be predicted for a number of years with assurance and considerable accuracy. A number of scholarly studies have shown that forecasts of earnings' growth beyond the near future are highly fallible, this didn't faze the superpros. They dubbed their favorites "one-decision stocks"; the only decision was at what price to buy because these stocks need never be sold. The tremendous buying channeled into the nifty fifty pushed their prices up to stratospheric levels. But when the market started to collapse in 1973, the "one decision" concept was instantly punctured. The institutions scrambled to sell, and the prices of their absurdly overvalued favorites went into a sickening and prolonged nosedive. In less than a year, IBM dropped 41 percent, Disney 63 percent, and "second team" favorites such as Clorox and Tropicana showed losses of 75 percent to 90 percent. In early 1982, most of the nifty fifty were still trading at prices far below their 1973 highs.

Another aspect of institutional conformity — and a contributing factor in the institution's poor investment performance — is the cult of limitless information. It rests on the notion that the greater the number of so-called "inputs," the better the "output" — the investment decision — will be. But a variety of experiments designed to test man's cognitive capabilities have confirmed what common sense tells us — namely that the information-processing capabilities of the human mind are strictly finite. At a certain level, additional information becomes useless or clouds the recipient's judgment. When I worked on Wall Street, I observed that the most highly specialized analysts — those who follow relatively few companies and whose knowledge of them is encyclopedic — were often poor judges of when to buy or sell their companies' stocks. Their preoccupation with detail, much of it trivial, blurred their perception of the crucial issues.

Since the 1960s, the brokerage industry has provided institutions with ever-increasing quantities of "in-depth research." Some of it is valuable, but much of it simply creates "information overload" and is therefore a hindrance to effective decision-making.

Having argued that institutional investors have at times displayed shocking wrongheadedness, it's only fair to add that — *through no fault of their own — institutions collectively stand little or no chance of beating the market. The reason is simple: they can't beat the market because collectively they* are *the market, or a very large part of it.* Their share of the dollar volume of public trading on the New York Stock Exchange has soared from 39 percent in the early 1960s to 70 percent and that of individuals has shrunk from 61 percent to 30 percent.

(Public volume excludes the trading that members of the Exchange do for their own accounts.)

THE PYGMIES' NEW EDGE ON THE GIANTS

It should be clear by now that individuals have no valid reason to doubt their ability to compete with the big institutions. In fact, they have a basic advantage — the advantage that a nimble pygmy has over ponderous giants.

Sheer size has long been a serious handicap in the market to leading institutions such as the big city banks, and their resources keep on growing. The larger institutions have such huge sums of money to invest that they are forced to concentrate their major stock holdings in some 200 of the nation's largest companies. They can and do buy stock in smaller companies, but not on a scale that's significant in relation to the size of their portfolios. If they were to invest significant amounts in small companies, they would drive up the price of the stock by their buying and force it down when they sell. This constraint on their freedom of choice creates a problem for the money managers. The 200 companies in which they make their big investments constitute the most exhaustively analyzed sector of the market. They are so closely followed by so many of Wall Street's top analysts that just about everything there is to know about them is known, and new information is promptly reflected in the price of the stock. Consequently, the chances of detecting sharply undervalued issues in the institutional sector of the market are slim.

In contrast, an individual's investor is free to choose from a universe of more than 7,000 companies, the majority of which are neglected by analysts in the major brokerage houses. And it's within this universe of underanalyzed companies that undervalued stocks are most likely to be lurking. A study made by John C. Groth and Donald R. Fraser, professors in the Department of Finance at Texas A. & M. University, tracked the monthly performance of 64 stocks followed by 15 or more analysts and 64 followed by only one analyst over the period January 1972 through December 1977. The study's conclusion: "There appear to be much greater opportunities for speculative gain among the securities followed by few analysts." The underanalyzed universe isn't composed exclusively of companies that are small or little known. It includes large, long-established companies that are not intensively covered by Wall Street analysts because they happen to be out of favor with the institutions. At certain periods in the second half of the 1970s, a list of underanalyzed companies would have included Woolworth, the New York Times Company, and Sperry and Hutchinson (later merged into Baldwin United), all of which were among the nation's 500 largest corporations.

In addition to having greater freedom of choice than the large institutions, the individual has another important advantage — superior mobility in the marketplace. Managing a big institution portfolio is like maneuvering a battleship in a canal. After the managers of billion-dollar portfolios have decided to buy or sell a stock, it may take them months to accumulate the half-million or more shares they want, or to unload their holdings, without sharply altering the stock's price by their buying or selling. The average individual doesn't trade enough shares to be bothered by this problem; he can jump in or out at a moment's notice, an especially valuable advantage at times of crisis or exceptional opportunity.

Private investors are free from yet another constraint that applies to institutions, the Employee Retirement Income Security Act of 1974. Under ERISA, managers of a pension fund can be sued by the fund's beneficiaries for behavior construed as imprudent; the definition of prudence boils down to doing what so-called prudent men are doing. Thus ERISA made groupthink and conformism more or less mandatory for money managers handling pension funds. In August 1979, new regulations promulgated by the Labor Department seemingly gave pension fund managers considerable latitude in their choice of individual investments so long as the overall policy was in accord with the concept of prudence. But even though ERISA is no longer the straitjacket it used to be, it still withholds from pension fund managers the total freedom that individuals enjoy.

Of all the changes on the investment scene, none has helped individuals more than the proliferation of specialized mutual funds, many of which have no sales charge and are known as no loads. The specialized funds have made it possible for small investors to own securities previously beyond their reach — for example, tax-exempt bonds and high-yielding money-market instruments that sell in denominations of $10,000 to $100,000, or securities that would be risky to invest in without the diversification that a fund provides — in particular, offbeat, speculative stocks.

Another tremendous benefit to individuals has been the introduction by mutual funds of the "switching" privilege. This allows investors to move from one type of fund to another within the same organization, usually without charge. The not-so-rich investor has thus gained a flexibility he never had before. When he becomes optimistic about the stock market, he can jump into an aggressive stock fund; when he turns pessimistic, he can take refuge in a money-market fund; and he can vary the proportions of his capital invested in stocks, fixed-income securities, and even gold mining shares as his perceptions of the economic look change. Switching no-load funds (see chapter 23) makes these moves possible at a moment's notice and without incurring brokerage commissions.

HOW ARE THE PYGMIES PERFORMING?

Investment clubs are groups of the smallest investors who pool their resources and pursue a common investment policy. Many members are school teachers, housewives, and middle-echelon executives, and six out of seven have had no investment experience before joining a club. Over the average lifetime of the clubs belonging to the National Association of Investments Clubs — ten years and seven months in 1980 — the clubs' average annually compounded rate of return (including reinvested dividends) was 8.2 percent; this was 44 percent above the return on the S&P index over matching periods. The top performing club over a five-year period ending April 30, 1980 — Grove City (Pennsylvania) Stockyard Club — achieved the phenomenal annually compounded return of 32.9 percent!

So take heart. While making money in the market isn't easy, it isn't as difficult as the scared cats and the losers would have you believe. As one successful amateur investor has said, "You don't have to be a genius. You just have to avoid being a fool." The first step toward avoiding foolishness is to get to know the market better — to understand its language and what makes it tick.

I

STARTING POINTS

1. What, Precisely, Is "the Market"?

The U.S. stock market is composed of more than a dozen markets: the New York Stock Exchange, on which about 1,600 companies are listed; the American Stock Exchange (950 companies); the Boston, Philadelphia, Midwest, Pacific, and other smaller regional exchanges; the Over-the-Counter market, which isn't a place but a nationwide network of 2,800 dealers through whom stocks not listed on the registered exchanges are bought and sold; and the so-called Third Market, which consists of firms that deal in listed securities (mainly with financial institutions) away from the floors of the regular exchanges — they sell from and buy for their own inventory of stocks.

The three major markets — the New York Stock Exchange (or Big Board), the American Stock Exchange (often referred to as the Amex) and the Over-the-Counter market (OTC) — differ considerably in character. The New York Stock Exchange list includes most of the nation's largest and most mature companies; at the beginning of 1981, the market value of NYSE stocks — their price multiplied by the number of shares outstanding — was nearly one and a quarter trillion dollars, *about 86 percent of the market value of all actively traded stocks*. The companies on the Amex are smaller and younger; a salient feature of the Amex is the large number of oil and gas exploration companies traded on this exchange.

The OTC is the market for some 30,000 unlisted companies, and it's here that new issues — companies making their first public offering of stock — are launched. Of the OTC's huge population, fewer than 5,000 companies are actively traded. They fall into two categories, of which by far the larger one, numerically, consists of small to medium-sized companies, many of them relatively young. These include a large number of avant-garde technological companies with scientific-sounding names such as Avantek, Cyclotron, Sci-Tex, and Xidex. The other category is made up of large, often well-known companies that include American Greetings and Tampax, a raft of banks and insurance companies, the South African gold mining companies and a handful of huge foreign concerns such as Burmah Oil Co., Ltd., and

Tokyo Marine and Fire. At the close of 1981, nearly 3,400 actively traded OTC companies met the requirements for registration of their stock on the National Association of Securities Dealers Automated Quotation System, NASDAQ, which came into being in February 1971. More than 60 metropolitan newspapers now carry NASDAQ price quotations daily or weekly. This has given the OTC market much greater visibility than it used to have. Moreover, this market, which had a somewhat disreputable reputation in the 1960s, has gained respectability thanks to improved surveillance procedures by the National Association of Securities Dealers and increased disclosure requirements for its companies. It's the market in which an astute, aggressive investor has the best chance of detecting undervalued issues, because so many of its companies are too small or too obscure for most analysts to bother with.

2. Taking the Market's Pulse, or How to Read the Indexes

If you ask anyone, "How did the market do today?" his answer will almost certainly be that the Dow Jones Industrial Average was up or down so many points. The Dow is the oldest and best known of the market indexes, and it's the easiest to follow because it's so widely quoted in the media. But it's a mistake to assume, as some investors do, that the Dow's behavior accurately reflects the behavior of stocks in general.

The Dow Jones Industrial Average dates back to an 11-stock average first compiled by Charles H. Dow, editor of the *Wall Street Journal*, in 1884. It has since expanded to 30 stocks, and there have been many changes in its components; the most recent at this writing were the replacement in mid-1979 of Chrysler and Esmark (formerly Swift & Co.) by IBM and Merck. The 30 Dow stocks are all of them "blue chips" — stocks of large, long-established companies that are leaders in their respective industries. Originally, the Dow's level was computed by adding up the prices of its component stocks and dividing the total by the number of stocks in the average. But, in order to maintain historical continuity, an adjustment had to be made for stock splits and changes in the composition of the average. Suppose, for example, that the 30 stocks' aggregate price at the close of trading on a given day was $1,500; the average would then have stood at 50 (1,500 divided by 30). But after the close, a $100 stock split 2 for 1, giving it a new price of $50, or a stock selling at $100 was replaced by one priced at $50; either change would have lowered the aggregate price of the 30 stocks to $1,450, even though no real decline had taken place. The simplest way of maintaining the average at 50 is to change the so-called divisor from 30 to 29. (1,450 divided by 29 equals 50). This was the method chosen by Dow Jones & Co., which computes the Dow averages. Over the years, adjustments in the divisor of the DJIA have caused it to keep on shrinking; in August 1981, it was 1.314. With the divisor at 1.314, a 10-point change in the average represents an actual price change of $13.14.

The divisor is also used in computing the Dow's "earnings per share," a figure that some investors have trouble understanding. If you read in a newspaper or brokerage house report that the Dow's latest 12 months' earnings were, say, $120, it means that the aggregate earnings per share of the 30 companies were $120 *after being adjusted by the divisor;* with the divisor at 1.314, the actual earnings were $157.68.

The total market value of the 30 Dow stocks in mid-1981 was $231 billion, or roughly 15 percent of the market value of all actively traded stocks. While the Dow encompasses a hefty segment of the U.S. economy, it significantly underrepresents the growth industries of the present and the future and it overrepresents cyclical industries, those tied to the ups and downs of the economy. Analysts often refer to the Dow companies as "Smokestack America," because a significant proportion of them are in basic industries such as autos, chemicals, paper, and steel. Moreover, the Dow companies are among the aging or elderly giants of American industry.

The Dow's critics also point out that its behavior can be misleading because it's a "price-weighted" index. The movements of an "unweighted" index are measured by taking the *percentage* price changes of each of its components and calculating the average change, *a method that gives equal weight to the behavior of every* issue; when a $10 stock moves to $11 (10 percent), the impact on the average is the same as when a $60 stock moves to $66. But the Dow Jones Industrial

Average is computed by adding up the actual dollar price changes of its components, the result being that high-priced stocks influence the average more than low-priced stocks because they have larger dollar fluctuations. The disproportionate impact of a few high-priced stocks was largely responsible for the Dow's surge to its all-time high of 1,052 on January 11, 1973. And when the Dow was at a three-year low of 742 in February 1978, 60 percent of the drop from its high was due to fewer than one quarter of the stocks in the average.

I've dwelt on the anatomy and dynamics of the Dow because it's the average you hear about most, and it's the handiest index for the average investor to use; but keep in mind its shortcomings. Let's now take a look at ten other indexes that are often referred to in the financial press and investment advisory services. Each of them has a story to tell. And the divergences between their behavior can sometimes furnish useful insights into the mood of investors.

The Dow Jones Transportation Average (formerly the Railroad Average) consists of 20 companies — airlines, railroads, and truckers. It's closely followed by exponents of the "Dow Theory," a market-forecasting system first formulated at the beginning of the century. The theory starts out with the observation that stocks usually fluctuate within a well-defined price range or "channel" for anywhere from several months to several years. Dow theorists hold that when BOTH the Industrial and the Transportation averages break out of an established channel, they are signaling a new trend in the market — an uptrend if they penetrate the upper end of the range and a downtrend if they fall below the lower end. However, if a breakout by one of the averages is not "confirmed" by similar action by the other, the Dow Theory holds that the breakout is "false" and the average will drift back into its previous range. The rationale is that the Industrials represent the producing sector of the economy, and the Transportation Average represents the distributing sector; so it is only when both averages break out of their trading range that they are signaling a change in economic expectations that will change the major trend of stock prices. The trouble with the Dow Theory is that its exponents differ in their interpretations of what constitutes a real breakout, and when they do agree, the advance or decline in stock prices is already well under way. Nevertheless, the theory is worth knowing about, because its signals get attention in the press and its followers sometimes have a temporary influence on the market.

The Dow Jones Utility Average is composed of 15 public utilities; you'll find a chart showing its behavior over the past three months on the next to last page of the *Wall Street Journal*, below similar charts of the Industrial and Transportation Averages. The Utility Average is widely considered a barometer of the anticipated trend in interest rates: it tends to rise when rates are expected to decline and to fall when rates are expected to rise. The reason: utility companies must continually borrow huge sums of money to finance plant expansion, so higher interest rates hurt their profitability and they benefit when rates fall. The Utility Average flashed a prophetic signal when it peaked at 162 in early 1965 and then went into a long downtrend. We now know that 1965 marked the end of an era of low inflation and low interest rates and the beginning of a new era of recurring hyperinflation and surges in interest rates.

Standard & Poor's 500-Stock Index is much more representative of the general economy and the market than the Dow Jones Industrials; in addition to its 400 industrial companies, it includes 20 transportation, 40 utility, and 40 financial companies. Originated in 1923, the S&P Index was subsequently carried backward and linked to the Cowles Commission Index stretching back to 1893; thus it provides a continuous record of stock prices spanning nearly a century. Because it combines breadth and longevity, it's the index generally used by stock market professionals and academic researchers, and it's the benchmark against which institutional money managers measure their performance.

Like the Dow, the S&P 500 is a weighted index, only it's weighted by market "capitalization." (A company whose stock is selling at $20 and has 10 million shares outstanding has a market capitalization or market value of $200 million.) The index is computed by adding up the market capitalizations of its components and dividing the total by the average market value of the index in the period 1941–1943, which stands for a level of 10. Thus the early 1982 level of 123 meant that the current market value was 12.3 times that of the base period. The weighting system causes the index to be strongly influenced by fewer than 40 stocks with huge capitalizations, such as Eastman Kodak, Exxon, General Motors, and IBM. The justification for weighting by capitalization is that an index so constructed reveals whether *the aggregate value of all the issues in it is rising or falling*. There is no such justification for price-weighting, as used in the Dow, because the market value of a company depends more on the number of its shares outstanding than on the price of its stock. In short, a capitalization-weighted index — though it does not accurately reflect the *average* percentage change in the prices of all stocks — reflects changes in *the total flow of investment funds* much more reliably than an index that is unweighted or price-weighted.

The New York Stock Exchange Composite Index, first published in 1966, includes all stocks on the Big Board and it's a capitalization-weighted index, computed in the same way as the S&P 500; it was initially set at 50, which represents its market value at the end of 1965.

The American Stock Exchange Market Value Index replaced earlier Amex indexes on August 31, 1973; its base value was set at 100 (and it has been computed retroactively to January 2, 1969). Its flaw is that most of the Amex companies have small capitalizations, so a mere half-dozen large-capitalization stocks (out of 950) account for roughly 25 percent of the weight of index, and this can be misleading. For example, in the first nine months of 1979, the Amex Market Value Index rose nearly 50 percent, whereas the gain registered by an *unweighted* index of all Amex stocks was only 22 percent. The unweighted index is compiled by *Indicator Digest*, an investment advisory service that also publishes an unweighted index of New York Stock Exchange stocks known as *The Indicator Digest Average*. The best known of the unweighted averages is the *Value Line Composite*, which tracks some 1,700 stocks analyzed by the Value Line Investment Survey, a leading advisory service that is profiled in chapter 14. About 85 percent of the stocks are listed on the Big Board and the rest are traded on the Amex or over the counter.

The NASDAQ Composite Index, a market value index that includes about 3,400 over-the-counter stocks, was started on February 5, 1971 with a base value of 100. In early 1982, it stood at 192, up 250 percent from its 1974 low. This shows how well the smaller and less-known companies performed over that six-and-a-half-year period; the Dow's rise from its '74 low was only 73 percent.

The most representative of all the indexes are those compiled by Wilshire Associates of Santa Monica, California, because they cover 5,000 stocks. The capitalization-weighted index (there's also an un-weighted one) is published in *Barron's* and in *Forbes*. It's known as the

Wilshire Equity Index, and its market value at the beginning of 1982 was about 1.3 *trillion* dollars, up 138 percent since the end of 1974.

Let me try to sum up, now, what some of the leading indexes reveal about different sectors of the market. The Dow Jones Industrial Average, an all-blue-chip index, tells you how the mature giants of American industry are performing; most of its stocks are widely held by institutions and wealthy, conservative individuals. The behavior of Standard & Poor's 500, because it's strongly influenced by big capitalization stocks, is the best indicator of whether the major financial institutions are buying or selling. The American Indicator Digest and the NASDAQ Composite represent the small-company sector of the market; these indexes reflect the behavior of aggressive investors — individuals, or professionals managing relatively small pools of money. The Wilshire is by far the broadest of the indexes; it comes pretty close to representing the universe of stocks that are actively traded.

3. A Company and Its Stock: A Case of Mistaken Identity

Inexperienced investors often make the mistake of thinking, "If I invest only in top-quality companies, I can't go too far wrong." It would take pages to list the top-quality companies that have been bad investments for long periods of time. A stunning example is American Telephone, the bluest of the blue chips, which made its all-time high of 75 way back in 1964; nine years later, when the Dow was at its peak, A.T.&T. had fallen to 55. In 1980 it sank as low as 45.

To identify a company's reputation with the current investment merits of its stock is a dangerous fallacy. The quality ratings that Standard & Poor's assigns to a stock are, to be sure, based on the company's historical sales, earnings, and dividend record and present financial condition, but S&P warns that a high-rated stock "may be so overpriced as to justify its sale" and a low-rated stock may be on the bargain counter. The fact that IBM is the colossus of a global growth industry and that its stock has the highest S&P rating (A+) doesn't mean that IBM is a sound investment at whatever happens to be the current market price. Eastman Kodak has long been and continues to be a superlative company, but the investors who bought Kodak stock anywhere near its 1973 high of 151¾ made a whoppingly bad value judgment; six years later, the stock was selling at 50, a loss of 67 percent. On the other hand, the stock of Avco Corp., which like other conglomerates was rated a "junky" company in the early 1970s, soared from a price of 2 in 1974 to 35 in 1978, a gain of 1,650 percent.

A company may be great, good, mediocre, or lousy, but at any given moment, there is really no such thing as a "good stock" or a "bad" one; *a stock is either overpriced, underpriced, or fairly priced in relation to stocks in general.* Stocks can be judged only in terms of *value*, which of course is a matter of opinion. But value invariably hinges on price.

How to analyze stocks and judge their worth is the subject of a later chapter. But there's a yardstick used in valuing stocks that I'll discuss now, because it's a basic term in the language of investing and will keep cropping up throughout this text. It's the price/earnings ratio.

4. All You Need to Know about Price/Earnings Ratios

Price/earnings ratios are the yardstick most commonly used — and misused — in valuing stocks. A stock's price/earnings ratio is its current market price divided by the company's annual earnings per share; if the price is $20 and the earnings per share are $2, the stock has a P/E ratio of 10 and is said to be selling at 10 times earnings.

You can find the P/E ratios of stock traded on the New York and American stock exchanges, but not of those traded over the counter, in the daily stock-market tables in your newspaper. (When you see a stock with no P/E ratio, it means the company is operating at a loss.) Every Monday, the *Wall Street Journal* publishes on its next-to-last page the price/earnings ratio of the Dow Jones Industrial Average at Friday's closing prices and its P/E ratio one year earlier.

The P/E ratios you'll find in the press are based on the company's latest reported earnings for the previous twelve months, which are known as "trailing earnings." But investors are vastly more concerned with the future than with the past—stocks rise and fall largely on the basis of *expectations*. So the P/E ratios most commonly used in stock valuation are based on estimates of earnings for the current year, and sometimes the year to come as well. The catch is that earnings estimates are fallible, however skillful the analyst who's making them may be. Here, then, is one of the limitations of P/E ratios: those based on trailing earnings are somewhat academic because they refer to the past, and those based on estimates of future earnings are frequently unreliable. That means they should never be the sole basis for valuing a stock but should be used in conjunction with other analytic tools discussed elsewhere in this book.

Before going any farther, it might be helpful to explain precisely why price/earnings ratios, which are commonly referred to as "valuations," are a measure of value. Ownership of a share of stock gives you a claim to its earnings; typically, a portion of the earnings will be paid to you in the form of a cash dividend, and the balance, known as "retained earnings," will be invested by management in the company's business to finance future development and contribute to the goal of future earnings' growth. The price you are willing to pay for a stock is, basically, a reflection of the value you place on ownership of its earnings, and that value will vary according to the rewards—increased dividends and/or a higher price for the stock—that you think ownership will bring you. A stock whose earnings grow at an average annual rate of, say, 15 percent for the next five years will normally rise much more in price and have larger dividend increases than one whose earnings grow at a rate of 5 percent. If 15 percent and 5 percent are the growth rates you anticipate for two different stocks, you will be willing to pay significantly more for each dollar of the current earnings of the high-growth stock than for each dollar of earnings of the low-growth stock. The different values that investors, collectively, put on a dollarsworth of the current annual earnings of different companies are expressed in the price/earnings ratios of their stocks; hence the term *valuations*. Another term for P/E ratios is *multiples*, because they represent a multiple of each dollar of earnings.

Historically, stock valuations or multiples have ranged from less than two times earnings to one hundred times and more. But at any given point in time the range is not nearly that wide; at the start of 1982 most stocks were selling in a range of 5 to 15 times earnings.

The level of a stock's price/earnings ratio is influenced by all of the factors that determine the judgment of investors about the stock's investment merit. These include the company's past record of sales, earnings, and dividends; its prospects for the year ahead and for the longer term; the reputation of its management; its financial condition and its accounting procedures; the principal industry or industries in which it operates and the extent to which its business is subject to government regulation; *and the current level of stock valuations in general.* A stock whose P/E ratio is 12 when the average P/E ratio for all stocks is also 12 is likely to sell at about 8 times earnings if the average multiple falls to 8 — unless, of course, there's a significant change in the relative position and prospects of that particular company.

The general level of price/earnings ratios tends to be low (in relation to the recent past) at the peak of a boom and high at the bottom of a recession. This may sound wacky, but it's perfectly logical and is easily explained. Investors, as I noted earlier, are concerned with the future rather than with the past, and in actual practice they value stocks on the basis of estimates of future earnings. Thus, in the depths of a recession, P/E ratios based on the past twelve months' depressed earnings are high, because investors are expecting earnings to bounce back and move into an uptrend. Similarly, P/E ratios based on twelve months of boom earnings are low, because investors expect earnings to start heading downward. At the end of 1974, for example, the Dow's earnings for that year were at a cyclical high point of $99.04 and its P/E ratio had fallen to 6.2 in anticipation of a sharp earnings decline in 1975. In 1975, the Dow's earnings fell to $75.66 and its P/E ratio, at the year's end, was up to 11.3.

Like the Dow Jones Industrial Average, the stocks of companies that are in highly cyclical industries — notably the airline, automobile, copper, rubber, textile, and steel industries — tend to sell at their lowest valuations when earnings are booming and at their highest valuations when earnings are acutely depressed. For example, from 1971 through 1979, the P/E ratio of General Motors stock averaged 6.3 in the years when earnings were high and 11.7 in the years when earnings were low.

The behavior of price/earnings ratios is altogether different in the case of so-called growth stocks — the stocks of companies whose earnings have increased even during recessions and are expected to remain in an uptrend for the foreseeable future. Since the valuation of a growth stock is closely linked to a projected rate of growth, the valuation normally drops — often sharply — if that rate is not achieved. And the valuation tends to rise if the growth rate is higher than investors anticipated. When there is a bull market for high-growth issues, their P/E ratios typically range from twice to four times the P/E ratio of the Dow Jones Industrials.

A BRIEF HISTORY OF PRICE/EARNINGS RATIOS

To use P/E ratios intelligently in valuing stocks you need to be familiar with how they have behaved historically. Over the hundred-year period 1871–1970, the overall level of P/E ratios averaged 13.9 times earnings, but variations from this norm have been frequent and wide. (All P/E ratios cited in this chapter and elsewhere in the text are based on the previous twelve months' earnings, except when I refer specifically to "estimated earnings.") Multiples were at their highest sustained level in history from 1961 through 1965 — the John F. Kennedy and early Lyndon Johnson era. During those years, the average P/E ratio of the Dow was about 19, but many stocks sold at 25 to 50 times earnings and multiples of 50 to 70 times earnings were not particularly rare. The euphoria underlying those unprecedented valuations stemmed from a then-prevailing myth that "fine tuning" of the economy by the administration would abolish recessions and keep business activity and corporate profits on a course of high growth.

Historic lows in P/E ratios were registered in mid-1949, when the Dow's valuation fell to 7 times earnings; in late 1974, when it fell to 5.8 times earnings; and in late 1979, when it fell to around 6 times earnings. In 1949, it was widely feared that the initial recovery from World War II would be followed by a global depression. When these fears proved totally unfounded, price/earnings ratios went into a long uptrend and stocks enjoyed their greatest bull market in history; with a few sharp but short-lived setbacks (in 1957, 1962, and 1966), that bull market lasted for roughly 20 years.

The 1974 collapse of P/E ratios was caused by runaway inflation, the Arab oil embargo, and drastic credit-tightening by the Federal Reserve Board, which together aroused fears that a major depression was in store. This time, too, the doomsday scenario did not unfold and stock prices shot upward at the beginning of 1975. But recurring spells of accelerating inflation, accompanied by uptilts in interest rates, kept P/E ratios at the low end of their historical range from 1975 through 1981. Over that period, the valuation of the Dow Jones Industrials averaged less than 9 times earnings.

It's unlikely that the overall level of P/E ratios will revert to the historic norm of about 14 unless inflation and interest rates recede to less than double-digit levels. But consider this: if the Dow Jones Industrial Average were to be valued at even 10 times earnings, and its earnings were to register only moderate growth, the average would rise to 1,500 or higher by the mid-1980s.

II

WHAT MAKES STOCK
PRICES MOVE

5. Every Share Bought Is a Share Sold

Unless some event of shattering importance occurs, the daily behavior of stock prices is the outcome of a tug-of-war between dozens of forces, some positive, some negative. These include economic, monetary, and political developments and rumors of developments; everything that's happening or believed to be happening in the corporate world; rulings by governmental regulatory agencies; court decisions that affect industries or individual companies; crop reports; scuttlebutt about what superstar money managers are buying or selling; the cash needs of investors (to pay bills or buy yachts), and so on. So trying to come up with specific reasons for the market's daily behavior is usually an exercise in futility. *Nonetheless, all changes in stock prices have an underlying rationale.*

Have you ever asked yourself what, basically, determines the price of a stock? The answer is: investors' expectations of the future returns — dividends and capital growth — that the stock will provide. So what makes stock prices move is changes in investors' expectations about future returns. What causes those changes can be summed up in three words: "Just about everything." *The behavior of the stock market reflects the collective knowledge, beliefs, hopes, fears, and fantasies of all investors. Facts, rumors, judgments, and emotions give rise to conflicting opinions about future risks and rewards. And those opinions assume concrete shape and size in the form of orders to buy and sell stocks; they are translated into demand and supply.*

There's a stockbrokers' saying about how to deal with a tiresome client who, whenever a stock of his falls even half a point, wants to know the reason why — "Tell him there were more sellers than buyers." In the markets where stocks are traded, prices move in accordance with the law of supply and demand. When sellers wish to unload more shares of a stock than buyers are demanding at a given price, the price declines. When buyers are seeking more shares than sellers are willing to part with at a given price, the price rises. *Every share of stock bought represents a share of stock sold, which means that every transaction reflects a conflict of opinion.* When you buy a stock that you think is probably undervalued, it's been sold to you by somebody who thinks it's probably overvalued.*

The factors that influence investors' expectations of future returns — and thus determine supply and demand — fall into three categories: fundamental, technical, and psychological. The *fundamentals* include the earnings, dividends, and financial condition of companies, and trends in the general economy and the monetary system. *Technical* factors are those that most directly determine the potential demand for and supply of stock; the most important — others will be considered in chapter 16 — is the size of the cash reserves in the hands of all investors. The *psychological* factors are, simply, fear and greed, and their influence on stock prices can hardly be exaggerated. We'll take a closer look at each of those factors in the chapters that follow, *focusing on specific information that can help you to anticipate movements in stock prices.*

6. The Business Cycle, Profits, and Interest Rates

Investors' expectations of a stock's future returns hinge largely on the trend in the company's profits. So the trend in overall corporate profits is the most important of the fundamental factors that influence stock prices, and it's closely related to the ups and downs of the general economy. The economy's cycles, from peak to peak, have averaged about 48 months. Since World War II, recessions or contractions have lasted on the average 11 months, and the subsequent recoveries and expansions 37 months; only one postwar expansion (1958–1960) lasted less than 3 years. Since investors try to anticipate the future, major declines in the stock market usually start while the economy is still booming and major advances usually begin in the very depths of a recession. *In the 5 business cycles between 1953 and*

---

*I have excluded from this discussion the important role of the exchange Specialist, who is charged by the exchange's governing body with maintaining a "fair and orderly market" in the stocks assigned to him. The Specialist can mitigate the impact of sudden drastic changes in supply and demand — but only temporarily. For a fuller description of his functions, see Appendix D, The Language of Investing.

1976, stock prices peaked and started to decline 6 months on the average before the onset of the recession; the shortest lead time was 1 month, the longest 12 months; *prices bottomed and started to rise about 5 months on the average before the beginning of the recovery.*

Those Influential Interest Rates. The relationship between interest rates and stock prices is in principle quite simple. Rising interest rates are normally unfavorable for the stock market for two reasons: (1) they increase the yields offered by fixed-income securities such as Treasury Bills, money market mutual funds and bonds, causing investors to switch money funds toward themselves out of the stock market into these securities, thereby depressing stock prices; (2) if interest rates rise steeply enough, they slow down business activity by making borrowing expensive and perhaps difficult, and this causes corporate profits to decline. A sustained downtrend in interest rates has, of course, the opposite effects and is therefore extremely bullish for the stock market.

Major advances in stock prices usually begin either not long before or not long after an upward cycle in interest rates reaches its final peak and long-term rates start declining. But there's a long time lag between an upturn in interest rates and a major downturn in the market, and the lag varies considerably; the major market advances since World War II have lasted anywhere from seven to forty-four months *after* interest rates bottomed and started rising. Moreover, in 1980 and early 1981, the principal market indexes (except for the Dow) climbed to all-time highs in the face of steep upsurges in interest rates. This unprecedented behavior suggested that, since inflation became recognized as our number one economic problem, investors have developed a certain tolerance for rising interest rates. They sometimes view them, or so it would seem, not simply as bad news for the economy, but also as reassuring evidence that the Federal Reserve Board is really committed to sticking with an anti-inflationary policy. However, when interest rates climb into the stratosphere and persist in staying there — as they did in the summer and fall of 1981 — investors finally become discouraged and stock prices drop. The reason: the persistence of extremely high interest rates is bound to cause a slowdown in business activity and could lead to a serious recession.

7. Inflation and Stock Prices: Are Stocks a Hedge or Aren't They?

In the 1950s and early 1960s, when inflation averaged less than 2 percent annually, the conventional wisdom was that stocks were a "hedge against inflation," because they represent ownership of real assets — property, plant, and equipment — whose values rise along with prices. This concept was seemingly demolished in the first half of the 1970s, when upward spirals in inflation were accompanied by two horrifying tailspins in stock prices. The disastrous losses suffered by most investors between 1969 and 1975 prompted some 5,000,000 individuals to liquidate their stock holdings. By the mid-seventies, the consensus was that inflation is poison for the stock market.

The behavior of stock prices tended to support this view until 1978; prices rose when inflation declined and they dropped when inflation tilted upward. Then something extraordinary happened: although inflation continued to heat up, the stock market embarked on a major advance that carried some of the popular averages to record-breaking levels in November 1980 and others (the Amex market value index and the NASDAQ composite) to their all-time peaks in May 1981. Some analysts concluded that the view of stocks as an inflation hedge was back in favor. The question — are they or aren't they? — can best be answered by looking at the historical data on inflation and stock prices.

According to a study co-authored by Roger G. Ibbotson and Rex A. Sinquefield — *Stocks, Bonds, Bills, and Inflation: Historical Returns (1926–78)** — the total return on Standard & Poor's 500-stock index over the 53-year period was 8.9 percent compounded annually, and the annual inflation rate averaged 2.5 percent. So stocks provided a real return of 6.4 percent (before income taxes) and they were indeed a hedge against inflation. The real return on U.S. Treasury Bills was zero — their annual return of 2.5 percent exactly matched the rate of inflation. And long-term corporate bonds provided a nominal return of 4 percent and a real return of only 1.5 percent. However, the data

*Published by the Financial Analysts Federation, Charlottesville, Va., 1979.

on stocks for a recent 10-year period of high inflation — March 1970 through February 1980 — tell a very different story: the annual return on the S&P index was nearly 1 percent *less* than the 7.5 percent annual increase in the Consumer Price Index. And over the four-year period, 1973 through 1976, the rate of return on common stocks, adjusted for inflation, was *minus* 6.2 percent annually.

The Ibbotson-Sinquefield figures show that, over the very long haul, the total return on common stocks has substantially exceeded the rate of inflation. *But stocks have not been an inflation hedge in periods when inflation has persisted at exceptionally high levels.* These conclusions are supported by Steven Leuthold's book *The Myths of Inflation and Investing* (Chicago: Crain Books, 1980), which tracks stock prices and inflation rates all the way from 1872 through 1979. During those 108 years, there were 14 years of exceptionally high inflation (8 percent to 18 percent), and in 9 of them, the total return on stocks was lower than the inflation rate. Stocks achieved their best annual rates of gain in periods of price stability or mild deflation.

There are several reasons why, in principle, high levels of inflation have an adverse effect on stock prices. One is that *inflation has a negative impact on real corporate profitability,* a subject that became a burning issue in the accounting profession in the 1970s. There is still no end of controversy as to how the so-called nominal profits that corporations report (and pay taxes on) should be adjusted to take into account the effects of inflation. But two adjustments made by the Department of Commerce are now generally considered standard procedure. The Inventory Valuation Adjustment, or IVA, adjusts nominal profits by subtracting from them profits on inventory that are strictly due to rising prices; such profits are in effect illusory, because the company has to replace inventory at the current, higher prices in order to stay in business. The Capital Consumption Adjustment, or CCA, reduces nominal profits by increasing depreciation charges, which are based on the original costs of plant and equipment and are, therefore, too low in light of current replacement costs. Together, these adjustments take a big slice out of reported profits. In 1970, there was only a 10 percent difference between total corporate profits before and after IVA and CCA; the figures were $37 billion and $33.4 billion. But in 1979, profits totaled $144.1 billion before IVA and CCA and $85.6 billion after; *the difference had widened to 40 percent.*

A second reason why high inflation tends to hurt stock valuations has already been mentioned; as inflation escalates, interest rates rise, making fixed-income securities more competitive with stocks.

Thirdly, a persistently high and rising level of inflation arouses fears that the Federal Reserve Board will resort to drastic credit-tightening measures that could cause a recession, a "credit crunch," or both. A credit crunch — a critical shortage of available cash — is one of the worst possible disasters for the market. When credit crunches have occurred — as, for example, in 1970 and 1974 — the downtrends in stock prices that were already under way turned into catastrophic nosedives. On both those occasions, investors feared that the Fed's policies would result in "overkill" and throw the economy into a depression. Moreover, a credit crunch combined with rising prices forces many investors, particularly those running businesses of their own, to raise cash by withdrawing funds from the stock market — and money is the market's lifeblood.

8. The Federal Reserve Board: A Fed-Watcher's Guide

At the corner of 20th Street and Constitution Avenue in Washington, D.C., stands a massive neoclassical building with floors of travertine marble and walls adorned with paintings of museum quality. Imposing and aloof, this structure is an appropriate setting for its tenant, the Federal Reserve Board, which is responsible for managing the nation's supply of money and credit. Nowadays, no government agency is so closely watched and so much discussed by Wall Street professionals as the Federal Reserve Board, commonly referred to as the Fed. Interest rates, inflation, and corporate profits are all of them strongly influenced by the policies of the Fed. Indeed some economists consider the Fed's policies the most important single influence on the behavior of the stock and bond markets.

The Federal Reserve Board, created by Congress in 1913, is a government agency independent of the administration and the legislature. As the manager of monetary policy, the Fed has the awesome responsibility of trying to smooth the ups and downs of the economy, while fighting inflation and keeping an eye on the foreign exchange rate of the U.S. dollar. The Fed prides itself on its independence, and it has sometimes persisted in a course that was objectionable to the White House and Congress. But it is by no means insensitive to political pressures. A study by Robert Weintraub, a staff economist for congressional committees concerned with monetary policy, suggests that Presidents since World War II have usually received from the Fed the policies they wanted. It's arguable that there's nothing wrong with this, since the Fed, by cooperating with the incumbent administration, is in effect being responsive to the wishes of the electorate. But the Fed's critics have accused it of playing politics. They charge, in particular, that in presidential election years, the Fed is apt to pursue policies designed to stimulate the economy and thus to improve the incumbent's image in the eyes of the voters.

According to textbook theory, monetary policy should be stimulative when the economy is ailing and it should be restrictive when the economy is booming and threatens to become overextended. A stimulative policy is one that provides ample growth in the supply of money and credit, thereby pushing down interest rates. Easy credit boosts the demand for automobiles, housing, appliances, and other goods and services, and it encourages borrowing by industry for investment in plant and equipment, which creates jobs and thereby increases consumer income and spending. A restrictive policy tightens the supply of money and credit, which pushes interest rates upward. Tight credit curbs consumer demand and discourages business investment, thereby causing unemployment and reducing consumer income and spending. For many years, the Fed's top priority as manager of monetary policy was to smooth the course of the U.S. economy and thus help to maintain a high level of employment. But when inflation became the nation's number one economic problem, the Fed found itself confronted with a taxing dilemma, which I will try to explain as simply as possible.

A policy of easy money, which in principle promotes economic growth, can become highly inflationary when—as in many of the past seventeen years—the federal government incurs huge budget deficits. The government finances these deficits by selling Treasury securities, an action that is popularly though not quite accurately known as printing money. When Treasury offerings are larger than investors (mainly financial institutions) are willing to buy at the current rate of interest, the Treasury has to raise interest rates to attract buyers. Thus exceptionally heavy Treasury financing tends to push interest rates up to levels that could have stifling effects on the economy. The Federal Reserve, normally a big buyer of government securities, can help to prevent this by significantly stepping up its buying, thereby shrinking the amount that has to be absorbed by the public. But Fed purchases of Treasury securities release cash into the nation's monetary system, and when the purchases are extraordinarily large, their effects are inflationary. Thus by helping the government to finance huge deficits without pushing interest rates too high, the Fed frustrates its own efforts to dampen inflation by curbing growth of the money supply—the total of all money sloshing around in the economy. One way out of this Catch-22 situation, some economists believe, is to reduce the size of the federal deficit. But solutions to our macroeconomic problems are beyond the scope of this book. My concern here is simply to explain the Fed's functions and influence in order to show how Fed-watching—which need only take a few minutes a week—can help the average investor to anticipate the behavior of the securities markets. So let's take a closer look at how the Fed manages monetary policy and at the specific signals that investors should watch for.

The Fed's chief policy-making body—its twelve-member Open Market Committee—meets in Washington, on a Tuesday, eight to ten times a year under conditions of secrecy that would do credit to the CIA. However, a so-called record of policy actions taken at a meeting is released to the press three days after the *subsequent* meeting—that is, usually with a time lag of about a month.

The most important and most flexible of the Fed's tools for managing monetary policy is *"open-market operations"*: buying U.S. government securities from banks and other dealers in these securities and selling to them; these operations account for at least 90 percent of the Fed's daily activities. Banks are required by law to maintain a certain ratio, determined by the Fed, between their reserves and their deposits, which they use to make loans. For example, when the reserve requirement for demand deposits at large banks is 12 percent, $1,000 deposited in a checking account permits the bank to loan out $880. When the Fed's Open Market Desk in New York City buys, say,

$400 million of Treasury bills, its payments are deposited in member banks of the Federal Reserve System, increasing the banks' reserves and thus permitting them to increase their lending. On the other hand, selling of government securities by the Fed siphons cash out of the money market, decreases the banks' reserves, and thus reduces their lending power. Through its open-market operations the Fed seeks to expand or contract the money supply so as to achieve a targeted rate of growth, determined annually by its policymakers.

There are several measures of the money supply. The one that gets the most attention because it's considered the best measure of spending money in the hands of the public is M1 (previously M1-B) — currency plus most checking accounts, including interest-bearing checking accounts at banks and thrift institutions. Changes in the money supply are made public weekly after the close of the stock market on Fridays. They're reported in leading newspapers in financial centers and in *Barron's* on Saturdays, and in the *Wall Street Journal* on Mondays, along with an analysis of whether M-1 ran above analysts' expectations and the Fed's own annually announced target range. If the money supply is moving above target, there's a good chance that the Fed's open-market operations will seek to reduce money-supply growth, causing interest rates to tilt upward. Conversely, if M-1 is expanding at less than the targeted rate, the Fed may ease up on restraints, and this would allow interest rates to fall. At times when inflation is at exceptionally high levels, bulges in the weekly figures for the money supply are thoroughly bad news for the stock market, since they show that the Fed isn't succeeding in holding down inflationary pressures and will probably be tightening its reins on credit. By the same token, it's good news for investors when the weekly money-supply figures are in accord with, or below, the targeted growth rate. So by keeping an eye on these figures you can get worthwhile insights into how well the Fed is coping with inflation and also into the probable trend of short-term interest rates.

A second weapon in the Fed's arsenal is its power to change *bank reserve requirements* — the minimum level of cash reserves that banks must keep in relation to their deposits. Over the past forty-five years, the Fed has changed reserve requirements for large city banks fewer than thirty times. When it does change them, here's what investors can expect: *the market will rise over the eighteen-month period following a decrease in reserve requirements and it will almost certainly decline over the eighteen months following an increase.* Writes Norman G. Fosback in *Stock Market Logic* (Fort Lauderdale: The Institute for Economic Research, 1976): "It may be stated categorically that a reduction in reserve requirements . . . for large city banks is the single most bullish event in the world of stock price behavior."

Another important indicator for investors is a change in the *discount rate,* the lending rate charged by a Federal Reserve District bank to its member banks. (Since 1960, the discount rate has ranged from a low of 3 percent in 1960 to a high of 14 percent [plus a 4 percent surcharge for big borrowers] in May 1981.) A decrease (or increase) in the discount rate is a signal that the Fed intends to ease (or tighten) credit, and *the historical record shows that the return on stocks has usually been higher than the average in the twelve months following a decrease and slightly lower than the average in the twelve months following an increase.* Changes in the discount rate occur relatively infrequently and are prominently reported in the financial pages, so it's easy to keep track of them.

Since the Fed limits the amount of borrowing that banks may do at its so-called discount window, banks tend to use it only as a last resort. They do most of their borrowing from other banks that have more than the required amount of reserves. The rate charged for such overnight loans is known as the *federal funds rate.* It's published in the *Wall Street Journal,* and *it's a key indicator of the demand for credit and therefore of the trend in short-term interest rates.*

A Fed-watcher's guide wouldn't be complete without a reference to *margin requirements.* The Securities Exchange Act of 1934 empowered the Fed to regulate the minimum amount that investors must put up when they buy securities on margin—that is, using in part funds borrowed from their broker. Since 1934, the margin requirement has been as low as 40 percent and as high as 100 percent (which means no borrowing is permitted). When the rate is, say, 50 percent—as it was when this book was written—an investor can buy $10,000 worth of stock by putting up $5,000. In theory, a margin rate hike should reduce the demand for stock by reducing the amount that investors can borrow, and a reduction should stimulate demand. But the record shows that a change in margin requirements is of little value as a stock market indicator. The probable reason for this is that margin requirements are usually raised only *after* the market has been booming for some time, and they are lowered only *after* the market has been in a prolonged slump.

However, margin requirements are one of three elements in *an indicator whose forecasting record, as of early 1982, had been literally infallible for sixty-six years.* Its discoverer, Norman Fosback, calls this indicator "Two Tumbles and a Jump," and he formulates it as follows: *When any one of the Fed's three policy variables — the discount rate, bank reserve requirements, or margin requirements — is lowered twice in succession, stock prices will jump over the ensuing year. The "two tumbles" signal was given sixteen times between December 23, 1914, and November 1981. On every occasion, Standard & Poor's 500-stock index was higher six months and also nine months after the signal date, even though stock prices sometimes dropped before rising. The six-month gains averaged nearly 18 percent and the nine-month gains 23 percent. Except once, at the start of the Great Depression in 1930, the S&P was up nearly 32 percent on average twelve months after the second tumble.* Changes in the discount rate, reserve requirements, and margin requirements are reported in the *Wall Street Journal* and other leading newspapers. So a vigilant investor should be able to tell when the "two tumbles" signal has been flashed. And if he heeds the record, he'll load up on stocks.

9. The Cash in Institutional Coffers

Assessments of the market outlook in newspapers, brokerage house "letters," and advisory services periodically refer to the size of the cash reserves held by institutional investors. High cash reserves represent latent buying power that could push stock prices upward: low reserves mean that the institutions are already heavily invested in stocks and are therefore no longer a source of strong demand that could keep prices rising. The largest of the pools of institutional cash reserves is that of private (nongovernmental) pension funds. But pension fund figures are disclosed quarterly and may be out of date by the time they appear in the SEC's *Statistical Bulletin*. However, since financial institutions tend to behave roughly like one another, you can deduce whether pension and other institutional cash reserves are high or low from a figure that's published monthly — the mutual funds' Cash/Assets Ratio. This is the percentage of the total assets of mutual funds — excluding money market funds — that is currently in cash or so-called cash equivalents (Treasury bills, commercial paper, and other short-term securities). The Cash/Assets Ratio is compiled on the last day of each month by the Investment Company Institute (1775 "K" Street, Washington, D. C., 20006), the national association of the mutual fund industry; it is publicly released with a three-week time lag and appears in the *Wall Street Journal.*

Since the Cash/Assets Ratio was first compiled in 1954, it has fluctuated between 4 percent and 14 percent; typically it has been about 7 percent, of which about 3 percent is the minimum required to meet expenses and redemptions of fund shares. Consequently, brokerage-house market letters and advisory services will tell you that a ratio of, say, 10 percent is high and, therefore, bullish. This is misleading because it doesn't take into account the current level of interest rates; fund managers tend to maintain a Cash/Assets Ratio that's above the historical norm of about 7 percent when they can get big returns on money market securities. Here's a formula, developed by Norman G. Fosback, to determine whether mutual funds' cash reserves are *really* high or low in light of the current rate of interest: add seven-tenths of the current Treasury Bill rate to the 3 percent minimum reserve requirement, and you will come up with a Cash/Assets Ratio that can reliably be considered "normal." For example, if the T-Bill rate is 12 percent, the *normal* Cash/Assets Ratio would be 3 percent + 8.4 percent (seven-tenths of 12 percent), which equals 11.4 percent. The historical record shows that, *if the actual ratio reported by mutual funds is 2½ percent above the normal ratio, a substantial rise in stock prices is probable over the next three to six months.* On the other hand, a reported Cash/Assets Ratio that is below the normal one is usually a bearish portent for the market.

10. Fear and Greed

Fear or greed becomes the dominant influence on stock prices whenever investors cease to act as thinking individuals and surrender to herd psychology.* This occurs with unfailing regularity in the final stages of major bull or bear markets. In the euphoria generated by a long and powerful market advance, investors get carried away by the lure of instant profits, and greed takes command; even normally hardheaded professionals ignore rational yardsticks of valuation and join the frenzied buying that pushes prices up to preposterously high levels, from which eventually they come down with a crash. Similarly, at the tail end of bear markets, fear conjures up images of total catastrophe, and panic selling forces valuations down to fire-sale levels. Here are some examples of the enormous impact that greed and fear can have on stock prices.

In the eighteen months leading up to the historic crash of 1929, Anaconda rose from 54 to 162, Montgomery Ward from 134 to 467, Radio Corporation from 95 to 505 and Westinghouse from 92 to 313. In the subsequent bear market, Anaconda fell from 162 to 4, Montgomery Ward from 467 to 4, Radio Corporation from 505 to 18 and Westinghouse from 313 to 16. At their peak prices in the bull market of the late 1960s, thirty "growth stocks" widely favored by institutions sold at a stratospheric average valuation of eighty-four times earnings — about five times that of the S&P 500. In the bear market of 1969–1970, the prices of these issues dropped on the average 81 percent from their bull market highs. Donald T. Regan, then chairman of Merrill Lynch, later said in his book, *A View from the Street* (New York: New American Library, 1972): "Institutional buyers, alleged to be . . . pretty cool customers making emotionless decisions, were just as susceptible to panic, if not more so, as anyone else." Institutions acted even more irrationally in the bear market of 1973–1974; twenty-seven of the favorite institutional stocks dropped, on the average, 84 percent from their 1971–1972 highs. Avon Products plummeted from 140 to 18⅝, Walt Disney from 119⅛ to 16⅝,

*The history of mass irrationality in investing is richly documented in Charles Mackay's *Extraordinary Popular Delusions and The Madness of Crowds* (1841), and in Gustave Le Bon's small classic *The Crowd* (1895), both of which are still in print.

McDonald's from 77⅜ to 21¼ and Westinghouse from 54⅞ to 8. *Nothing was fundamentally wrong with these companies. Indeed, at their 1975 highs — that is, in less than a year — the twenty-seven stocks were up, on the average, 221 percent from their 1974 lows.*

Crowd psychology doesn't necessarily vanish from the marketplace at times when the market is neither booming nor collapsing. It can manifest itself in fads and fashions that generate speculative crazes for stock groups whose promise is either vastly exaggerated or entirely fanciful. Over the past two decades or so, such fad-followed stock groups have included small business investment companies, companies in the bowling business, copycat fast-food franchisers short on assets and know-how, real estate investment trusts, infant technology companies with no earnings and no markets for their products, and other so-called "concept" stocks that put stars into investors' eyes and eventually took the shirts off their backs.

In the hope of making a quick killing people often buy fad stocks or other market favorites that their reason tells them are dangerously overvalued. They rationalize their greed with the "greater fool theory," which says that you'll be able to sell an overpriced stock to a greater fool at an even higher price. Occasionally, the theory works. But never forget that, in the stock market, fear displaces greed with astonishing rapidity, and all those fools who were frantic to buy suddenly become scared cats who are frantic to sell.

11. The Market Discounts the Future

Even though all investors don't act as thinking individuals all of the time, many investors act as thinking individuals much of the time. And as such they are constantly seeking, in their buying and selling, to anticipate future developments. That's what is meant by the dictum "The market discounts the future." In that saying is wrapped a key to understanding the behavior of stock prices.

A favorable (or unfavorable) development that's anticipated by knowledgeable investors causes a stock to rise (or fall) weeks, and sometimes months, *before* it actually occurs; *by the time it does occur, it's been taken into account in the stock's current price.* For example, when a $20 billion program to encourage the development of synthetic fuels was legislated by Congress in June 1980, the stock of companies that stood to benefit had already moved up appreciably in anticipation that the bill would be passed. Another example: after the market's close on October 27, 1980, General Motors announced a third-quarter loss of $567 million, until then the largest quarterly deficit ever reported by a U.S. corporation; the news had been so fully discounted that the following day General Motors' stock actually moved up ⅜ to 49⅛. So don't rush to buy on good news or sell on bad news, as so many amateurs do; check first to see whether or not the news has probably been discounted. A recent runup in a stock's price is usually an indication that investors have anticipated good news, and a recent decline tells you that bad news has probably been discounted. Developments that are unexpected or unpredictable cannot, by definition, have been discounted. If the development is of such importance that it could significantly affect the company's future, it often pays to act promptly. A case in point was the nuclear accident at the Three Mile Island plant of General Public Utilities in March 1979. In the two weeks following the accident, the company's stock declined from 17⅞ to 13, and it subsequently sank as low as 3⅜. When unexpected catastrophe strikes, the quicker you sell the better.

Stock prices may also discount expectations related to the distant future. This is evident in the lofty and sometimes astronomic valuations placed on the stocks of young companies that are pioneering new technologies. Naive investors think they are getting into such companies "on the ground floor"; they fail to realize how stiff a price they are paying up-front for expectations of rewards that are still far distant and, in most cases, highly uncertain.

A historic example of reckless discounting of the future was the first public offering of Genentech, a pioneer in genetic engineering, whose prospects investors found intoxicating. Although the company had virtually no earnings when its stock went public at $35 a share in October 1980, investors who failed to get stock in the offering were so frantic to buy that Genentech opened for trading in the aftermarket at 80 and rose to a high of 89 on the day of issue. It closed at 71 — leaving everyone who bought in the aftermarket with a loss; three months later it had fallen to 36. The moral: even when a company's prospects are "Such stuff as dreams are made on," ask yourself coolly whether those dreams have not already been overdiscounted in the price of the stock. Whenever future promise grossly overinflates present price, the risks of future shock are large.

Once a novice has understood the market's discounting mechanism, he has taken a giant step toward losing his innocence. Among other things, this understanding will imbue him with a healthy skepticism about tips from a friend or broker who claims to know of an impending development that will make a stock jump. In such cases, you should immediately check on a stock's recent behavior; if it's had a runup, the development has probably been widely anticipated. If the stock hasn't been climbing, there are, as Talmudists say, two possibilities: your informant may know something that hasn't been discounted — or his information may be phony. Your decision on how to act has to depend on how reliable you consider your source to be. But remember this: the chances that highly significant information about a company is not widely known are exceedingly slim — unless the company happens to be an offbeat one that few analysts follow.

12. The Academic Gospel: What's of Value in It for the Layman

It's now time to consider two related doctrines about the behavior of stock prices that are gospel in academic circles and have had a huge influence on institutional investors: the Random Walk Hypothesis (or "Model") and its outgrowth, the Efficient Market Hypothesis. The former holds that the past price behavior of a stock affords no clues to its behavior in the future; stocks move randomly, they do not move in trends. The Efficient Market Hypothesis goes much farther. It maintains that at any given moment a stock's price is the best available estimate of its value; consequently all of the efforts of analysts and investors to unearth undervalued stocks and anticipate market movements are completely useless. According to the Efficient Market Hypothesis, a twenty-stock portfolio selected by a chimpanzee throwing darts at the stock tables in a newspaper has the same chance of outperforming or underperforming the market as a twenty-stock portfolio selected by the top brains in Wall Street. This thesis — understandably abhorrent to most people in the brokerage business — runs counter to common sense and large amounts of documentary evidence. Nonetheless, the Random Walk and Efficient Market hypotheses contain important elements of truth. A thorough understanding of these doctrines will provide inexperienced investors with a professional perspective on the workings of the stock market. And it will furnish them with insights that have a crucial bearing on the way they handle their investments.

THE RANDOM WALK THEORY OF PRICE MOVEMENTS

The theory gets its name from the unpredictable movements of microscopic particles suspended in fluids or gases. The concept that the random behavior of particles was paralleled by the price behavior of stocks and commodities was first formulated in 1900 by a French student of mathematics, Louis Bachelier. Bachelier's work was redis-covered by U.S. academic researchers around 1960 and tested by them in a succession of statistical studies. The evidence thus accumu-lated appeared to destroy the claims of technical analysis — a system for forecasting stock and commodity prices on the basis of past patterns in their price behavior. The academicians' studies appeared to prove, again and again, that changes in stock prices occur indepen-dently of previous changes; consequently, past price movements offer no information that's of use in forecasting future movements. Accord-ing to the Random Walk Model, a rise in a stock's price for five days in a row gives no indication of what it will do on the sixth day; the odds that it will rise rather than fall are 50/50 — just as the odds are 50/50 that a tossed coin that's come up heads five times will come up heads a sixth time. To put it more graphically, the behavior of stock prices resembles the walk of a drunk. No matter how closely you watch a drunk lurching this way and that, you can't predict in which direction or how far his next step will take him. The random walkers' conclu-sion: technical analysis is bunk.

This verdict has failed to shake the strongly entrenched position of technical analysis in the investment community. To the contrary, brokerage houses have expanded their budgets for technical research, and technically oriented advisory services have a larger following than ever before. In subsequent chapters, I'll cite persuasive evidence that stocks do not move randomly all of the time; over the long term, trends in the market develop and persist. However, the Random Walk studies make it hard to reject the conclusion that *short-term price fluctuations* are random and unpredictable. I therefore believe that the efforts of technical analysts to anticipate short-term ripples in stock prices are worse than worthless; they're financially damaging in the long run to those who follow them. Typically, technical analysts who make short-term recommendations tell you to buy a stock at (say) $34 "for a possible move to 38," and to limit your losses by simultaneously placing an order to sell the stock if it drops to 32⅛. That kind of advice leads to incessant in-and-out trading, which makes brokers rich and leaves investors poor.

THE EFFICIENT MARKET HYPOTHESIS: HOW TO PROFIT FROM INEFFICIENCY

Efforts by academic researchers to account for the supposedly random behavior of stock prices led to formulation of the Efficient Market Hypothesis. The EMH carried the academic blitzkrieg into the realm of fundamental analysis, which seeks to determine the intrinsic value of stocks and project their future value on the basis of economic and financial fundamentals. The EMH holds that all available information that affects stock prices is known to and continuously analyzed by large numbers of investment professionals and concerned investors, and that all incoming information is evaluated almost instantly. Thus, at any given moment, a stock is "efficiently" priced, which means that its price reflects all of the facts, opinions, and expectations that have a bearing on its value. As James Lorie and Richard Brealey, leading exponents of the EMH, succinctly put it, "current prices reflect what is knowable." A stock's price may be too high or too low, but it's the best available estimate of what the stock is worth, because it represents the collective judgment of large numbers of informed investors, all of them competing in the search for values. Thus the EMH argues that there are no undiscovered values, precisely because analysts and informed investors work so hard at discovering them. And since stock prices at all times reflect what is knowable about values, no individual or team of professionals can consistently outperform the market. An investor may get lucky for a few months or even a couple of years, but over the long haul his rate of return will be about the same as that of a broadly-based market index such as Standard & Poor's 500 — unless he's willing to assume above-average risks.

By taking above-average risks an investor can and indeed should obtain better than average returns, according to the Efficient Market Hypothesis. Its basic assumption is that investors act rationally at all times — that is, they constantly seek to minimize risk and maximize returns. Consequently, they would not invest in high-risk stocks or other high-risk securities, unless such securities provided larger returns than those considered to be less risky. The argument applies only to a well-diversified portfolio of high-risk issues; it doesn't imply that *every* high-risk issue is likely to provide above-average returns. It recognizes, too, that a high-risk portfolio will have much larger price swings than the S&P index; indeed, there will be times when the portfolio shows a lower rate of return than the index or even alarmingly big losses. Nonetheless, in the long run, a market that prices stocks efficiently will provide superior returns to investors who assume greater than average risks — and manage to survive. For those who don't take such risks, there is no hope of outperforming the market for any length of time.

Proponents of the EMH recognize that it hinges on a paradox. Beating the market is an impossible dream only because so many smart investors are dumb enough to keep trying. If they recognized the futility of their efforts, they'd cease to work so hard at digging for undiscovered values and evaluating incoming information, and the market's pricing mechanism would then cease to be efficient — prices would no longer reflect what is knowable. *Thus for the Efficient Market Hypothesis to be true, investors and analysts must believe that it isn't true.* That paradox does not, in itself, refute the EMH. But there are compelling reasons for believing that the concept of efficient pricing — though it applies to part of the market much of the time — doesn't apply to all of the market all of the time.

1. For stocks to be efficiently priced, the collective judgment of investors must invariably be rational — an assumption whose absurdity was documented in an earlier chapter, "Fear and Greed." As the

figures cited there show, it is farcical to maintain that stocks were efficiently priced at their 1972–1973 highs, their 1974 lows, and their 1975 recovery levels. Clearly, there are times when the collective judgment of investors goes haywire and the market as a whole becomes spectacularly inefficient.

2. The EMH assumes that all available information about stocks is known and all incoming information is instantly assimilated. This assumption—common sense tells us—can apply only to stocks that have been thoroughly analyzed and are closely followed by analysts and informed investors. Some proponents of the EMH concede that the stocks of small, offbeat companies—ignored by analysts, and lacking a large body of shareholders—may be inefficiently priced; so it may be possible to discover among them issues that are undervalued. But supporters of the EMH generally contend that such companies constitute a tiny and inconsequential subsector of the market. There's convincing evidence to the contrary; the requirements for efficient pricing apply, at most, to one-fifth of the 7,000 companies whose stocks are actively, or fairly actively, traded.

The intensive research done by brokerage firms is focused on fewer than 200 companies with large market capitalizations. Another 300 companies (including public utilities) have been thoroughly analyzed and are closely tracked by brokerage firms. Thus, there are roughly 500 stocks about which nearly all that can be known is probably known; these constitute the hard core of the efficient market (which, as I've pointed out, becomes spectacularly inefficient when investors get carried away by euphoria or panic). An additional 800 companies are covered by two or three analysts and are closely followed by a substantial number of informed stockholders. So it's arguable that their stocks are priced relatively efficiently.

The numbers just cited account for only 1,300 out of 7,000 regularly traded companies. Of the remaining 5,700, 5,000 are not covered by brokerage house research departments and about 700 are followed by not more than one analyst, according to Walter R. Nelson, publisher of the *Directory of Securities Research.* Moreover, the companies ignored by analysts include roughly one-quarter of those on the New York Stock Exchange and half of those on the Amex. Thus, there are about 850 listed and 4,850 unlisted companies whose stocks are not closely followed by analysts. And it's unreasonable to assume that all available information about them is continuously known, evaluated, and efficiently reflected in the prices of their stocks. *These companies constitute an inefficient sector of the market.* Admittedly, their total market value is only a fraction of that of the companies in the efficient sector. But, unlike the institutions, the individual investor doesn't have to invest in companies with large capitalizations. So, for individuals, the inefficient sector of the market is neither tiny nor inconsequential.

3. A third weakness in the Efficient Market Hypothesis has been forcefully exposed by David Dreman on his books *Psychology and the Stock Market* and *The Contrarian Investment Strategy*. Dreman cites a succession of scholarly studies that prove that stocks with low price/earnings ratios have outperformed stocks with high price/earnings ratios over a large variety of time periods dating back to 1937. This shows that unpopular stocks — those on which investors put low valuations — tend to be underpriced. But if all stocks were efficiently priced, unpopular stocks would perform no better (or no worse) than popular stocks. *And there's decisive evidence that unpopular stocks, over the long term, have provided higher returns.*

4. The concept that all stocks are efficiently priced is also refuted by abundant evidence that many investors — individuals, investment counselors and managers of small-to-medium-sized mutual funds — have beaten the market for periods long enough to rule out luck and without taking inordinately high risks. A few examples: Over-The-Counter Securities Fund outperformed the S&P index by a margin of three to one over a 23-year period, stretching from late 1956 to 1980. (The fund is so widely diversified — it owns 350 stocks — that its overall level of risk is not especially high.) A fund run by Hugo Koehler of Train Smith, a top-echelon New York investment counseling firm, increased about tenfold in value between 1964 and 1980 — more than 13 times the increase in the S&P 500. Between 1975 and the spring of 1981, the less risky of two supervised lists of growth stocks recommended by Rauscher Pierce Refsnes, a Dallas brokerage house, achieved an average annual gain of 33.5 percent versus an average annual gain of 13.5 percent for the S&P index; the average annual gain of the riskier list was 61.2 percent. Few investors are likely to come close to matching the kind of performance I've cited, but

achieving appreciably higher returns than the S&P 500 is certainly not an unrealistic objective.

This exposition and critique of the Efficient Market Hypothesis suggests conclusions and precepts that I'll sum up here and now.

• It's reasonable to assume that the stocks of the nation's largest and most exhaustively analyzed companies are probably efficiently priced much, if not most, of the time. *This has reassuring implications for the average investor. If you're contemplating purchase of a stock in the efficient sector of the market* — General Motors, Kodak, ITT, Mobil, Xerox, and the like — *you shouldn't consider yourself at a disadvantage because you know so much less about the stock than the experts do; everything that the experts know is reflected in the stock's current price, and the price that you pay will represent a fair estimate of the stock's value at that particular moment.*

• Be skeptical if your broker advises you to switch from one efficient market stock to a similar one in the same industry — for example, from Exxon to Mobil or vice versa; it is virtually certain that your broker's reasons (other than earning a commission) for recommending the switch are part of the "available information" that's already reflected in the prices of both stocks. It may make sense, however, to switch from one efficient market stock to another in a *different* industry in order to achieve better diversification.

• If you set your sights on outperforming the market, your best chances of succeeding lie in following one or more of the following basic approaches (or variants thereof).

1. The Intrinsic Value Approach: you try to find sharply undervalued stocks in the inefficient sector of the market (which contains large companies as well as small ones).

2. The Emerging Growth Stock Approach: you try to find small high-growth companies that are strongly positioned in growth industries *before* their potential has been widely recognized and their price/earnings ratios are forbiddingly high.

3. The Contrarian Approach: you invest in large, well-known companies whose stocks are out of favor and are therefore selling at conspicuously low price/earnings ratios.

4. *The Market Timing Approach:* you confine your buying and your selling to periods when the market as a whole is inefficiently priced —that is, you buy when you think investors have surrendered to panic and you sell when you think that investors are getting carried away by euphoria. (How to implement these approaches will be fully discussed in later chapters.)

MODERN PORTFOLIO THEORY: A PSEUDOSCIENCE

There's one more academic contribution to investment theory and practice that merits scrutiny; it's an outgrowth of the Efficient Market Hypothesis and it's called Modern Portfolio Theory (MPT). MPT defines risk as volatility — the extent of a stock's price swings (over a selected period of time) in relation to those of a supposedly "representative" market index, Standard & Poor's 500. A stock's volatility, which is calculated by computers, is expressed by name of the Greek letter beta; the S&P index, the benchmark, is assigned a beta of 1. Thus, a stock that has risen or fallen 15 percent whenever the index has risen or fallen 10 percent has a beta of 1.5; this means that its risk is 50 percent greater than the overall risk of the index. A stock that has risen or fallen 7 percent when the index rose 10 percent has a beta of 0.70; it's considered to be 30 percent less risky than the S&P 500.

A stock's beta measures only that portion of its risk which is contingent on the behavior of the market. But stock prices also rise and fall because of company and industry developments. This type of risk, *not reflected in beta,* can be minimized by proper diversification, because price fluctuations caused by factors other than the market's behavior vary from industry to industry and company to company. For example, energy and computer issues will at times perform better and at times worse, in relation to the market, than stocks with the same betas in the food and cosmetics industries. Consequently, an efficiently diversified portfolio of, say, 15 stocks with an average beta of 1.5 is considerably less risky than a single stock with a 1.5 beta.

Constructing an efficient portfolio is what investing is all about, according to Modern Portfolio Theory, which assumes that it's futile to look for undervalued stocks or try to anticipate advances and declines in the market. The portfolio manager's function (the theory holds) is to examine various combinations of stocks (or stocks and other securities) until his computer—which has been programmed with betas and other measures of risk and return—comes up with the most efficient combination. That combination is the one that provides the largest expected return* for the degree of risk the manager is willing to assume.

An extreme form of applied MPT is known as "passive management" or "indexing." The portfolio manager settles for the risk and expected return of Standard & Poor's 500 index, and he builds a portfolio that reflects as accurately as possible the composition of that index without including all 500 of its stocks; the portfolio gives each industry the same "weight" or representation as it has in the S&P 500.

The strategy (or rather, nonstrategy) of indexing was enthusiastically seized upon by a good many large institutions as a remedy for their dismal performance. An indexed portfolio can't quite match the returns of the S&P index because of management costs and other expenses. Nevertheless, institutions managing billions of dollars have a justification for indexing; it doesn't make much sense for them to try to beat the market because, in effect, they *are* the market. On the other hand, individuals can beat the market, and I see no point in their investing in an index fund—a mutual fund whose portfolio is geared to the S&P 500; they will be paying management fees simply to achieve guaranteed mediocrity. They would be far better off in one of the many growth funds that have fairly consistently outperformed the market.

Modern Portfolio Theory represents an attempt by academics to replace qualitative judgments in investing with a supposedly "scientific" approach that consists in playing complicated statistical games with computers. But investing is not a science like physics or mathematics, and the scientific method has limitations when you apply it to a human activity that's concerned with crowd psychology

---

*"Expected return" is a theoretical formulation crucial to MPT and one most laymen will find difficult to grasp. Defined as simply as possible, the expected return of a security is the riskless yield offered by a Treasury Bill (T), *plus* the difference between the rate of return on the S&P index (RSP) and the Treasury Bill yield, *multiplied* by the beta of a given security: expected return = T + (RSP - T) multiplied by beta. Thus if T-Bills are yielding 8 percent, the rate of return on the S&P index is 14 percent and a portfolio's beta is 1.5, its expected return is: 8 percent + (14 percent - 8 percent) x 1.5, which equals 17 percent.

and the uncertainties of the future. After losing a bundle in the notorious South Sea Company, a red-hot stock speculation of 1720, Sir Isaac Newton said, "I can calculate the motions of heavenly bodies, but not the madness of people."

Notwithstanding its shortcomings, Modern Portfolio Theory highlights an important truth that many investors are either not aware of or unwisely disregard — namely, that proper diversification reduces the type of risk that is not contingent on the market's behavior but stems from industry and company developments. Most of the portfolios of individuals are not adequately diversified, according to surveys cited in *The Changing Role of the Individual Investor* (New York: John Wiley & Sons, 1978) by Marshall E. Blume and Irwin Friend, professors at the University of Pennsylvania's Wharton School. Predictably, small investors, excluding those who invest in mutual funds, diversify the least. For example, Blume and Friend found that the typical $13,000 portfolio contained only two stocks. They also found that over a twelve-month period in the early 1970s, 63 percent of the investors who owned one or two stocks suffered losses but only 32 percent of those who owned ten to nineteen issues were losers.

How to achieve good diversification is discussed in a later chapter dealing with portfolio strategy. The good news is that, if you put an equal amount of money into five stocks in different industries exposed to different types of risk, you will eliminate about 80 percent of the diversifiable risk involved in owning one stock.

III

GETTING ADVICE AND INFORMATION

13. How to Pick and Use a Broker

I've been a client of brokers — at last count, nine of them — and a broker myself for roughly equal periods over the past thirty years. My experience has left me with strong but impartial views about the broker-client relationship. As a client, I have often felt that brokers are a miserable breed. As a broker, I have often felt that clients — with a few treasured exceptions — are an exasperating species.

Before going any farther, let me remind you of a prickly truth about the brokerage business: *since brokers don't charge fees, their earnings come solely from commissions, so they earn money only when a client buys or sells.* There's a cynical Wall Street joke about a sale of stock on which the client has lost a bundle: "The broker made money and the firm made money — and two out of three ain't bad."

The brokerage industry's compensation system saddles brokers with a conflict of interest from which the Wall Street Establishment steadfastly averts its eyes. The conflict is flagrantly obvious. Basically, a broker is a salesman; he serves his employers and earns his living by generating commission business. But from a client's standpoint, a broker is supposed to be a professional investment adviser, and as such he shouldn't encourage clients to incur excessive commission expenses.

To play down the image of salesmanship, brokerage firms publicly refer to their brokers as "account executives" or "registered representatives" (because they're registered with the exchanges and/or the National Association of Securities Dealers). But intramurally, brokers are usually called salesmen or "producers." And to prosper or even to stay in business, a producer must produce; he must devote most of his working day to getting and executing orders. On the other hand, to serve his clients well, he should devote a lot of time to activities that don't directly put a nickel into his pocket — for example, studying research material and keeping track of companies that he's recommended to clients. To achieve an ideal balance between his roles as salesman and investment adviser, a broker needs to be a well-organized workaholic, with a vast knowledge of the investment world, a flair for making wise decisions for investors with widely different objectives, and a strong sense of responsibility about the handling of other people's money. Such paragons are extremely rare, but probably no rarer than paragons are among insurance salesmen or real estate agents.

The attention you can reasonably hope to get from a broker — and the attention you can rightfully demand — is obviously related to the commission dollars you put into his pocket. So it's helpful to know precisely what you are paying a brokerage firm for its services and what portion of your commission dollars goes to your broker.

Since May 1, 1975 — when the system of "fixed minimum commissions" was abolished by the SEC — brokerage firms have been free to set their own rates, and investors, if they have sufficient clout, can negotiate discounts from these rates. The standard rates for individual investors in early 1982 were about 20 percent higher than the old, pre–May Day fixed commissions. Rates vary considerably, depending on the firm, the price of the stock, and the size of the order. Many firms have a minimum charge — it's usually anywhere from $25 to $40 — so you may wind up paying a murderous 20 percent commission if you buy, say, 50 shares of a $4 stock. Rates are highest on small orders and they decline as the amount traded grows larger. For example, when this book was written, the commission on a 100-share order of a $12 stock was typically about $36, or 3 percent; the commission on a 1,000-share order of a $35 stock was typically about $455, or 1.3 percent. The overall rate averages roughly 2½ percent,* with two-thirds usually going to the brokerage firm and one-third to the broker. Brokers with a sizable business get a slightly larger cut.

As a rule of thumb, most investors can assume that their broker's take is roughly 90 cents for every $100 worth of stock they buy or sell. So if an investor's annual trading averages $20,000 a year, his broker's annual earnings from his account are about $180. Most investors trade much less than that. A major brokerage house reported that, in 1979, 80 percent of its retail clients — 957,000 individuals — generated on the average $130 each a year in commissions, which implies a trading volume of about $5,200. So typically a small

---

*Commission rates are higher on tax shelters and mutual fund shares that are sold through brokers.

investor is worth about $45 a year to his broker. And, nowadays, $45 buys barely *one hour* of service from professionals in most fields, including acupuncture and hair styling. So it's obvious that very small investors* can't expect a lot of tender loving care from a broker.

There are several ways of coping with this problem. For people of a strongly self-reliant bent, the most satisfactory course is to acquire sufficient investment know-how to make decisions without being overly dependent on a broker's time and guidance. An alternative course — one that's been chosen by many novices who are socially inclined — is to form an investment club or join an existing one. These clubs — of which there are an estimated 20,000 with about 15 members each and an average investment of $3,500 per member — are groups of compatible people who get together to buy securities on a small scale and to learn about investing. They make a modest start-up contribution to a common fund, select a broker, and commit themselves to investing a fixed amount monthly — typically about $25 each — in securities chosen by the club's members at their monthly meetings. Approximately one-quarter of the clubs belong to the National Association of Investment Clubs (1515 East Eleven Mile Rd., Royal Oak, MI 48067), a nonprofit organization whose annual dues are $25 per club plus $4.50 for each club member. For this, members get a 64-page manual on investing, a monthly magazine, a model portfolio containing about 40 stocks selected and followed by a committee of 7 investment professionals; plus other services. Since investment clubs for the most part don't lean on a broker's advice, they can save on commission expenses by using a discount broker. As I pointed out in my Introduction, investment clubs on the average have outperformed the S&P 500. The club members I have met shared the sentiment voiced by Elizabeth Martz of Royal Oak, treasurer of the Investment Club of Michigan: "A club is a place where you can have fun, learn about the market, and make money."

The easiest course for small investors — and for many of them the soundest — is to buy shares in one or more "no-load" mutual funds:

Regardless of how size is defined, the vast majority of this country's 32.3 million stockholders are small or very small investors. According to a 1980 survey made by the New York Stock Exchange, 57 percent of all investors then had stock portfolios worth under $5,000 and another 26 percent had portfolios worth $5,000 to $25,000. Only 17 percent of stockholders owned portfolios worth $25,000 or more.

funds that have no sales charge and are not marketed through brokers. (My only reason for favoring no-load funds is economy. The load funds marketed through brokers typically charge an 8½ percent sales commission.) No-load funds deal directly with investors, who must contact them by writing for a prospectus. Their shares are sold, and can be redeemed at any time, at their current net asset value per share — the market value per share of the fund's portfolio. Annual management fees and expenses, which are taken from income received on the fund's holdings, average less than 1 percent of an investor's share of the fund's total assets. For that modest charge, an investor gets the benefits of diversification and professional manage-ment. Moreover, the fortunes of no-load fund managements are closely linked to the results they achieve for their shareholders. The earnings of these management firms depend on the size of the assets they manage; and since no-loads aren't promoted by brokers, they can increase their assets only by making gains in the market and by gaining new shareholders through superior performance. In sum, even for investors who aren't in the "very small" category, no-load mutual funds, which are more fully discussed in chapter 23, make a great deal of sense.

There are, however, some good reasons for using a broker in preference to mutual funds, provided your capital is not minute. When an investor buys mutual fund shares, he's buying a piece of a large and usually widely diversified portfolio, and there may be many stocks in it that he might reasonably not want to own, assuming that he has strong and informed opinions. With a broker, he can concentrate on the stocks that he likes best; he can move quickly into stocks he thinks will be winners and out of those that seem to have turned sour; and he can use options either to speculate or to hedge (see chapter 25). In addition, some people share my feeling that investing, for all its headaches and hard knocks, is an exhilarating challenge, and letting a fund manager call the shots for you takes away most of the fun.

The more an investor knows about brokers, the better equipped he'll be to use their services intelligently and guard against their shortcomings. So let's take a closer look at the species that numbers about 50,000 men and women.

A composite profile drawn by the New York Stock Exchange depicts the "typical broker" as a 40-year-old college graduate with a degree in business and 10 years' experience in the securities industry. He or she — there are many women brokers — handles more than 300 accounts, but only a small portion of them are active. The average annual earnings of brokers who deal with individual investors were $55,654 in 1980, according to the Securities Industry Association. But a supersuccessful broker makes upward of $200,000. Small to medium-sized investors are likely to be best served by a broker who's earning a good living but not a fortune or a pittance. Big producers usually give most of their attention to their larger clients, and a marginal producer may be so hungry for commissions that he'll try to "churn" (that is, overtrade) his clients' accounts.

Anyone of average intelligence and so-called good character can become a broker in a mere four months, provided he can convince the sales manager of a brokerage firm that he has the makings of a good securities salesman. To qualify as a registered representative, you have to take a four months' training course in a brokerage house and pass a six-hour multiple-choice test, most of which has to do with stock and bond trading procedures and industry regulations. James J. Needham, when he was chairman of the New York Stock Exchange in 1973, made the startling admission that a large percentage of brokers were "not adequately trained or sufficiently knowledgeable" to give investment advice.

Since Mr. Needham's day there has been some improvement in the training of brokers and a substantial improvement in the research available to them. But nowadays registered representatives in the big brokerage houses have a wider range of wares to sell — and therein lies a problem. The giant brokerage firms have transformed themselves into financial supermarkets, whose "products" (in addition to stocks, bonds, and mutual funds) include options, commodities, gold coins, financial futures, tax shelters such as real estate partnerships, deferred annuities, and life insurance. It stands to reason that a broker who handles a broad line of goods is spreading himself thin. "How on earth can you keep up with the stock market when you're selling Krugerrands and partnership units in a shopping center in Albuquerque?" says a brokerage house executive who deplores what he calls "the deprofessionalization of Wall Street." No less worrisome is that broadening of the product line creates fresh conflicts of interest; brokers with underdeveloped scruples tend to promote the types of investment which are the most lucrative to them—for example, options and tax shelters—but which may not be suitable for a particular client.

In spite of the present system's flaws, good brokers do exist, though they are heavily outnumbered by the mediocre and poor ones. To qualify as "good," a broker should be scrupulous, wise in the ways of the market, and truly anxious to do well for his clients. He should also give good service; that would include careful handling of orders, prompt action to correct clerical errors—which are appallingly frequent in the brokerage business—supplying clients with research material, keeping them informed about their stocks, advising them when to sell, and ensuring that checks due to them are mailed without delay.

The obvious first step in looking for a good broker—whether you're doing it for the first time or making a switch—is to ask friends, relations, and business associates whether they have a broker they can confidently recommend. Tax accountants are a good source of referrals; they see how their clients are doing in the market and sometimes know the names of their brokers. And here's a tip worth heeding: a broker who's strongly endorsed by a doctor or dentist is probably a winner, because medical men are often avid players of the market.

You shouldn't fail to interview the recommended broker or brokers. A good broker will start out by asking you for a full picture of your financial situation and investment objectives; the "Know-Your-Customer" rule requires him to obtain this information. You, in turn, should try to find out as much as you can about his professional credentials, modus operandi, and approaches to investing. Questions you might ask include the following: How long has he been in the brokerage business? Does he have a large and varied list of clients or does he concentrate on a limited number of substantial investors? Does he deal mainly in stocks, options, and bonds or is he also heavily involved in commodities and other investments? Does he rely mainly on the recommendations of his firm's research department or does he do much stock-picking on his own—and if so, what are his sources? Does he consider himself conservative or aggressive and what are the investment strategies he favors?

His answers should tell you whether he's the right sort of broker for an investor in your particular situation. For example, even if he accepts small accounts, a high-powered broker with a stable of wealthy clients might not be the best choice for a small investor; a broker who does his own research could be valuable to investors with the analytic know-how to check out his suggestions, but a novice would probably be better served by a broker who follows his firm's recommendations, which are made by trained analysts who devote all of their time to research and keep in close touch with the companies assigned to them. Whatever your situation, try to get a broker with experience, preferably one who's been through a few market debacles; a neophyte may give you more attention, but he'll be learning his lessons with his clients' money, including yours.

Asking a broker about his track record is as silly as asking a maître d' whether the plat du jour is good. The broker will either tell you he's a winner or he'll take the modest tack: "We do OK." You can't expect him to give himself a failing grade. Most brokers, however, will supply references, and it's worth giving them a call.

If, for some reason, you aren't able to find a broker through referral, just walk into a brokerage house and ask to see the person who handles prospective clients; it may be the branch manager or the so-called broker of the day. You can get the names of firms in your area from the Yellow Pages, under "Stock & Bond Brokers." Or you can write to the Public Information Office of the New York Stock Exchange (11 Wall St., New York, NY 10005) for its free pamphlet, *Investors Service Bureau Directory*, which lists more than 300 NYSE member firms that deal with individual investors. As a walk-in prospect, you will probably be assigned one of the firm's younger or less solidly entrenched brokers. If the interview leaves you with serious misgivings, ask if it's possible to see a different broker, or try a different firm.

Investors like to gripe about their brokers, but they seldom take the trouble to run a precise check on their performance, a chore that's worth doing once a year. Investment performance can be judged only in relation to the overall behavior of the market and the degree of risk an investor has chosen to take. Investors who are taking average risks should compare the performance of their portfolios to that of Standard & Poor's 500-stock index, preferably over a period of 12 months or longer. A broker whose recommendations match the performance of that index (taking into account commission expenses) is doing an acceptable job; a broker who keeps on beating the index should be considered outstanding. But if your broker, assuming that you hew to his advice, underperforms the S&P 500 consistently and by an appreciable margin, start looking for a replacement.

However badly a broker performs, he can't be held accountable for a client's losses, unless the client can show that he's been victimized by professional misconduct.* Such misconduct typically involves "churning" (overtrading an account) or ignoring "suitability" — that is, recommending investments that are too hazardous in light of a client's personal and financial circumstances. When such misconduct is flagrant, a client stands a good chance of obtaining at least partial restitution of his losses — provided he hasn't explicitly or implicitly approved the broker's course of action. His case will be shaky if his account shows a history of excessive trading and high-risk speculation and he failed to holler until he was badly burned. So act promptly if you think your broker is churning or otherwise mishandling your account.

If you have a complaint that you can't settle with your broker, your first move should be to write to the chief executive of his firm. If that doesn't work, you can turn to the New York Stock Exchange's Investor/Broker Liaison Section (45 Water St., New York, NY 10041), which handles more than a thousand complaints a year. And if the Liaison Section fails to get results, you may ask it to refer your complaint to the Exchange's arbitration department, whose decision you must agree to accept as binding. Your alternative is to sue the broker and his firm. But arbitration costs little and you'll probably get a verdict faster than by going to court.

A MINI-GUIDE TO BROKERAGE FIRMS

When they are looking for a broker, most investors are more concerned about the qualities of the individual who'll handle their

---

*When an investor has been accidentally penalized by a broker's goof such as failure to execute an order, any decent broker will make good on his mistake, provided it's brought to his attention promptly. If, for example, he has forgotten to enter a sell order and the stock's price has declined, he'll make the sale in his firm's "error account" and credit you with the price at which the stock was trading when you placed your order.

account than about the firm he works for, so long as its financial condition is sound. However, there are several different types of brokerage houses, and it's well worth considering which might suit you best. Here's a rundown of the main types that are hospitable to individual investors.

THE WIREHOUSES

The best-known brokerage firms are the giant "wirehouses" with networks of branch offices throughout the country. The largest are Merrill Lynch, Shearson/American Express, Dean Witter Reynolds (now owned by Sears Roebuck), Paine Webber, E. F. Hutton, Bache Halsey Stuart Shields (now owned by Prudential Insurance), Thomson McKinnon Securities, and Smith Barney Harris Upham.

The big wirehouses are financial supermarkets that offer a full range of investment services. They have large research departments that follow anywhere from 300 to (in the case of Merrill Lynch) more than 1,100 companies, and some of them are ranked in the top bracket for research by institutional money managers, according to the annual surveys made by *Financial World.* In a recent survey, 6 of the big national brokerage houses were among the 15 firms rated the best for research; they were (in the following order) Merrill Lynch, Smith Barney, Paine Webber, Dean Witter, Shearson/American Express, and E. F. Hutton.

The wirehouses are hospitable to small investors because economics of scale permit them to turn a modest profit on accounts too small for many firms to handle on a break-even basis. Several of the national giants have special plans that enable small investors to buy and sell, subject to certain conditions, at discounts from the regular commission rates. And some — Merrill Lynch, Bache, and Paine Webber, for example — have modestly priced programs, whose management fees are tax-deductible, tailored for small investors who need investment information and guidance.

THE REGIONALS

The major regional houses offer a narrower range of investment services than the nationals, and they follow far fewer companies. But their knowledge of local industry is a valuable asset. It enables them to spot emerging growth companies whose stocks are still cheap because they haven't yet been touted on Wall Street. In addition, the regionals, since they concentrate on a limited number of companies, are able to keep especially close tabs on the stocks they recommend. The regional firms whose research I've followed closely and consider excellent are Rauscher Pierce Refsnes in Dallas, Prescott Ball & Turben in Cleveland, and Interstate Securities in Charlotte, N.C. Among the other regionals with a reputation for high-grade research are Robinson-Humphrey in Atlanta, Rotan Mosle in Houston, Wheat First Securities in Richmond, Va., Boettcher & Co. in Denver, Robert W. Baird Co. in Milwaukee, Crowell Weedon and Bateman Eichler Hill Richards in Los Angeles, and Piper Jaffray in Minneapolis.

THE "CARRIAGE TRADE" HOUSES

A third type of brokerage firm is the New York City "carriage trade" house that caters mainly to investors with six-figure portfolios (though accounts smaller than that are generally accepted). The carriage trade houses maintain low profiles and high standards of service and professionalism. This league includes Morgan Stanley, Neuberger & Berman, L. F. Rothschild Unterberg Towbin, and Wertheim.

THE SMALL FRY

A fourth category is made up of a multitude of smallish to very small firms, most of which welcome small investors. Their drawbacks are lack of expertise in many investment areas and minimal budgets for research — weaknesses that put them at a disadvantage in competing with stronger firms to obtain the better brokers. The attraction of small firms — a big one to some investors — is personalized service. In the brokerage business, small firms are analogous to the small-town general practitioner or family doctor in the field of medicine.

THE DISCOUNTERS

The fifth category of brokerage firm is the discount house, which came into being when fixed minimum commissions were abolished in 1975. There are now more than 100 discounters with offices all over the country, and their share of the business done by individual investors — it was 8 percent in 1981 — is steadily growing. The discounts they offer on the standard rates charged by regular brokers range from 35 percent to 75 percent, depending on the size of the order and the volume of trading done by the client. (It doesn't pay to use discounters for orders involving less than about $800, because they generally have a minimum charge of $25 to $35.) The discounters don't provide research or investment advice; they simply execute orders, using salaried registered representatives who don't receive commissions. Most of the discounters now offer custodial services — that is, they'll keep your securities and collect dividends or interest, generally at no charge.

The discounters make a lot of sense for investors well equipped to do their own research and make their own decisions. The nation's largest discounter is Charles Schwab & Co., a boldly innovative firm with headquarters in San Francisco; early in 1982, its expanding network of more than 35 offices included branches in Manhattan, Chicago, Los Angeles, and Washington D.C. The conveniences that Schwab offers its clients include exceptionally long business hours — 8:30 A.M. to midnight, eastern time; price quotations 24 hours a day, 7 days a week via a toll-free number; and *automatic* investment of idle cash in brokerage accounts in a money-market fund. At this writing, Schwab is the only discount broker that provides a special service similar to the Cash Management Account introduced by Merrill Lynch and now available from some other wirehouses. Investors who deposit cash or securities or both in a Schwab No. 1 Account can withdraw cash or borrow against their securities by using a Visa card or writing checks, and any cash in the account earns interest at money-market rates. The minimum initial investment is only $1,000, whereas the handful of regular brokers offering similar accounts require $5,000 to $25,000.

Among the other major discount brokers, several of whom have branch offices in different parts of the country, are the following firms (with their home base in parentheses): Quick & Reilly, Andrew Peck and Muriel Siebert (New York City), Rose & Co. (Chicago), Kahn & Co. (Memphis), and Stock Cross and Fidelity Brokerage Services (Boston), an affiliate of the company that manages the Fidelity group of mutual funds. (The toll-free numbers of these firms can be obtained from directory assistance, 800-555-1212.)

The clients of all brokerage firms, including the discounters, are insured against loss resulting from a firm's bankruptcy by the

Securities Investor Protection Corporation; the SIPC is a nonprofit organization created by Congress in 1970, funded by the brokerage industry, and backed by borrowing power of $1 billion from the U.S. Treasury. The maximum amount covered by the SIPC is $500,000, but some firms have taken out added insurance on their own. Thus, nowadays, investors can entrust their securities to the custody of a brokerage house without fear of being wiped out if it founders. Nonetheless, they should check carefully into the firm's reputation and financial condition. When the Manhattan brokerage house of John Muir — an aggressive underwriter of small, highly speculative companies — foundered in 1981, some of its clients suffered losses they couldn't recover through insurance because their accounts were "frozen" until they could be transferred to another firm. These clients were not able to sell stocks that they thought would decline — and which in fact did decline, at least temporarily. But assuming that the brokerage firm you deal with is thoroughly sound, there are considerable advantages in keeping your securities in a custodian account, especially if you are an active investor. You don't have to receive or send stock certificates through the mail whenever you buy or sell, and your monthly statement shows the market value of your portfolio and provides you with a documented record (for your tax return) of all the income you receive. Moreover, a custodian account with a brokerage firm that has its own money-market fund (or an arrangement with an outside one) enables you, if you so wish, to have your dividends, interest, and cash from the sale of securities automatically invested in the money fund — a service that's of value to many investors and for which there's no charge.

14. Information, Please

Information is the raw material out of which investment decisions are shaped, and the individual investor usually gets too little of it. (The problem of "information overload" that I referred to in a previous chapter mainly afflicts institutional investors.) Two kinds of information are indispensable — background information that provides you with a frame of reference for your investment decisions, and up-to-date information about the general economy, the major industries, and individual companies. Much of the background information that you are likely to need is provided in this book. How much current information you require—and how much you should spend on it—depend of course on your financial situation, your investment objectives, and the extent to which you wish to be your own investment manager. An aggressive do-it-yourself investor who's hunting for neglected, undervalued stocks obviously needs more sources of information than a conservative investor whose goal is high income. Keep in mind that unfocused, intermittent perusal of a welter of investment publications is more likely to create confusion than to bring enlightenment. Your information-gathering should be concentrated on sources closely related to your individual requirements.

A great deal of investment information is available free of charge —far more than most people realize. It includes brokerage-house research, company annual reports, and economic and financial publications issued by some of the leading banks. I'll first discuss how to make the most of this material, then I'll review selected sources of information and advice that you have to pay for—but fortunately with tax-deductible dollars. Subscriptions to financial publications and investment advisory services are a tax-deductible business expense, provided your tax return shows that you have investments.

RESEARCH FROM THE BROKERAGE FIRMS

Getting research material should be no problem for investors who do business regularly with a broker. A broker who gives good service will be pleased to send you reports on the types of investment in which you are particularly interested, and he can usually get his firm to put you on a mailing list for some of its "retail" research. ("Retail," in Wall Street terminology, refers to business with individual investors as opposed to institutions. Some retail reports are digests of much longer reports prepared for institutions; others—often reports on companies not large enough to be of interest to major institutions —are conceived and written primarily for a firm's individual clients.) Whether you have a regular broker or not, you can get research material simply by walking into the nearest office of any major brokerage house. You'll generally see a table or display rack on which recent reports and other pamphlets are stacked, and they're yours for the taking.

Another way to get brokerage-house research is by writing in for the free reports advertised from time to time in big city newspapers or the *Wall Street Journal*. The purpose of these ads is to furnish leads to potential customers, so be prepared for a follow-up call from one of the firm's brokers, soliciting your business. However reputable the firm may be, it's generally unwise to do business with a broker who calls you up cold. If the caller touts a specific investment without inquiring fully into your financial situation, you can turn him off pronto: ask him to repeat his name, then tell him he's violating rule 405 of the New York Stock Exchange, the so-called Know-Your-Customer rule.

Some people mistakenly dismiss brokerage-house research as simply a sales tool of the brokerage industry. It certainly is a sales tool — in Wall Street, research reports are sometimes referred to, intramurally, as "merchandise" — but it is not *simply* a sales tool. It is also a fruitful source of factual information and professional insights, and as such it can be valuable to investors who know how to use it intelligently. Remember, too, that the effectiveness of research as a business-getter is generally related in the long run to its quality. That's why major firms spend several million dollars apiece on their research departments and are willing to pay outstanding analysts anywhere from $80,000 to more than $150,000 a year.

Over the past twenty years, I have read several thousand research reports, and currently I read or scan a couple of dozen a week. Many analysts appear to be incapable of expressing themselves in straightforward, grammatical English. But the quality of Wall Street research is better than it was, say, fifteen years ago. There are several reasons for this: (1) Sobriety in stock valuation — a rarity in the exuberant climate of the 1960s — came back into style in the 1970s. (2) The training of analysts has been upgraded by the Chartered Financial Analysts program of the Financial Analysts Federation; to earn a C.F.A. diploma an analyst has to pass a rigorous examination requiring at least three years of part-time study. (3) Because of greatly increased corporate disclosure, analysts now have official company figures to work with in certain areas where they previously relied on educated but often inaccurate guesstimates.

Brokerage houses put out two kinds of report that focus on individual stocks — technical and fundamental. Technical reports, which usually contain charts, pick stocks whose chart "formations" (patterns of price behavior) suggest that they are in an uptrend or about to enter one. When a technical analyst rates a stock a "buy," he usually suggests a "target" price at which traders should cash in their profits, and he also gives an exact "stop loss" price; this is a price at which the stock, if it declines, should automatically be sold in order to limit losses. The fundamental reports concern themselves with a company's sales, earnings, profitability, financial condition, and other such basics. A fundamental analyst makes his recommendations primarily from a long term standpoint; he's usually looking ahead anywhere from nine months to a couple of years or longer.

The most common complaint of investors about brokerage-house research — they're referring to fundamental research — is that it keeps on telling you what to buy but seldom tells you when to sell. The gripe is valid, but there's one good reason why outright sell recommendations aren't made more often in fundamental reports. An analyst who removes his buy rating from a stock — either because it's risen in price or its immediate prospects look less promising — may still think that in the long run it will go higher and therefore shouldn't be sold by long-term investors; so he puts the stock on "hold." Other reasons why analysts are somewhat reluctant to make blunt sell recommendations: they may be leery of ruffling their relationships with corporate managements, on whom they're vitally dependent for information; and they know that a "sell" opinion is more dangerous than a "hold" or even a "buy." If a recommended stock drops, an analyst can always argue that it will recover, so the price drop has made it an even better buy — and time may eventually prove him right. But investors — and sometimes the analyst's employers — are apt to be unforgiving when a stock whose sale he urged at 20 has climbed briskly to 30.

Brokerage-house reports employ a variety of phrases that enable them to express negative opinions while sidestepping the naked four-letter word *sell*. Here are some examples, quoted in the unretouched jargon of Wall Street: "We would not expect the stock to be a better than average performer over the intermediate term." "We feel the stock lacks appeal at this time." "We would avoid the stock until

the current uncertainties have been resolved." When you read comments such as these about a stock you own, you have only yourself to
blame if you don't sell and it performs badly.

How good—or bad—are brokerage-house recommendations?
Several academic studies have concluded that their overall performance (not taking into account an investor's commission expenses) is
roughly the same as that of the overall market. This finding was
predictable, because the brokerage houses collectively recommend so
many stocks that they are, in effect, recommending "the market."
However, some firms have better research than others or are especially strong in certain areas. In chapter 13, I named six national and
eleven regional firms which have a good reputation for research. A
dozen firms at most—not counting those that cater only to institutions or very rich investors—might be added to that list; among
them are Drexel Burnham Lambert, Kidder Peabody, Oppenheimer &
Co., and L. F. Rothschild Unterberg Towbin.

HOW TO READ A RESEARCH REPORT

A report may have been issued anywhere from a few days to several
weeks before you get your hands on it. So start out by comparing the
price at which the stock was recommended with its current market
price; then look at its price range for the past twelve months, which
should be in the front or back of the report. (If it isn't, you can find it
in the stock tables in your daily newspaper.) If the price has risen
appreciably since the report was issued, remember that every point
gained has lessened your profit potential and has made your possible
loss larger. And if the stock has had a large runup over the previous
twelve months, you can assume that its merits have been widely
recognized and it's no longer cheap. Buying stocks that are already
big winners can work well for a quick-footed trader when the
market's off and running, but it's not a prudent policy for long term
investors.

Assuming that the stock's price is not out of sight, your next step is
to determine how good is the report's claim to credibility. That
doesn't require expertise; it simply calls for careful scrutiny and
common sense. A report is not to be trusted if its flavor is more
promotional than analytic. To test its credibility, just ask yourself the
following questions: Has the analyst taken a searching look at the

company's problems? Do you feel that he has made a thoughtful assessment of how and when management expects to overcome them? Has he pointed out the unfavorable factors in the company's outlook and uncertainties that are *potentially* unfavorable? Has he built his earnings estimate by making specific estimates of how much each segment of the company's business will contribute? Has he clearly stated the assumptions — about the economy, the success of new products, raw material prices, and other matters — on which his estimates are founded? In short, has he presented a tightly reasoned and well-documented case for his optimism about the company and his belief that its stock is undervalued? If all of your answers are "yes," it's highly probable that the analyst has done his homework and that his opinions have been conscientiously arrived at.

It doesn't follow, of course, that his recommendation will prove to be a good one; opinions conscientiously arrived at can be flawed by errors of judgment or invalidated by unforeseeable events. Nor does it follow that the stock meshes closely with your investment policy; it could be either too tame or too risky. So it's advisable to do some further checking. You should be able to handle this on your own after reading the coming chapters on stock valuation and investment strategy. And with a credible and well-documented report in hand, it takes far less time and effort to determine whether a stock's worth buying than if you're analyzing it from scratch.

There's one simple check you shouldn't fail to make if your strategy is to avoid overanalyzed companies: find out what percentage of the total number of its shares outstanding is held by institutions. The figures are given in Standard & Poor's (monthly) *Stock Guide*, and your broker can look them up for you in less than a minute. If institutional holdings amount to more than 20 percent of the shares outstanding, you can assume that the stock is widely followed by analysts. An overanalyzed issue such as IBM may be a sound long-term investment, but the chances that it's undervalued in relation to other stocks are exceedingly slim.

THE (NOT SO) HIDDEN ASSETS OF ANNUAL REPORTS

You can usually obtain a company's annual report free of charge by writing to its Corporate Secretary. (The addresses of major corporations can be found in directories available in libraries.) Most annual reports are based on results for the calendar year and on the company's financial condition at the close of business on December 31. But fiscal years (reporting periods) ending at the close of other months are quite common. The time lag between the end of a company's fiscal year and the publication of its annual report is typically about twelve weeks.

As a starting point for this chapter, I asked professionals involved in the preparation and analysis of annual reports — corporate executives, security analysts, and consultants who advise companies on their relations with investors — how useful these reports can be to the layman. Here's the gist of what they said.

• The conventional wisdom that annual reports are "puffs" for management and say little that's worth knowing is largely out of date. To be sure, the annual (as it's commonly referred to on Wall Street) is a biased document; it's designed to convey the company's story as favorably as the realities permit. But nowadays most chief executives, especially those of large companies, are leery of excessive sugar-coating that could cost them their credibility with investors; distrust is damaging to a company's stock. Moreover, increased disclosure requirements mandated by the SEC have made annual reports far more revealing. Second to meetings with management, the annual is considered by security analysts to be their best source of company information — better and more comprehensive than the company's 10K, a report containing the financial data that corporations are required by law to file with the SEC.

• Most investors don't learn a fraction of what they could from annual reports. A layman with a feel for figures can wrest a lot of valuable information and useful insights from an annual, if he makes some effort to acquire the know-how.

• The annual report, by itself, is not a sufficient basis for making investment decisions; further research is necessary.

Investors typically spend five to ten minutes reading a report, according to Richard A. Lewis, president of Corporate Annual Reports, a New York investor relations firm; that isn't nearly long enough to find out what a report is really saying. Many lay investors skimp on their reading of annual reports because they find them hard to understand. Annuals have been made longer and more complicated by the SEC's widened disclosure requirements plus a slew of rulings by the Financial Accounting Standards Board (FASB), a professional body that sets accounting standards.

The SEC now requires companies to publish, among other things, a breakdown of sales and earnings by type of business, a five-year statistical summary of operations, a "discussion and analysis" by management of the company's operations in the year just ended and the year before that, and quarterly dividends paid and quarterly highs and lows for the stock price over the past two years. In addition, rulings by the FASB have made the "Notes to Financial Statements" very much longer and more complex. These footnotes now disclose long-term lease commitments, properly considered a form of long-term debt, because they are obligations to make payments in the future. Pension obligations, too, must be revealed and investors shouldn't ignore them; if sufficient funds to meet future claims have not been set aside, the unfunded obligations could be a potential burden on future profits. About a thousand of the nation's largest corporations are also required to show the effects of inflation on their assets and income, using two different methods. The "Constant Dollar" method adjusts financial data for "general inflation," which is measured by changes in the Consumer Price Index, with 1967 as the base year. The more complicated "current cost" method adjusts financial data on the basis of the estimated costs of replacing plant, inventory and equipment at current prices. An example: In the 1979 annual of H. J. Wilson Co., a catalogue showroom merchandiser, reported earnings per share were $2.17; they came to $1.85, adjusted for general inflation, and to $2.04 under the "current cost" method.

All of the new disclosures are potentially valuable to discerning investors, but some of them — in particular, the adjustments for inflation — can be infernally confusing. The problem is that the nitty-gritty of annual reports is composed by accountants, lawyers, and financial executives, a troika with an inbred hostility to clarity. This chapter, used in conjunction with Appendix D, starting on page 281, should help you to cope. And help is on its way from the companies themselves; a growing number of large corporations are working hard at making their annual reports more intelligible and more readable. And some have put them on cassettes and may get around to putting them on video cassettes. I doubt that annual reports will make "socko" viewing material, but some people may prefer to do their investment homework by staring at the small screen instead of struggling with the fine print.

The annual report is a company's single most important communication to the public. To get the maximum mileage out of their reports, corporations include material that serves a variety of purposes — giving the company a more recognizable identity, building its image as a socially conscious concern, pitching its major products, throwing bouquets to its employees, or advocating political and economic ideas. Two examples: McCormick & Co., a specialty-food company, proclaimed its identity to the reader's nose by impregnating its 1978 annual with vanilla. And in one of its annual reports, MacMillan Bloedel, a Canadian forest products concern, listed the names of 19,000 of its 24,000 employees.

There's a Wall Street saying that amateurs read annual reports from front to back and professionals read them from back to front, beginning with the footnotes. Like most smart-aleck generalizations, this one shouldn't be taken as gospel. A sensible approach for a layman is to let his most pressing concerns as a stockholder or prospective investor determine the sequence in which he studies the report.

For example, financial condition should probably be the primary concern in the case of a young company whose growth could be aborted by a shortage of funds, or of a large company that's wobbling under a huge burden of debt. But with a mature, gilt-edged company such as IBM or Merck, the crucial concern would be its prospects of sustaining its rate of growth. The rest of this chapter takes a closer look at the most important sections of an annual report, focusing on what they can tell you about the four primary concerns of investors: a company's finances, performance, prospects, and management.

MANAGEMENT'S MESSAGE TO THE STOCKHOLDERS

Often called the chairman's or president's "letter," this opening section is where current problems and major developments are most likely to be discussed. It's usually easy to tell when management is being candid and when it's dishing out blah. Eastman Kodak was visibly pouring molasses on a sour story when it said, "The spirit and skill with which Kodak people went about their work was, without question, the highlight of 1977." The real highlight was that earnings per share were below their 1973 level for the fourth consecutive year, a distressing performance for a company long noted for its growth.

A good example of the kind of candor that generates confidence is the comment made by the president of the L. S. Starrett Company, a leading industrial tool producer, in its 1979 report: "On a per-share basis, fiscal 1979 earnings amounted to $5.65. Now, so as not to kid anybody, I want to point out that . . . about $0.09 was due to the fact that there were some fewer outstanding shares, and $0.39 was due to a reduction of Scotland's income tax."

The "message" is also the place where you'll find management's comments on the company's prospects and, occasionally, a specific earnings forecast. For example, chairman Charles F. Luce predicted in Con Edison's 1977 annual report that earnings in 1978 would be below the 1977 level; as it turned out, they were $4.29 per share as against $4.53 in 1977. By studying the messages in a company's three most recent annual reports, beginning with the earliest, you can get a good fix on management's credibility and prescience.

INCOME STATEMENT

Also called the "profit and loss" (P & L) statement, this table sums up the company's performance — what it took in, what it paid out, and the crucial bottom line. Two sets of figures — for the year just ended and the year before — tabulate sales and other income, costs and other expenses including interest charges and depreciation* (a book-keeping charge that doesn't involve any outlay of cash), "extraordinary" gains or losses (such as those resulting from sales of property), income taxes, net income after taxes, and earnings per share.

You will sometimes find two different figures for earnings per share — "primary" and "fully diluted." Dilution occurs when convertible issues (bonds and/or preferred stock) are converted into common stock and when stock options and/or warrants† are exercised; this increases the total number of shares outstanding, thereby reducing the earnings per share. Fully diluted earnings are based on

---

*Depreciation is generally not itemized on the income statement. You can find the exact figure in a section of the annual report entitled "Consolidated statements of changes in financial position."

†See glossary for definition of all these terms.

the number of shares that would be outstanding if all convertible issues were to be converted and all options and warrants exercised. Since dilution could have an adverse effect on earnings per share in the future, it should be taken into account when you're considering a stock's price/earnings ratio. A $30 stock that has a P/E ratio of 5 based on primary earnings of $6 per share may not be as modestly valued as you think, if its fully diluted earnings are only $4 per share.

An analysis of the income statement is now provided in a mandatory section usually headed "Management's analysis and discussion." The SEC requires it to be strictly factual, and it's generally terse to a fault — but it does state reasons for the increases and decreases in items on the income statement. It also records significant developments such as major borrowings or repayments of debt.

FIVE-YEAR SUMMARY OF OPERATIONS

"The summary," as it's called, offers much of the same data as the income statement, but five years is a sounder basis than two for judging how a company is doing. First, look at the earnings record; in addition to showing past performance, it can provide important clues to the company's prospects. It could indicate that growth is accelerating or slowing down or that a troubled company is making a comeback. It can also tell you something about the capabilities of management, provided you take into account conditions in the industry or industries in which the company is operating. For example, the dismal record of Chrysler from 1974 through 1978 was a strong warning that the company had serious management problems. (In 1979, the directors brought in a new chief executive, Lee A. Iacocca. But by that time the automobile industry was sinking into a protracted slump.)

You should now check two basic measures of profitability. One is the *net profit margin* — the percentage of profit, after taxes, per dollar of sales. This figure is sometimes given in the summary; if not, it's easily computed with the help of a pocket calculator; divide net income (excluding "extraordinary" gains or losses) by total revenues. The five-year pattern of the profit margin is a vital indicator of the health of a business. A slippage in the margin, which can occur even when earnings are rising, could mean that management is doing a poor job of controlling costs, or is unable to raise prices sufficiently to cover rising costs, or is encountering other difficulties. An improvement in profit margins is generally something to cheer about. However, if a company's margin is already high for its type of business, a boom in profitability may flash a cautionary signal that the profit margin has reached a peak because of abnormally favorable conditions. In such cases the price of the stock, too, is likely to be close to a peak, and it might be wise for holders to cash in their gains.

The second basic measure of profitability is *return on stockholders' equity*, often referred to as ROE. The equity or ownership interest of stockholders in a company is their original investment in it plus all earnings not paid out in dividends but reinvested in the business. Stockholders' equity appears on the balance sheet as a *liability* because it represents a claim on the corporation by the stockholders. You will find it shown as the sum of three itemized figures: (1) the "par" value of the outstanding stock, par being an arbitrary figure (often $1 per share) that bears no relation to the asset value of a share; (2) "paid-in capital" — the difference between par value and the capital actually received by the company from the sale of its stock; (3) retained (reinvested) earnings.

The return on stockholders' equity is often given in annual reports; if it's not, you can compute it by dividing net income by stockholders' equity. ROE is a measure of how well management has performed for the stockholders. Some outstandingly successful stock-pickers have made it a rule only to invest in companies with a high return — 20 percent or more — on stockholders' equity. A high ROE generally indicates that the company is strongly positioned in areas of growth. Moreover, companies with a high ROE are better able to finance future growth out of their own profits than those with a low ROE; consequently, they are less dependent on borrowing.

BREAKDOWN OF SALES AND EARNINGS

These figures also cover a five-year period and they show what each major "segment" or division of the company has contributed. The breakdown tells you at a glance which are the strongest parts of a company's business and which, if any, are lagging or actually showing losses. A detailed discussion of each division's performance over the past year is found in the main text of annual reports.

BALANCE SHEET

The balance sheet is a photograph of a company's financial position at an instant in time, the close of its fiscal year. The relationship between different parts of the balance sheet provide indications of the company's financial strength, which in turn can furnish clues to future performance. The stronger a company's financial condition, the greater is its ability to finance aggressive marketing strategies, develop new products, embark on expansion programs, or make acquisitions.

The two balance-sheet relationships that you shouldn't fail to check on are the current ratio and the size of debt in relation to the total capitalization (stockholders' equity plus debt). The first is the ratio of current assets (cash, marketable securities, receivables, and inventory) to current liabilities (all items payable within a year); it's a measure of a company's ability over the coming twelve months to meet its obligations and still have ample resources to run its business effectively. These resources — current assets minus current liabilities — are known as "working capital." There's no single "correct" current ratio; 2 to 1 is widely considered a desirable minimum, but the figure varies from industry to industry.

The size of a company's debt in relation to its total capitalization has an important bearing on its ability to raise credit. In the case of a typical industrial company, there could be cause for concern if debt amounts to appreciably more than 40 percent of the total capitalization.

Two other balance-sheet items that deserve attention are *goodwill* and *book value*. The former is the cash value assigned to intangibles such as patents and franchises. Goodwill can also refer to the cost, over and above their tangible assets, of companies acquired before November 1, 1970. For acquisitions made after that date, the FASB has ruled that any excess of cost over tangible assets must be amortized over not more than forty years. If the figure for goodwill is large, it's a blemish on the balance sheet.

Book value is total assets minus total liabilities (including the redemption value of preferred stock) divided by the number of shares outstanding. Theoretically, book value represents the value of a share of common stock if the company were to be liquidated. But in the real world assets are valued largely on the basis of what they earn.

Historically, the stocks of flourishing companies have usually sold at prices substantially above their book values. When a stock's market price is significantly below its book value — as, for example, in the case of U.S. Steel, which in March 1981 had a book value of about $60 and was selling at 30 — it's usually an indication that a company's assets are obsolescent, or that they're being poorly managed, or both. Assuming that the low price of a stock is due to poor management and not to obsolescent assets, the company could become a takeover candidate; it may look bargain-priced to other managements who think they could run it more profitably.

AUDITOR'S OPINION

These few paragraphs signed by an accounting firm usually state that the financial data in the annual report "fairly" represent the company's financial condition, "in conformity with generally accepted accounting principles, applied on a consistent basis." Sometimes, however, the OK is a "qualified" one. It may be "subject to" the outcome of a major uncertainty such as the verdict in a lawsuit, or the auditor may express reservations about some of the financial data. A survey by Corporate Annual Reports Inc. of 1,226 annuals issued by large corporations revealed that 12 percent of the auditors' opinions were qualified ones.

NOTES TO FINANCIAL STATEMENTS

It's worth struggling to try to decipher these notorious footnotes; the information they contain about a company's accounting practices and other matters enables you to judge the "quality" of reported earnings — a crucial issue that laymen all too often ignore. A stock that seems to be a bargain on the basis of its low price/earnings ratio may no longer look cheap when you take into account the poor quality of its reported earnings. As a rule, the quality of earnings is good if a company charges to current expenses all research and development costs that it's allowed to (by accounting rules) and depreciates assets as rapidly as possible; *such conservative accounting tends to understate earnings. Reported earnings are of poor quality — that is, overstated — if a company depreciates assets relatively slowly and treats research and development costs as capital investments, which are amortized over a period of years.* Reported earnings of $3 a share based on conservative accounting practices could be inflated to $4 a share or more by permissive accounting. And in many cases reported earnings based on permissive accounting have been found to be nonexistent when recomputed on the basis of stringent accounting standards.

The quality of earnings is also affected by the method a company uses to price its inventory; this is disclosed in a footnote and is easily understood by a layman. The traditional method, FIFO (first in, first out), assumes that goods are sold in the order in which they entered the inventory. In a period of rising prices, the earliest items in the inventory are the lowest in cost; consequently the FIFO method results in profits that are exaggerated by inflation, because the lowest-cost goods have to be replaced at the current higher prices. Moreover, these exaggerated profits are subject to income taxes. Thus, many companies have wisely switched to the LIFO (last in, first out) method, which assumes that each item sold was the last to enter the inventory. This reduces inventory profits stemming from inflation and saves the company money on taxes.

With the disclosures now made in annual reports an astute layman has a fair chance of spotting serious trouble. The most revealing figure, many analysts think, is *return on total investment* — that is, net income divided by stockholders' equity *and* long-term liabilities. *If you find that over several years a company's total assets are producing shrinking returns, it's probably high time to sell the stock.*

Studying annual reports is vital for do-it-yourself investors. But it's hardly less valuable to those who lean on a broker's advice. Investors who have learned enough about a company to focus on the crucial questions can make the most of the services that a broker and the analysts behind him can provide.

THE INVESTMENT ADVISORY SERVICES: AN INSIDE GUIDE TO MARKET GUIDES

Through direct mail and eye-catching ads in the financial pages, investment advisory services claim they'll guide you along the path to profit — in stocks and options, commodities and precious metals, in down markets as well as up markets. Some make extravagant claims that blatantly appeal to gullibility and greed. Others, more plausibly, invite you to benefit from their extensive research and expertise. Subscriptions range from $40 to more than $500 a year, tax-deductible; typically they were $65 to $175 in late 1981.

According to George Wein, president of Select Information Exchange, which publishes a catalogue of the services, there must be as many as 1,000 of them. Wein's best guess is that they have a total of about 500,000 subscribers; the larger ones each have more than 30,000, while many have fewer than 100.

The services cover nearly every conceivable approach to investing. More than half of them are mainly or entirely technical — that is, they base their forecasts on past patterns of price behavior and trading volume and are primarily concerned with timing decisions. Many of the other services take the fundamental approach, including the three largest: the *Value Line Investment Survey,* Standard & Poor's *Outlook,* and *United Business & Investment Report.* And there's a profusion of specialized services devoted to options, stock charts, growth companies, foreign investments, mergers and acquisitions, mutual funds, and "insider trading" — purchases and sales of a company's stock by its own officers. (Such insider transactions are perfectly legal so long as they are not based on information, not publicly disclosed, which could significantly affect the price of the stock.) Finally, there are numerous services that cover nonstock areas — the bond and money markets, commodities, precious metals, real estate, coins and currencies.

Some services can influence the price of a stock — at least temporarily. For example, a stock often has a runup when it's featured in *Value Line* as the "stock highlight" of the week. A few timing services with a large and loyal following can even swing the market as a whole. Joseph E. Granville, a celebrated market soothsayer, flashed a sell-everything signal early in January 1981; the following day U.S. stocks lost $38 billion of their market value, and trading volume on the New York Stock Exchange rocketed to a record of nearly 93 million shares.

Anyone who publishes a paid advisory letter must register with the Securities and Exchange Commission, which requires him to report annually the service's financial condition, investment strategy, methods of analysis, and sources of information. But no qualifications or tests are required. In fact, publishers of advisory services have included high school dropouts, an electrician, a textile designer, and a hairdresser.

A 1963 Supreme Court ruling requires the services to disclose the holdings, if any, of their owners and employees in a stock they're recommending. And the SEC has obtained injunctions against services accused of "scalping" — buying a stock, featuring it as a hot tip, then taking a quick profit on the resulting runup. Unfortunately, the commission's staff isn't large enough to ensure that no flimflam goes undetected. But the leading services have strict rules of their own governing securities transactions by their employees.

The author of this book has been a reader of advisory services for nearly thirty years — first as a private investor, then as a securities analyst and research director on Wall Street, and since 1976 as a financial writer on *Money* magazine, where I scan several dozen services each month. Here are some points to keep in mind about the species in general.

• The services vary enormously in quality. Many are worthless and potentially harmful; some are excellent.

• The majority of the technical services are addicted to cloying self-congratulation. They often make fuzzy or cagily hedged forecasts and later boast that they've been "right on target." Some of the habitually bearish services even have the gall to go on saying they're right when the market has for months or even years proved them wrong. Predictably, services that go easy on self-praise and admit errors are among the best in the business.

• The published performance records of advisory services don't take into account buying and selling commissions; consequently they overstate gains and understate losses. The overstatement isn't significant in the case of services with a long-term investment strategy, because they don't do much trading. But ignoring commission expenses grossly inflates the results claimed by technical services that make short-term trades and recommend the use of "stops."* For example, a service that recommends buying a stock at $10 and later decides to sell it at $12 credits itself with a 20 percent gain. But typically, two-way brokerage commissions on 100 shares at those prices would add up to about $70. So an investor's real gain would be only $130, or 13 percent.

*A "stop" is an order placed with a broker (or simply one you give to yourself) to sell a stock if it declines to a specified level.

• The major services that focus mainly on fundamentals are the most useful for the average investor. They provide statistics, earnings projections, industry and company analyses, investment strategies, stock recommendations, and model portfolios — a package of investment materials that you can't find assembled elsewhere in one place.

• For a person with a few thousand dollars and a minimum of investment knowledge, an advisory service probably has no practical value; that kind of investor is better off letting mutual funds manage his money. For investors with, say, $15,000 and up, a good service can be helpful. Substantial investors — people with a stake of at least $100,000 — who are active in the market might benefit from taking several services. The most you can expect from a service is that it provide a sound basis for your own decision-making; no service can make all the decisions for you.

How good are the advisory services as stock-pickers? One of the few scholarly studies of their performance that I know of was made some years back by Harlan L. Cheney, a former professor of finance at Georgetown University's school of business administration. He found that from 1957 through 1968 the recommended lists of four leading (but unnamed) advisory services registered an average cumulative gain, including dividends, of 353.3 percent as against 225.7 percent for Standard & Poor's 500-stock index. These results can't, of course, be taken as representative of all services, but they do indicate that the better ones have been able to select stocks that provided higher than average rates of return. Between 1978 and mid-1981, the services that focused on emerging growth companies, little-known over-the-counter stocks, and new issues picked a lot of big winners, because such stocks were among the market's top performers.

In choosing a service, the first step is to ask yourself what type best meets your requirements — one that concentrates on stock selection or market timing, one that offers a broad range of information or a specialized service. A look at the ads can help you weed out probable phonies. As a rule, services that promise you the moon belong on the garbage heap. Before committing yourself to a year's subscription to one of the services, it's a good idea to sample as many as you can. Most services offer trial subscriptions — often for not more than $10 or $15 — and some will send you a sample copy at no charge. The cheapest way of getting to know a variety of services is to write for the free catalogue published by Select Information Exchange, 2095

Broadway, New York, NY 10023. The catalogue describes hundreds of services and offers you trial subscriptions to 20 services of your choice for $11.95. (Many services are not included in this offer.) If you then take a regular subscription to one of those you've sampled, your $11.95 is fully or partly deducted from the price.

There's no way of rating the advisory services because they're so varied in character. Moreover, personal convictions about investment strategy are bound to influence one's judgment. For example, my belief that for most investors in-and-out trading is a loser's game causes me to have a low opinion of technical services that cater largely to short-term traders. Another type of service that I have no use for is the messianic type, which preaches that the apocalypse is at hand and peddles a hard-and-fast recipe for survival. The favorite investment recommendations of the doomsayers — gold bullion, silver coins, and Swiss francs — did spectacularly well in the second half of the 1970s, but poorly over the first two years of the eighties. Moreover, these are investments that produce no interest or dividends and are therefore unsuitable for anyone who needs some income. And much of the doomsayers' advice has been zany or mischievous — for example, stockpiling a year's supply of canned goods, buying arms and ammunition, selling your real estate in order to buy silver (and "bury it in some safe place"), and obtaining a forged passport so that you can flee the country when it turns into a police state. In addition, the devastating stock market crash predicted by the doomsayers had failed to materialize as of January 1982.

My basic objections to the prophets of doom are, first, that they systematically promote fear and paranoia; second, they delude their loyal followers into thinking that a basket of their favored investments offers "safety" and removes the need for further investment decisions. This is pernicious nonsense. Putting most of your capital into gold, silver, and Swiss francs is a high-risk strategy. The precious metals are extremely volatile, and not only could they drop precipitously — as both gold and silver did in early 1980 and again in 1981 — they could also stay down long enough to make life nightmarish for people who've invested too heavily in them.

The services profiled in the rest of this chapter represent a cross-section of those that I consider to be the best for amateur investors. They were chosen because of their record for stock selection or market foresight, or because their coverage is broad and exceptionally informative, or because they perform a specialized function well. Limitations of space have prevented me from including many services that meet these criteria — it would take an entire book to cover the advisory industry thoroughly. Price, too, has been a factor in selection. With the exception of two services that I consider outstanding, I have excluded those that cost more than $300 a year. On the other hand, some services have been included because they are moderately priced and I rate them an excellent buy for investors who can't afford costlier ones. The subscription prices given are those in effect late in 1981.

THE BIG THREE

The Value Line Investment Survey. (Published weekly by Arnold Bernhard & Co., 711 Third Avenue, New York, NY 10017. One year, $330. Ten-week trial, $33.)

If I had to rely on one service only, I would unhesitantly choose *Value Line.* Its cost puts it beyond the reach of many small investors, but for anyone who can afford it — and who learns to use the incredible amount of information and guidance that it offers — the survey is invaluable.

With about 95,000 subscribers, *Value Line,* founded in 1936 by Arnold Bernhard, is by far the largest of the advisory services. Each week its staff of 70 analysts and economists feeds into two big computers more than one million statistics on the general economy, 93 industries, and 1,700 stocks. Stocks are given two separate rankings of 1 (best) to 5; one ranking is for "timeliness" — that is, probable price performance relative to the market over the next 12 months — and the other is for safety. Some years ago, *Value Line* made a test of its performance rankings and reported its findings at a conference at the University of Chicago. Over a five-year period (1965–1970) in which the Dow Jones industrials registered a 12 percent loss, the Rank 1 stocks showed a gain of 129 percent, and the Rank 5 stocks a loss of 41 percent; the performance of the other three groups was also in line with their rankings; Rank 2 outperformed and Rank 4 underperformed the Dow, and Rank 3 roughly matched it.

Subsequently, Professor Fischer Black, then at the University of

Chicago — a leading exponent of the Efficient Market Hypothesis, which holds that no method of stock analysis can outperform the market — tested a portfolio strategy based on the *Value Line* rankings for timeliness. He invested an equal amount in each of the stocks ranked 1, sold any of them that dropped to Rank 3, and reinvested the proceeds in the Rank 1 stocks. To Black's surprise, this strategy produced better returns than the overall market. His conclusion: "Most investment management organizations would improve their performance if they fired all but one of their security analysts and then provided the remaining analyst with the Value Line service."

The strategy that *Value Line* itself recommends is for an investor to pick from the stocks ranked 1 or 2 for timeliness those that best meet his safety and income requirements. For example, a conservative investor might confine his portfolio to the sometimes relatively few stocks in those groups that have a high ranking for safety and pay a respectable dividend; *Value Line's* weekly "Summary & Index" section will enable him to find them in less than 10 minutes. This section's useful listings include stocks with the lowest price/earnings ratios; stocks selling below book value; stocks with the highest growth rates; stocks with the highest probable long-term (3- to 5-year) profit potential; and stocks that have performed best and worst over the previous 13 weeks.

The main body of the *Value Line Survey* consists of more than 2,100 pages (in detachable sections) containing 1,700 continually updated company analyses that are both encyclopedic and compact. They assemble on a single page all of the data that an amateur analyst needs to size up the merits of a stock for himself. In sum, the *Value Line* offers a comprehensive overview of the economy and the stock market, fully documented company reports, and a portfolio strategy that each individual can adapt to his particular needs. Its chief limitation is that its coverage includes relatively few small or little-known companies. (That sector of the market is covered in a separate publication, the *Value Line O-T-C Special Situations Service*, which costs $300 a year extra.)

Value Line Investment Services also manages four common stock mutual funds that base their stock selections on the *Value Line* rankings and are oriented toward different degrees of risk. The Leveraged Growth fund and the Special Situations fund aim at large capital gains; the Value Line fund seeks growth and income, and the fourth is an income fund. They can be bought through brokers, and they have a low sales charge of 2½ percent.

The Outlook. (Published weekly by Standard & Poor's Corp., 25 Broadway, New York, NY 10004. One year, $145. Three-month trial, $39.)

Founded in the 1920s, this service—one that most brokerage houses subscribe to—is staidly conventional, with a cautiously bullish bias. Its strengths are that it's easy to read and digest, it doesn't encourage taking large risks, and it is backed by the large statistical and analytical staff of Standard & Poor's. Regular features include analyses of stocks "In the Limelight," lists of the best—and worst—acting stock groups, industry surveys, and a "Master List" of about 35 recommended issues graded in 4 categories on the basis of risk.

A study published in the *Journal of Portfolio Management* in 1977 concluded that over the previous six and a half years portfolios constructed from stocks recommended in the Master List had "generally outperformed the market on both an absolute and a risk adjusted basis," even taking into account buying and selling commissions.

Typical subjects covered periodically in the *Outlook:* stocks for high income, stocks with high prospective earnings growth, low-priced stocks that look attractive. A weekly summation of the service's forecast and policy tends to be as bland as Pablum. A characteristic forecast (made February 25, 1981): "Conservative investors would probably be well advised to stay with a cautious policy pending clarification of economic and monetary trends."

United Business & Investment Report. (Published by United Business Service, 210 Newbury St., Boston, MA 02116. One year, $150. Eight-week trial, $5.)

This 12-page service is similar in posture and coverage to *The Outlook* but devotes more space to Washington news and business trends and somewhat less to the stock market. Regular features include a page on commodities, industry surveys, and buy, hold, or sell opinions on stocks and on bonds. Its advice generally steers investors along a conventionally conservative course.

THREE GOOD BARGAINS

Smart Money. (Published monthly by the Hirsch Organization Inc., 6 Deer Trail, Old Tappan, NJ 07675. One year, $85, including special bulletins and the *Stock Trader's Almanac.* Three-month trial, $25.)

More like a small magazine for amateur investors than a typical advisory service, *Smart Money* is fun to read and has a hot record as a picker of highly speculative stocks, including a category that it calls "America's Most Undiscovered Companies." All told, the service recommended 82 stocks between March 1979 and February 1981; taking losses into account, the average gain on the prices at which the recommendations were made was 96 percent. In the ensuing twelve months, stock prices declined and *Smart Money's* track record slipped. But clearly the service has a flair for discovering dark horses that often finish up-front. It also provides its readers with periodic reports on wave-of-the-future technologies such as solar energy and fiberoptics.

Smart Money's editor and publisher, Yale Hirsch, doesn't concern himself with minor market fluctuations, but he tells you bluntly whether he's bullish or bearish on the major trend of the market. His forecasting record has been mixed since the service started in 1973, but that hasn't stopped him from guiding his readers into profitable stocks. Subscribers to *Smart Money* get a free copy of the *Stock Trader's Almanac* (retail price, $20), which contains a fascinating potpourri of historical lore and miscellaneous information about the stock market, including useful commentaries on seasonal and cyclical patterns of price behavior.

Market Logic. (Published twice a month by the Institute for Econometric Research Inc., 3471 N. Federal Hwy., Fort Lauderdale, FL 33306. One year, $95, two-issue trial, free.)

Based on econometric models (which apply mathematical formulas to forecasting) and on computer research, this inexpensive service provides in every issue projections of where Standard & Poor's 500-stock index will stand three, six, and twelve months hence, a review of what the market indicators are indicating, a list of the industry stock groups that are performing best and worst, and a forecast of the trend in the gold price. Other sections offer a digest of advisory service opinions, a guide to mutual fund selection, an extensive report on trading by corporate "insiders," an options portfolio, and a "Master Portfolio" of recommended stocks, which has a respectable record. By dialing a hot-line number, subscribers can tune in to a recorded stock market commentary that's updated twice weekly.

The Johnson Survey. (Published monthly by John S. Herold Inc., 35 Mason St., Greenwich, CT 06830. One year, $78. Three months, $25.)

Formerly named *America's Fastest Growing Companies,* this service has evolved and expanded into a publication of 40 pages or more with widely diversified coverage. Its centerpiece is a "Guide to Investment Selection," which tabulates investment data on about 200 growth stocks and rates them on a scale of A to C. This guide is supplemented by 15 or more pages of company progress reports. A section headed "Investment Opportunities and Insights" summarizes brokerage house, advisory service, and newspaper reports on a wide variety of investment topics — for example, international investing, "best commodity bets," Standard & Poor's "10 stocks for action," the outlook for bonds, and a list of the best-performing mutual funds. Another useful monthly feature focuses on the South African gold stocks. The *Johnson Survey*'s policy is not to make investment recommendations or forecast the market's behavior. It presents a large amount of well-organized information and opinion and invites you to decide for yourself.

GROWTH STOCK SERVICES

Equity Research Associates. (Published twice a month by Equity Research Associates, a division of Ladenburg, Thalmann & Co., 540 Madison Avenue, New York, NY 10022. One year, $360.)

ERA is the top service on "junior" growth companies — high-growth enterprises whose revenues, for the most part, are under $100 million. ERA's founder and president, John Westergaard, has been a leading analyst of junior growth companies for more than two decades. A keen observer of the American scene, he is as concerned with ideas as with numbers: he primarily seeks underanalyzed companies whose growth is linked to changes in American life-styles and to changes in the techniques and technologies used by American business. For example, he was among the first to recognize the exceptional growth potential of Flight Safety International, the leading independent supplier of pilot training services; Community Psychiatric Centers, which operates hospitals for acute psychiatric cases; and Datapoint, a pioneer in the development of data processing terminals linked to a central computer.

Westergaard monitors about 200 junior growth companies and focuses his reports on those he considers most promising. In recent years he has carried about 50 stocks on his recommended list (including some that have grown out of the "junior" category). At the end of 1980, the recommendations made since 1976 showed an average gain of 140 percent (not including dividends). Westergaard's overall strategy and specific criteria for selecting stocks are discussed in detail in chapter 21.

Growth Stock Outlook. (Published monthly by Growth Stock Outlook Inc., P.O. Box 9911, Chevy Chase, MD 20815. One year, $95. Three-month trial, $40.)

This service tracks about 100 growth companies that it has recommended since it was started in 1965; new recommendations are introduced with a concise analysis. A company whose earnings decline for two consecutive quarters is deleted — unless editor Charles Allmon believes its earnings are about to turn upward. The data tabulated in each issue include the stock's price range and earnings per share over the past six years, its latest twelve-month and quarterly earnings, and its book value, return on stockholders' equity, and four-year annual growth rates. In addition, stocks are ranked for attractiveness on a scale of A to C. As a possible model for its subscribers, *Growth Stock Outlook* manages a portfolio of selected growth stocks; when he considers the investment outlook unfavorable, Allmon sells stocks and parks the proceeds in money-market securities. Started in mid-1973 with an investment of $50,000, the model portfolio had a value of $189,409 (including reinvested gains and income) on January 15, 1982. Allmon is a brilliant stock-picker who takes a conservative approach to investing for growth; his policy is to ferret out growth stocks that have not yet achieved wide recognition and are still selling at low price/earnings ratios.

Growth Stock Outlook has a sister publication, *Junior Growth Stocks* (twenty-four issues a year, $115; three-month trial, $50). It tracks about 150 junior growth companies plus 70 companies that went public during the previous 18 months. But it doesn't make recommendations. Its purpose is to provide basic information to investors who wish to make their own decisions.

AN INCOME-ORIENTED SERVICE

Income Investor (Published monthly by Indicator Research Corp., 1 Fair Street, Palisades Park, NJ 07650. One year, $95. Two-month trial, $15.)

This well-produced 24-page booklet draws on the resources of an advisory company that also publishes *International Gold Digest* and *Indicator Digest* (twice monthly, $78 a year), a respected, inexpensive, all-round service whose coverage includes interpretation of 18 market indicators, features devoted to investment tactics and stock recommendations, and unweighted indexes of all stocks on the New York and American stock exchanges, which give an accurate picture of the *average* price changes in these markets.

Income Investor provides a compact appraisal of the outlook for the stock market, interest rates, and precious metals. It also suggests in what proportions income-oriented investors should distribute their portfolio assets between money-market securities (or funds), common stocks, gold mining shares, and different types of bonds. The service makes specific investment recommendations, and it tells you when to sell. Subjects covered in special features have included convertible bonds, foreign government bonds, high-yielding common stocks that could become takeover targets and options strategies for increasing your portfolio's income. This is a well-rounded, imaginative, reasonably priced service.

MUTUAL FUND SERVICES

Switch Fund Advisory. (Published monthly by Schabacker Investment Management, 8943 Shady Grove Court, Gaithersburg, MD 20877. One year, $85. Three-month trial, $30.)

Editor James M. Schabacker has a market forecasting system that uses a combination of more than a dozen fundamental and technical indicators. Each issue of his service gives fund-switchers two kinds of market timing advice. One is based on the traditional concept of increasing or decreasing exposure to risk in accordance with market conditions; it tells investors in what proportion they should split up their assets between stock funds and money-market funds. The other tells those who take the all-or-nothing approach whether they should currently be fully invested in aggressive funds or completely out of the market. Schabacker also reports the performance and current yields of about 150 no-load and load funds of all types, including tax-exempts and golds. And he runs a model portfolio that is invested in four different categories of funds. His service is particularly helpful to investors who wish to follow a "balanced portfolio" approach, using mutual funds rather than individual securities.

The Superyield Reporter. (Published monthly by Growth Fund Research Inc., Growth Fund Building, Yreka, CA 96097. One year, $100. Sample copy, free.)

Started in 1979 and directed primarily toward the small income-oriented investor, *The Superyield Reporter* concentrates on closed-end stock and bond funds (whose shares are traded like stocks on the regular exchanges and over the counter) and also on money-market funds.

Growth Fund Guide. (Published monthly by Growth Fund Research Inc., Growth Fund Building, Yreka, CA 96097. One year, $65. Sample copy, free.)

Regular features include the best- and worst-performing funds over the past one, three, six, nine, twelve, and twenty-four months, performance ratings in rising markets and in declining markets for thirty funds followed on a continuing basis, and current fund recommendations. A useful chart section shows the price performance, on a monthly basis, of the thirty funds over the past three and a half years, and it gives their addresses, telephone numbers, objectives, and investment requirements.

TECHNICAL SERVICES

The Professional Tape Reader. (Published twice a month by Radcap Inc., P.O. Box 2407, Hollywood, FL 33022. Editor: Stan Weinstein. One year, $250. Three issues, $30.)

Systems and Forecasts. (Published twice a month by Signalert Corp., 185 Great Neck Rd., Great Neck, NY 11021. Editor: Gerald Appel. One year, $120. Three-issue trial, $25.)

The Zweig Forecast. (Published every three weeks by Martin E. Zweig, 747 Third Ave., New York, NY 10017. One year, $165. Three-month trial, $25.)

These three services — edited by three well-known specialists in market timing — are among the best of their kind but are useful only for investors with faith in technical analysis and a grasp of how to use it. Appel, Zweig, and Weinstein address traders primarily, and their services are similar in format and content. They lead off with a commentary on the state of the market, a forecast (sometimes hedged) of its short, intermediate, and long-term trends, and a recommended portfolio strategy. Each service then gives its reading of numerous market indicators, makes brief stock recommendations based mainly on technical analysis and follows up on previously recommended issues. The *Professional Tape Reader* and the *Zweig Forecast* (in that order) devote the most space to stocks. *Systems & Forecasts* has a proprietary feature: a rating system for mutual funds based on their performance both in market downswings and upswings. It covers 26 funds and gives exact "signal" prices at which traders should move into a fund or out of it.

MISCELLANEOUS SERVICES

Consensus of Insiders. (Published weekly by the Consensus Group, P.O. Box 10247, Fort Lauderdale, FL 33305. One year, $180. Six-issue trial, $20.)

This unimpressive-looking service is designed for investors who wish to take their cue from corporate and stock market insiders. Its stock selection section is simply a list (unaccompanied by investment data) of 20 or so companies whose stocks have been most widely bought by their own officers. Several academic studies have found that strategies based on following insider buying produced higher returns than stocks in general (even though there's a time lag of 30 to 60 days before insider transactions are made public). Since 1962, editor Perry Wysong has tracked the record of a model portfolio in which he buys stocks strongly favored by insiders and typically holds them for about six months. The results have dramatically outperformed the Dow Jones Industrials.

For market timing, Wysong uses two indicators based on the buying and selling of stocks by market insiders (Specialists and traders on the floor of the New York Stock Exchange) and investment professionals (mutual fund managers). The indicators' rationale is that these people — particularly the Specialists — are closer to the forces at work in the market than the general public is, so their behavior can be helpful in anticipating price trends. When both of Wysong's indicators turn from "neutral" to positive, his service flashes a buy signal; when they turn to negative, it puts out a sell. His signals have an excellent but by no means infallible record for calling substantial swings in the Dow.

New Issues. (Published monthly by the Institute for Econometric Research, 3471 North Federal Hwy., Fort Lauderdale, FL 33306. One year, $78. Two-issue trial, free.)

Started in September 1978, this service has done a good job of covering the treacherous new issues market. By November 1981, the 96 stocks it had recommended out of 300 initial public offerings had shown an average gain of 67 percent on their offering prices. Editor Norman G. Fosback describes forthcoming offerings, analyzes those he recommends, and draws attention to buying opportunities in the "aftermarket" — that is, after a new issue has been launched and is trading over the counter. Fosback isn't averse to *not* making any recommendations when he considers upcoming issues overpriced or is leery about the condition of the market. His service provides a calendar of forthcoming offerings that gives the underwriter's name and address, the number of shares to be sold, their probable price, and the expected date of the offering.

Investors Intelligence. (Published every two weeks by Chartercraft Inc., 2 East Avenue, Larchmont, NY 10538. One year, $60. Two-month trial, $10.)

This publication is the *Reader's Digest* of the advisory services. Each issue provides one-paragraph summaries of the market views of 30 services, culled from the 95 it monitors, and it gives a selection of their stock recommendations. Other features include advice to fund-switchers on the allocation of their assets between stock funds and money-market funds, and a list of stocks that have been bought or sold by more than three corporate insiders.

Investors Intelligence is known for its "Bearish Sentiment Index," which shows the percentage of services that expect the market to decline. The number has been consistently largest (60 percent or more) at market bottoms and smallest (usually 10 percent or less) at market tops. Reason: most of the technical services are trend followers, so they tend to be wrong at major turning points in the market. The "Bearish Sentiment Index" has become widely recognized as a contrary opinion indicator: investors should be buying when sentiment among advisory services is exceptionally bearish and selling when it's strongly bullish.

IV

ANALYTIC APPROACHES

15. The Fundamental Approach: Judging What a Stock Is Worth

Investment analysis seeks to answer the questions *what* should I buy, or sell? *when* should I buy, or sell? The chapters that follow will show you how to use the three principal analytic approaches and a fourth that in recent years has attracted attention. The *Fundamental Approach*—the oldest and the dominant one in the investment world—concerns itself with value. The *Technical Approach* focuses on supply and demand, and concerns itself mainly with timing. The *Psychological Approach*, generally referred to as Contrary Opinion theory or Contrarian investing—concerns itself with groupthink and crowd psychology. Its goal is to discover opportunities for profit created by the irrational behavior of large numbers of investors. The connection between presidential politics and the stock market is the basis of a relatively new approach to market timing, which is known as *Political Cycle Investing*.

Security analysis is an art that's struggling to become a science, and isn't likely to succeed—because you cannot put a stock in a test tube. What security analysis can do is enable investors to separate realities and probabilities from vague hunches and unfounded hopes and fears. Through systematic assessment of the available facts, it arrives at specific estimates which, though fallible, are vastly preferable to uninformed guesswork.

A stock's investment value or "intrinsic" worth as determined by fundamental analysis may be approximately the same as its market price, in which case the stock is said to be "fairly" or "reasonably" valued. If a stock is found to be undervalued or overvalued, fundamentalists assume that its market price will sooner or later come into line with the intrinsic value. That could happen in a few months or possibly a year, but it usually takes longer. Consequently, fundamental analysis is basically oriented toward long-term investing, though it also concerns itself with the intermediate term (three to twelve months).

The practical function of fundamental analysis is to determine (1) which issues, at their current prices, are undervalued or overvalued *in relation to others;* (2) whether stocks in general are undervalued or overvalued on the basis of their projected returns (dividends and price gains) and the returns offered by competitive investments — in particular, bonds and money-market securities such as Treasury Bills.

A MINI-REFERENCE LIBRARY FOR AMATEUR STOCK ANALYSTS

Professional analysts draw on vast amounts of information, for which a major brokerage house typically spends upward of $500,000 a year, if you include computerized data services. But for less than $40 (at late 1981 prices) you can assemble the reference materials described below. They provide the data you need to follow the analytic procedures described in this chapter and the investment strategies discussed later. There's one essential addition — the brief but extraordinarily comprehensive stock reports issued by Standard & Poor's. Your broker can usually supply you with an S&P report on a company you wish to analyze. Here's my suggested kit of reference materials for amateur analysts.

The Fortune Directory contains investment data on the nation's 1,000 largest industrial corporations and 300 leading nonindustrial companies; included are sales, net income, assets, return on stockholders' equity, earnings per share, and 10-year earnings growth rates. The directory appears serially each year in *Fortune* in May, June, and July, or it can be ordered for September delivery by sending $7 to Fortune, Double 500 Directory, P.O. Box 8001, Trenton, NJ 08650.

The *Forbes Annual Report on American Industry* appears in the early January issue of *Forbes* magazine, which can be bought on newsstands; it cost $3 in 1981. A prodigious compendium of information for the do-it-yourself investor, this special issue starts out with reports on 50 industries and then measures the performance of more than 1,000 large companies over the previous 12 months and the previous 5 years. The data for individual companies include sales and earnings for the past 12 months and their 5-year growth rates; the past year's return and the 5-year average return on stockholders' equity and on total invested capital; the number of shares outstanding and their total market value. The issue also ranks the 1,050 companies on the basis of (1) profitability, (2) growth, and (3) market performance.

Barron's is a financial weekly that usually runs to more than 100 large pages; at this writing, it sells on newsstands for the bargain price of $1. My $40 budget for reference materials allows $12 for the purchase of one issue of *Barron's* in the first week of each month. Here's a partial list of what you'll get, in addition to the excellent general articles: several reports on individual companies, a review of the past week on the stock and bond markets, a department on options, and about 40 pages of statistics. These include the prices and earnings of all stocks on the New York and the American stock exchanges, and of the over-the-counter issues quoted on NASDAQ; the prices and current yields of all bonds traded on the New York and the American stock exchanges; the prices and yields of U.S. Treasury bonds and notes; the past week's high, low, and closing prices of all options traded on the options exchanges; the past week's closing level, and the percentage gain or loss for the year to date, of the Dow Jones Industrials, the S&P 500, the NYSE Composite index, the Amex index, and many other useful stock and bond averages and indexes; the market prices and net asset values per share of closed-end stock and bond funds; the past two weeks' reported figures for the money supply; all of the key short-term interest rates; and the past week's figures for short sales by odd-lotters, the public, exchange members, and exchange Specialists — their significance is explained in chapter 16. For a do-it-yourself investor, *Barron's* is invaluable.

The *Dow Jones Business & Investment Almanac* (Dow Jones–Irwin, $15.95; available in bookstores) contains surveys of 20 industries with financial data on major companies in them; data on the 100 fastest-growing smaller companies; the market performance of some 25 stock groups; the historical investment returns on stocks, bonds, and money-market securities; charts of the Dow Jones averages since the late 1940s and tables showing the behavior of other major stock averages; and sections devoted to mutual funds and to options.

The *Investors Information Kit* published by the New York Stock Exchange consists of several useful pamphlets including *Income Leaders on the Big Board*, which gives you the dividends paid by common and preferred stocks yielding 6 percent or more, *Understanding Convertible Securities*, and *Understanding Financial Statements*. (New York Stock Exchange, Publication Section, 11 Wall Street, New York, NY 10005. $3.95 postpaid). Other background materials published by the New York Stock Exchange are distributed, free of charge, through brokerage houses.

Stock Guide, issued monthly by Standard & Poor's, is a basic investment tool that brokers constantly refer to. Its $50 annual subscription cost is not included in the budget for my suggested reference library; however, if you have a friendly broker, he'll be glad to send you an issue from time to time free of charge. This compact booklet covers 5,100 companies, and by running your eye across a single line you'll get most of the key investment data on a stock — its S&P quality rating; the size of institutional holdings; the price range since the early 1960s and over the previous and current year; the dividend yield and price/earnings ratio; the earnings per share over the past 5 years, the past 12 months, and recent quarters; and the company's financial position and market capitalization. A separate section provides investment data on nearly 400 mutual funds. (Standard & Poor's Corporation, 25 Broadway, New York, NY 10004).

A source of free information that thrifty investors might welcome is bank publications that discuss the state of the economy. These include *Business in Brief*, issued bimonthly by the Economics Group of the Chase Manhattan Bank (1 Chase Manhattan Plaza, New York, NY 10081); the weekly *Financial Digest* and monthly *Economic Report* of Manufacturers Hanover Trust (350 Park Avenue, New York, NY 10022); Citibank's monthly *Economic Letter* (Citibank, Box 1251, New York, NY 10043); and the monthly *Business and Economic Review* published by the First National Bank of Chicago (Business & Economics Research Dept., One First National Plaza, Chicago, IL 60670).

There are many other valuable sources of investment data, but the package of reference materials described above gives you, I think, the best mileage you can hope to get for $40. If your budget for investment research is elastic, I suggest you take one or more of the investment advisory services described in chapter 14 and/or a periodical that covers the investment scene. The magazines that, in my opinion, can be most helpful to individual investors are *Financial World* ($36 a year), *Forbes* ($30 a year), and *Money* ($21.95 a year), with the last of which this writer is associated. (P.S. Of course you won't forget that documented expenses on research materials are tax-deductible, provided your tax return shows you to be a bona fide investor.)

Having assembled an adequate information bank, an amateur investor is equipped to tackle the nitty-gritty of security analysis. The procedures may at first sound forbidding. But all it takes to acquire a functional grasp of them — I'm not suggesting that you aim at professional expertise — is common sense, patience, a command of simple arithmetic, and above all a strong desire to be self-reliant rather than blindly dependent on the judgment of others. Once you've mastered the basic procedures, they'll enable you to make educated value judgments about a stock in much less time than you spend doing your income tax. This know-how is a tremendous asset for the layman. But even with it, inexperienced investors shouldn't try to operate entirely on their own. Do-it-yourself analysis will often raise questions that you should refer to your broker. If he doesn't know the answer himself, he may be able to get it from an analyst in his firm's research department or from the *Value Line Investment Survey*.

VALUATION APPROACHES

Present Value: The reigning academic theory of stock valuation is that a stock's intrinsic value is "the present discounted value of its expected future cash returns" — that is, the future stream of dividends and the eventual sale price, discounted by the risk-free return on money plus an appropriate premium for risk.* The present-value concept has many applications in finance, and as a model for stock valuation, it's totally logical. The catch is that the model makes assumptions that are totally divorced from practicality. Analysts' estimates of earnings for the next 12 months are notoriously fallible. It's therefore highly unrealistic to judge a stock's worth on the basis of projections of earnings and dividends stretching far out into the future. To come up with the correct total cash return over, say, a 10-year period, an analyst would have to assess accurately a multitude of variables on a year-by-year basis — sales, profit margins, market reception of new products, strength of competition, state of

*The formula for discounting is as follows: if the discount rate is 14 percent, the present value of $1 one year hence is $1/1.14 = $0.88.

the economy, and so on. He would also have to project correctly how much an investor would receive from sale of the stock 10 years hence. The present-value model ducks these real-life difficulties by expressing uncertain projections in algebraic symbols. It then constructs an equation out of those symbols, and — hey presto — comes up with a mathematically "correct" figure for present value. But unless all of the projections are right, the present-value figure is phony. Like computers, present-value equations are subject to the "GIGO" principle: garbage in, garbage out.

The Ben Graham Approach: The late Benjamin Graham (1894–1976) pretty much founded the discipline of security analysis in the mid-1930s when he and David L. Dodd published their monumental work *Security Analysis,* which has gone through four editions (New York: McGraw-Hill, 4th edition, 1962). Ironically, in his later years Graham concluded that the more elaborate approaches to security analysis were of dubious value. In an interview with Patricia Dreyfus that appeared in *Money* magazine in July 1976, Graham distilled the insights of a lifetime devoted to analyzing stocks into two simple methods. One of them starts out by looking for stocks with low price/earnings ratios; Graham's requirement was about seven times earnings at a time when that valuation was 40 percent below the P/E ratio of the S&P index. Then comes the decisive test: *the company's current assets must exceed its current liabilities together with its long-term debt.* The second method ignores price/earnings ratios and focuses exclusively on current assets. The first step is to find companies whose current assets exceed their *total* liabilities — current liabilities plus long-term debt and the market value of their preferred stock (if any). The next step is to divide the difference between current assets and total liabilities by the number of shares outstanding; this gives you "net net working capital" per share. If the net net asset value per share is higher than the market price, the stock is undervalued. It's easy to see why. An investor is getting the company's property, plant, and equipment at zero cost, which means that he is buying the stock at less than its liquidating value.

Graham also provided simple — though controversial — guidelines for selling. He recommended setting a profit objective of between 50 percent and 100 percent and selling when it's reached; if it isn't reached within three years, the stock should be sold anyhow.

Graham's simplified valuation methods are fairly easy to use; all of the data required (except for the stock's current price) are in Standard & Poor's monthly *Stock Guide. Both methods are bargain-oriented ones that focus on assets and ignore growth prospects.* They're well suited for investors who concentrate on tangible value. But if you're venturesome, you're likely to find their requirements constricting. They will assuredly keep you out of the great growth companies of your era, because such companies have the kind of romance that commands high valuations. By Graham's yardsticks, the growth stocks of the 1950s and 1960s that are now mature giants — an Avon Products, an IBM, a Texas Instruments — were never undervalued. But thousands of investors made enormous profits in them.

The Value of Book Value: A company's book value is its total assets minus total liabilities (including the redemption value of preferred stock), divided by the number of shares outstanding. Since the difference between total assets and total liabilities is common stockholders' equity, book value is the same as stockholders' equity per share.

Book value has several uses in security analysis. For one thing, it can be an indicator of whether the general level of stock prices is abnormally high or low. There have been only a few periods between World War II and 1981 when the Dow Jones Industrial Average was priced below its book value — 1949, late 1973 and 1974, early 1978, and early 1980. Each of those periods was followed by a major rise in stock prices. On the other hand, from the late 1950s through 1968, the Dow sold on the average at 65 percent *above* book value. And that decade was followed by a long and severe bear market, at least for the vast majority of stocks. So it would seem that most stocks are undervalued when the Dow is selling at or below book value, and they are probably becoming overvalued when the Dow rises 40 percent above its book value. Your broker can get you the Dow's book value and you need to update it only once a year. It was in the area of $900 in late 1981 (when the Dow stood at 860).

Book value is also the basic tool of some analysts who specialize in ferreting out sharply undervalued stocks. Unless the market is severely depressed, the stocks of companies that are prospering sell at appreciably more than book value; most of the stocks selling substantially below book value are deadbeats or weaklings — but not all of them. A well-known New York analyst, Ray Dirks, has written a book — *Heads You Win, Tails You Win* (New York: Stein and Day, 1979) — which argues that focusing exclusively on stocks selling below book value is the safest and most profitable investment strategy. Dirks has a formula for avoiding the trash and homing in on the treasures: the stock must have an earnings yield* of 14 percent or more — which simply means a price/earnings ratio of about seven or less — and, preferably, it should have a "respectable" though not necessarily consistent or impressive earnings growth rate. Dirks's approach is somewhat similar to the first Ben Graham method described earlier, but it's not quite so exacting. Even so, a stock with a decent earnings record that is selling below book value and at seven times earnings or less is apt to be undervalued.

Bargain-priced Growth: An approach to stock valuation that's bargain-oriented but takes into account growth has been developed by Barry Ziskin, a New York money manager whose firm is called the Opportunity Prospector. Four times a year Ziskin screens 8,000 stocks to find out which ones meet his seven exacting and undeviating criteria. Two of them are related to consistency and magnitude of growth: pretax income from operations must show a growth rate of *at least 10 percent in each of the previous 6 years and total growth over the 6-year period amounting to 20 percent compounded annually.* Three criteria are designed to establish that the company is in tip top shape financially. The main requirements are: (1) the current ratio must be at least 2 to 1, or working capital per share must exceed market price per share; (2) long-term debt must be covered by working capital or by the latest 12 months' cash flow (net income plus depreciation and amortization); (3) accounting procedures must be conservative. (These terms and ratios are explained in the discussion of annual reports in chapter 14.) The remaining criteria ensure that the stock has not achieved wide recognition — institutions must own less than 10 percent of the shares outstanding, and the P/E ratio must be less than 10 times estimated earnings for the current year.

The merit of Ziskin's system is that it excludes subjective judgments. When a stock meets all of the criteria, it's a buy. It is then held

---

*A stock's earnings yield — its earnings per share divided by its price — is the reciprocal of its price/earnings ratio (price divided by earnings). So if a stock's earnings yield is 14 percent, its P/E ratio is 14 divided into 100, or 7.2.

until it flunks any one of the tests, at which point it's automatically sold. In the majority of cases, stocks are sold either because they've achieved wide recognition and their valuation has risen above 10 times earnings, or because their growth shows signs of faltering. According to Ziskin's records for the period between mid-1973 and December 1979, 112 issues that qualified as buys were subsequently disqualified and sold. Two were losers, 3 broke even, and 108 showed gains averaging 78 percent (before allowing for brokerage commissions); during that period the S&P index was up less than 2 percent. Clearly, this valuation system achieves remarkably good results. And even though amateur investors can't apply it to the letter — it calls for too much work — they will find its basic requirements an excellent guide to discovering undervalued growth companies. In sum, those requirements are: (1) a vigorous *and* consistent growth rate; (2) a strong financial condition; (3) low institutional sponsorship and a P/E ratio under 10.

Stock Valuation—Casting a Wider Net: While they have a proven record of success, the systems discussed thus far are limiting; relatively few stocks meet their requirements. A wider-angled approach to finding attractive stocks is to start by checking whether a stock appears to be overvalued or undervalued in relation to others. Then, if it seems to be undervalued, you try to analyze the company in the conventional way — that is, by looking into earnings record, its profitability, its product line, the competition it faces, the prospects for the industry it's in, and so on. The specifics of that approach will be described in the rest of this chapter.

The preliminary check — finding out whether or not a stock's relative valuation seems attractive — can be a tremendous time-saver. Why go to all the trouble of studying a company if its relative valuation shows that it's probably overpriced? There are two ways of establishing relative valuation. I'll explain both of them, step by step, because they serve somewhat different needs.

The yardstick of valuation most widely used by analysts is the price-earnings ratio, which was fully explained in chapter 4. The P/E ratios given in newspaper stock-market columns are based on a company's latest 12 months' earnings. Professionals, however, base their P/E ratios on *estimates* of earnings for the current year, which you will find in brokerage house reports and investment advisory services. Though fallible, such estimates are usually a better guide to evaluating a stock than the previous year's results. For example, the stocks of fertilizer companies such as International Minerals & Chemical Corp. looked cheap in early 1976 on the strength of their booming earnings in 1975. But the outlook for the fertilizer industry suggested that earnings were about to decline — and they did, in 1976 and 1977. A P/E ratio based on past results is also highly misleading when a company has suffered a sharp drop in earnings due to temporary difficulties — for example, a strike; or when it's started to show a small profit after a period of losses. In such cases, the P/E will look forbiddingly high, but the stock may not be really overvalued on the basis of the company's "normal" earning power — its average earnings over the past 5 years.

Amateur investors (aided and abetted by stockbrokers, who should know better) often make the mistake of concluding that a stock is cheap simply because its price/earnings ratio is low — say, 5 times earnings. But P/E ratios vary from industry to industry and often from company to company within the same industry. Moreover, the overall level of stock valuations and the valuations of industry groups have varied greatly over the past 30 years. So, a stock's current price/earnings ratio does not, on its own, provide significant clues as to whether the stock is undervalued, overvalued or fairly valued. *What security analysts want is to know is whether the P/E ratio is higher or lower in relation to the overall level of P/E ratios than it has been in the past.* With the proper information at your fingertips, figuring out a stock's relative P/E takes only a few minutes.

First you calculate (from a Standard & Poor's company report, the *Value Line Survey*, or some other source), the stock's average P/E over the past five years. Let's take, as an illustration, the stock of Carolina Freight Car (traded on New York Stock Exchange); its average 5-year P/E ratio in mid-February 1981 was about 6. Now you measure this figure against the average P/E of a leading market index over the past 5 years. Professionals use Standard & Poor's 500, but for most laymen it's easier to use the Dow, because its current P/E is published every Monday in the *Wall Street Journal*. The 5-year average P/E of the Dow — a calculation you need make only once a year — was 8.5. So the historical ratio of Carolina Freight Car's valuation relative to the Dow's was 6 divided by 8.5, or 71 percent.

The final step is to measure the stock's current estimated P/E against the P/E of the Dow. (It's preferable to base the Dow's P/E on the prevailing estimate of its earnings for the current year, which your broker or his research department can give you.) In mid-February 1981, Carolina Freight Car, then selling at 14, had a P/E of 4.7, based on estimated 1981 earnings. The Dow's P/E based on estimated 1981 earnings was about 8. So the ratio of Carolina Freight Car's current P/E relative to the Dow's was 4.7 divided by 8, or 59 percent. Now you've discovered whether your stock is selling at a lower or higher relative valuation than it has in the past. In the case of Carolina Freight Car, it was lower — 59 percent against 71 percent. So there appeared to be a possibility that the stock was somewhat under-valued.*

A different and quicker way of determining relative valuation has been devised by George Lasry, the author of *Valuing Common Stock*, and I've found it enormously valuable. The Lasry test is a lot simpler than it may appear at first sight to an inexperienced investor; with the necessary data at hand and a little practice, you can apply it to a stock in less than one minute. Before telling you how it works, I should explain its rationale.

The Lasry test uses two yardsticks — a company's return on stock-holders' equity (ROE)† and the price/earnings ratio of its stock. Return on equity is a measure of profitability (of how well the company is performing) and the price/earnings ratio is the valuation investors put on a company's stock. So if you divide ROE by the P/E ratio you get a number — Lasry calls it the "ranking number" — *which tells you whether a stock's valuation is high or low on the basis of its profitability*. The higher the ranking number, the lower the valuation, and vice versa. Let's assume, for example, that stock A has a return on equity of 21 percent and a P/E of 7; ROE divided by P/E gives us a ranking number of 3. Stock B has a return on equity of 14 percent and a P/E ratio 7, so its ranking number is 2. A is undervalued in relation to B because it's selling at the same valuation of seven times earnings but its profitability is much higher — 21 percent as against 14 percent.

---

*The stock subsequently rose nearly 27 percent to 17¾ and then slipped back. At the end of 1981, it had performed somewhat better than the Dow.

†The *Forbes* issue included in my suggested mini-reference library gives the recent and the five-year average ROE for more than a thousand companies. If you need to calculate a company's ROE, the easiest method is to divide earnings per share by book value.

The Lasry test begins by establishing the average ranking for stocks in general; you do this by dividing the median ROE for American industry (or the S&P 500) by the median P/E for stocks in general. The 5-year median ROE for American industry at the end of 1980 was 15.8 percent. The median P/E ratio for all stocks in early 1981 was about 8. So the median ranking number was about 2.

The next step is to calculate the ranking number of the stock you're investigating. If its return on stockholders' equity doesn't vary greatly from year to year, you can simply divide last year's ROE by the current estimated P/E ratio; in the case of companies with sharp swings in profitability, you should take the average return on equity over the past five years.

The final step is to compare the ranking number of your stock with the median ranking for the market in general. If, for example, the median ranking is 2, here is what the Lasry test tells you: (1) stocks with a ranking of anywhere from 1.7 to 2.4 are probably not appreciably overvalued or undervalued in relation to others; (2) *a stock begins to look undervalued if its ranking number is close to 3 and it could be a bargain if the ranking is 3.5 or higher;* (3) *there's a strong possibility that stocks with a ranking of 1.5 or less are relatively overvalued.*

From my standpoint, the Lasry test has one important drawback: the stocks of high-growth companies selling at fairly high price/earnings ratios almost invariably come out either overvalued or at best fairly valued. If the median ranking is 2, a stock selling at 16 times earnings would have to have an ROE of 32 percent merely to match the median ranking—and relatively few companies have a return on equity of more than 30 percent. So the Lasry test will keep an investor out of high-growth issues with relatively high P/E ratios. But there are periods when such issues are the stellar market performers—for example, from 1978 through mid-1981. Lasry's rejoinder to this objection is that most high P/E stocks are always relatively overvalued. They may indeed be stellar performers at times when the market environment is favorable, and provided that their earnings growth at least matches expectations. But, Lasry argues, high P/E stocks are apt to get clobbered when their earnings are disappointing or the market suffers a major setback. His test, he says, was devised to serve an investment policy based on discovering stocks that are *sharply undervalued*—not on the basis of uncertain estimates of future growth but on the basis of their *actual* return on equity. Judging from what I know about Lasry's record, his policy has been extremely successful. However, if you want to invest in stocks in the high-growth category, you should use the relative P/E method to check on their current valuations.

The Lasry test and the relative P/E test provide what lawyers call prima facie evidence that a stock may be undervalued or overvalued. But that isn't sufficient. For example, if a stock's relative P/E ratio is currently below its five-year average, you would want to know whether the change is justified by a deterioration in the company's position and prospects. The further evidence you need to reach a reasonable verdict on the merits of a stock must be pieced together by giving the company a general checkup. Here's how the average investor, who isn't in a position to visit the company and interview its management, might go about doing this.

A logical starting point is to determine whether the company is predominantly in growth sectors of industry or in cyclical ones, or whether it's about evenly involved in both. (See Appendix C.) You will find a breakdown by "sector" or industry of a company's sales and earnings in its S&P report or its annual report. If the company is cyclical, check on whether the underlying earnings trend is upward — that is, whether profits in recent up years were generally higher than profits in earlier up years and profits in recent down years were higher than profits in earlier down years. As a rule, a cyclical company that doesn't have an underlying pattern of growth should be avoided by long-term investors.

In the case of growth companies, the earnings record gives you instant answers — positive or negative — to several crucial questions. Has the annual percentage increase in earnings been accelerating or slowing down in recent years? How much has profit growth been affected by recessions — slightly or substantially? Has the growth rate been consistent or does it show pronounced variations? (Investors pay high premiums for consistency.)

Now compare the pattern of sales to that of earnings. If sales gains have not been keeping pace with profit growth, it's most unlikely that profit growth can be sustained. But what if sales have been increasing conspicuously faster than earnings? It's a warning that the company needs to trim costs or eliminate unprofitable operations.

Turn next to the dividend record and calculate the average percentage of earnings that the company has paid out in dividends over the years. A large dividend payout is attractive to investors whose primary goal is high current income, but for growth-minded investors it's undesirable. Dividend income is subject to double taxation. As a stockholder you have in effect paid the corporate income tax rate on your share of the company's earnings, and then you are hit with personal income taxes on the dividend payout. So the smaller the dividend payout, the greater is your share of earnings that escape double taxation and are reinvested for you in the business, causing your equity as a stockholder to grow.

Your next target is the company's earnings prospects, perhaps the most vital factor in stock valuation. For companies in highly cyclical industries, these prospects tend to be closely related to the future course of the economy. Since the behavior of stock prices tends to anticipate major moves in the economy by roughly six months, the time to consider cyclical stocks is when you think a recession has hit bottom or even sooner; their prices usually start rising well before economic recovery is discernible. Conversely, you should be thinking about selling cyclical stocks some time before the economy seems to be reaching a peak — unless you expect the next business slowdown to be mild and short-lived.

When you're assessing the prospects for a high growth company, you run into a problem if its previous 12 months' earnings gain was well below its average annual gain — or, worse still, if profits declined. In such cases, the stock has often dropped so far in price that it would be a bargain provided the company regains its momentum in the fairly near future. But if it doesn't — and this kind of prognosis is often tough even for the pros — the stock could be a catastrophic investment. Since the stocks of high growth companies usually pay inconsequential dividends and are therefore unattractive from the standpoint of income, there's not much limit to how far their stock can decline if earnings stop growing. A horrific example: when the profits of Levitz Furniture Corp. peaked in 1972, it was selling at 242 (adjusted for a subsequent 1-for-4 reverse split); by 1974, it had fallen to 6. Seven years later, it was selling at only 29, even though its profits started rising again in 1976.

Assuming that a high growth company is running true to form, you still have to ask yourself some questions about its future. Is it maintaining or enhancing its profit potential with new products, expansion programs and perhaps acquisitions? Is there a serious threat of mounting competition? (Xerox, for example, found the going tougher after IBM and Kodak joined its earlier competitors in the copier market.) Do its major markets continue to offer opportunities for robust growth? Is its growth menaced by changes in government policies or regulations? You can find the answers, or clues to them, by studying the company's annual report, by questioning your broker or knowledgeable business friends, and by combing through recent issues of business and financial periodicals in a well-stocked library.

A major factor in stock valuation is a company's profitability. The principal yardsticks: its operating margin (the pretax amount earned per dollar of sales, excluding both income from investments and outgoing interest charges); its net profit margin (income after taxes divided by total revenues); its return on stockholders' equity (net income divided by the total balance-sheet value of the shareholders' ownership in the company).

You can gauge the company's profitability by comparing its margins and return on shareholders' equity with averages for its industry (which you'll find in the suggested reference materials or in the annual *U.S. Statistical Abstract,* available in libraries). A company's profitability, together with its sales and earnings record, gives you a reliable reading on the quality of management. Meeting a company's top executives, as professionals do, is sometimes not a help in judging their competence. Many Wall Street analysts bear scars of the mistakes they've made by overrating, or being misled by, a charismatic chief executive.

Your next exercise is to run through the company's balance sheet, which shows its assets, liabilities, long-term debt, and other financial data at the end of the previous fiscal year (or most recent quarter). Your first checkpoint: *the ratio of current assets to current liabilities.* The excess of current assets over current liabilities is the company's working capital — the funds available to run the business. The adequacy of working capital depends on the industry in which the company is operating. As a rough rule of thumb, it's desirable for current assets to be twice as large as current liabilities, or nearly so, but utilities, supermarkets, and other industries that generate prompt cash payments get by on less. When in doubt, ask your broker whether a company's ratio is comfortable. A company that has impressed you with its earnings growth could prove to be strapped for working capital because it's expanded too rapidly—and that could spell trouble.

Another key ratio is that of long-term debt to stockholders' equity. A high debt-to-equity ratio makes earnings extremely volatile because of the high fixed charges for bond interest. Take, for example, a company with a million shares outstanding that's earning $1 million and has fixed annual charges of $500,000 for bond interest (computed after taxes): its earnings per share will be $1 million minus $500,000 divided by a million shares—that is, 50 cents. But if total earnings drop 20 percent, earnings per share will drop 40 percent. The math then becomes $800,000 minus $500,000 divided by a million shares, or 30 cents. Such companies are said to be highly leveraged, and their valuations tend to be relatively low because their earnings are extremely volatile. Moreover, a succession of losing years could drag such companies into bankruptcy. Chrysler, International Harvester, Lockheed, and Pan American World Airways are examples of companies whose survival has been endangered in bad times because they are so highly leveraged.

Your next checkpoint on the balance sheet is *book value;* it was discussed a few pages back as well as in chapter 14. That chapter also briefly covered a subject that's important in security analysis—a company's accounting practices and how they affect the "quality" of its earnings. Reported earnings may be overstated or understated depending on whether accounting practices are "permissive" or conservative.

You will need one more crucial piece of information before you weigh the evidence—*an estimate of earnings* for the company's current fiscal year and, if the year is halfway through, a tentative projection of earnings for the next year. Your broker can get you earnings estimates for companies that are well covered by analysts, but you may sometimes have to make an earnings estimate yourself.

There's a mechanical way of forecasting earnings that gives you what might be called a well-educated guesstimate: *simply multiply the current book value by the 5-year or 3-year average return on stockholders' equity.* If book value stands at $10 and average ROE was 20 percent, estimated earnings per share will be $2. If the company's ROE has been improving steadily, you can refine your estimate by using last year's ROE or even a slightly higher one instead of the average. The mechanical method shouldn't be applied, however, to highly cyclical companies whose earnings fluctuate sharply.

There's another rough-and-ready method for forecasting earnings. Look at the total revenues for the past few years and the net (after-tax) profit margin. Then, drawing on everything you've learned about the company, estimate revenues and the profit margin for the current year. By multiplying these two figures you'll get net income, which, divided by the number of shares outstanding, gives you earnings per share. If estimated revenues are $100 million, the net margin is 6 percent; and if there are three million shares outstanding, net income will be $6 million and earnings per share $2.

To wind up your analysis you should try to figure out *the ratio of risk to possible reward*, a crucial factor that amateur investors often fail to evaluate. There are several ways of doing this. I'll illustrate a crude but useful one, using a hypothetical stock, Testcorp. Inc., which had an EPS (earnings per share) of $3.65 last year, is expected to earn $4 a share this year, and is selling at $24.

First, you make a projection of a price to which the stock might drop within the next 12 months if things turn out badly; then you make a reasonably optimistic price projection; then you compare the possible percentage loss and gain. A moderately pessimistic projection for Testcorp. might be based on EPS of $3.50 and a P/E ratio at or close to the low end of its range for the past several years, which we'll assume was 5 to 9; that would give a price of $3.50 × 5, or $17.50 — 27 percent below the current price. A rational projection based on favorable assumptions might be that the stock will sell at eight times EPS of $4 or $32 — about 33 percent above the current price. The ratio of possible reward to risk — 33 percent to 27 percent — is *not* inviting. If you're trying to beat the market, you should look for stocks whose potential gain appears to be twice their possible loss.

Some of the procedures described in this chapter undoubtedly sound formidable to a beginner, and at the start he'll certainly find them taxing. But they really aren't difficult to learn. And even a novice, once he gets organized and has the data at hand, will quickly pick up speed and proficiency. Madelon Talley was a New York housewife with no financial experience when she joined the Dreyfus Corp., a large mutual fund organization. While performing statistical chores, she taught herself how to analyze stocks and so impressed management with her acumen that she was soon promoted to portfolio manager; within a few years, Mrs. Talley was a recognized star. Another brilliant stock-picker with no formal training in economics or finance is Charles Allmon, a money manager who became fascinated by the stock market while working as a photographer for *National Geographic*. The losses Allmon suffered through following brokers prompted him to develop his own investment strategy in the 1950s; the best opportunities, he concluded, lay in the smaller companies that analysts had overlooked. This strategy proved so successful that friends started asking him to manage their investments, and before long he found himself with a stable of clients. Clearly Madelon Talley and Charles Allmon are exceptionally gifted people; moreover, they didn't retain their amateur status. But I know amateurs who have learned to analyze stocks and have done their own stock-picking with remarkable results. One of them is Robert S. Morrow of Dublin, Ohio, an electrical engineer who had no interest in the stock market until his wife badgered him into joining an investment club that calls itself the MMMDCX Stock Club. I have seen a record of the 13 stocks bought and subsequently sold by the club on Morrow's recommendation between February 1976 and May 1981. The average holding period was 21 months. The total net gain — two stocks were losers — amounted to 1,746 percent, roughly 75 percent compounded annually over the 5-year period. How did Morrow achieve these phenomenal results? He used a market timing approach and confined his stock-picking to high-technology issues, which, as an engineer, he was well-equipped to understand. But you don't have to be a high-tech buff to outperform the market. Charles Allmon, for example, tends to avoid high-tech issues, because in most cases he considers their price/earnings ratios forbiddingly high.

A final word about stock valuation. Don't waste your time analyzing overanalyzed stocks that represent the most efficient sector of the market. The chances are virtually nil that you can discover anything about a Kodak, an Exxon, or a Texas Instruments that isn't known and reflected in the price of the stock. Confine your homework to lesser-known or underanalyzed companies, which are by no means always small ones. If you are good at handling numbers and have an inquiring mind, you should find stock analysis an intriguing form of detective work. And it can be a lot more rewarding than solving crossword puzzles.

16. The Technical Approach: Focusing on Supply and Demand

There's much in technical analysis that smacks of abracadabra, but its underlying premises are ones that common sense can readily accept: the behavior of investors tends to repeat itself, so past trends or patterns in buying and selling can provide valuable clues to future price movements. While the best policy for most amateur investors is to rely mainly on fundamentals in their choice of investments, an understanding of some of the tools of technical analysis can be of considerable help to them in deciding when to buy and when to sell. Before getting down to specifics, let me briefly review the case for and against technical analysis.

Technical analysts don't deny that fundamental factors — earnings, interest rates, trends in the economy. and so on — influence the actions of investors. But, the technicians claim, EVERYTHING that influences investors — including fear, greed, and crowd psychology — is precisely reflected in the behavior of stock prices and trading volume, recorded on charts or in the output of computers. The purists of technical analysis argue, further, that the fundamentals are "irrelevant" and indeed misleading, because they don't tell us anything about the dominant force in the market: the emotions of investors. It follows that the only winning approach is to go straight to the heart of the matter and focus on price and volume data, which are a mirror of what really makes stock prices move: the interplay of supply and demand. The messiahs of technical analysis insistently reiterate that the data they heed are "the language of the market," and "only the market tells the story."

The trouble with this credo is that the market speaks "with forked tongue"; its language is often so ambiguous that it tells different stories to different technicians. For example, when Joseph E. Granville flashed his notorious "sell everything" signal on January 6, 1981, the market was telling another cardinal of the technical hierarchy, veteran analyst Edson Gould, that its trend was still upward. Indeed Granville himself was bombastically bullish only three days before he pushed the panic button; his market letter of January 3, headlined "Straight Up," urged investors to do "some aggressive new buying." Thus from a practical standpoint, a major drawback of technical analysis is that the data it studies are subject to divergent interpretations. And when technical gurus give conflicting advice, you have to be an expert in the abstruse "language of the market" to judge which of their readings seems to be the more persuasive. In contrast, when fundamentalists differ, the evidence they present — earnings' records, product information, profit margins, and so on — is of a kind that an intelligent layman can weigh for himself.

The most far-reaching attack on technical analysis has come from the Random Walk Hypothesis (discussed in chapter 12). But the Random Walkers claim too much, or so their critics charge — in my opinion, rightly. The most that the Random Walk studies have proved is that the particular technical tools they tested — past patterns of price behavior — failed to produce worthwhile results. That does not prove that past prices *coupled with volume data — figures showing patterns of money flows into stocks and out of them —* are of no value in predicting future price movements. Nor do the mathematical concepts involved by the Random Walkers prove beyond a reasonable doubt that stock prices move randomly *all of the time.* Common sense and the perceptions of countless investment professionals suggest that stock prices, at least part of the time, do move in trends. That view is supported by a study* conducted at the Wharton School of the University of Pennsylvania by Edward L. Bishop III and John R. Rollins and later published in the fall 1977 issue of the *Journal of Portfolio Management.* Bishop and Rollins measured the results of buying and selling the shares of five mutual funds in accordance with the signals given by a well-known technical service, Lowry's Reports Inc., chosen because its timing system is clearly defined and all of its signals have been a matter of public record since 1938. The study covered nine different periods between 1950 and 1975 and led its authors to the following conclusions.

*"The Validity of Technical Stock Market Analysis: A Study of Lowry's Reports Inc.," December 30, 1975.

(1) Purchases and sales made in accordance with the Lowry signals "resulted in over double the gains achieved through buy-and-hold strategies" (taking into account commission costs). (2) "Trends in the market do seem to exist . . . and can be discovered in advance using weak form [technical] data." Complete randomness is not a correct description of how prices behave. (3) Trends develop and persist only when significant changes in investors' expectations substantially increase the flow of funds into or out of the stock market. The rest of the time stocks move randomly, and even during an extended uptrend or downtrend, there are trendless interludes when price movements are random.

TRENDS AND COUNTERTRENDS

A basic concept of technical analysis stems from Newton's First Law of Motion, which says that a body in motion, left to itself, will continue to move in the same direction. Applied to stock prices, this means that a trend in force will persist until a significant change in investors' expectations (about the market or an individual stock) causes it to reverse itself; the odds are better than even that a market (or stock) in a well-established uptrend will continue to advance, and that one in a clear-cut downtrend will continue to decline.

Technical analysts identify three kinds of trends: the long-term (also known as the "primary" or major) trend, which may last anywhere from nine months to several years or even longer; the intermediate-term or "secondary" trend, which typically lasts from two or three months to nine; and the short-term or "minor" trend, which is measured in days or weeks. A primary uptrend is usually interrupted by intermediate-term "corrections" (downtrends) and a primary downtrend by intermediate-term rallies (uptrends). Similarly, intermediate-term trends are punctured by short-term movements running counter to the trend. Some technical analysts concentrate on the primary and the intermediate-term trends; they wisely issue buy and sell signals only when they anticipate a swing of at least 50 to 100 points for the Dow. But many technicians address themselves to in-and-out traders; they try to catch minor fluctuations, which are probably unpredictable and certainly not predictable enough to make short-term trading a profitable strategy for amateur investors, taking into account the large brokerage commissions involved.

There are three main approaches to technical analysis that are not mutually exclusive. *One of them studies charts showing the past price behavior of a stock (or a market average);* bars at the bottom of the chart represent the volume of trading. *The second approach focuses on market indicators,* of which there are several dozen — for example, the Mutual Funds' Cash/Assets Ratio, discussed in an earlier chapter. To those who know how to interpret them, each of the market indicators gives a reading that is bullish, bearish, or "neutral," and taken together these readings are helpful in judging which way the market is headed. *The third approach focuses more directly than the others on supply and demand; it measures the flow of funds into or out of a stock or the market in order to determine whether greater pressure is being exerted by buyers or sellers.* The Lowry program, for example, measures (1) the total gains for all stocks closing at a higher price than the previous day's close and the total volume of transactions in those stocks, and (2) the total losses for all stocks closing lower than the previous day's close and the total volume of transactions. Out of these figures, Lowry's builds indexes from which it gets its buy and sell signals. (*Lowry's Weekly Market Trends Analysis Reports* [350 Royal Palm Way, Palm Beach, FL 33480] cost $200 a year plus postage when this chapter was written.)

The majority of technical analysts use charts (which show trading volume) together with market indicators. Here's a rundown on some of their basic concepts and tools, which — *used in conjunction with fundamental analysis* — could be of help to amateur investors, both in identifying market trends and in deciding when to buy and sell individual stocks.

A LOOK AT THE CHARTS

Two of the key concepts underlying the chartist approach — "support" and "resistance" — are rooted in the plausible belief that the behavior of investors tends to repeat itself. If you look at a long-term chart of the Dow Jones Industrial Average, you'll see clearly that, between 1966 and the close of 1981, the Dow backtracked when it approached, reached, or went slightly above the 1,000 level; that happened in 1966, 1968, 1973, 1976 (many times), 1980, and 1981. This tells us that throughout the 15-year period there was substantially more selling than buying whenever the Dow reached the area of 1,000. That's what is meant by resistance level; it's a level at which, in the past, supply has recurrently exceeded demand and pushed prices downward. Similarly, a "support level" is one at which previous declines have repeatedly been arrested because of more buying than selling. From 1976 through 1981, the 750 area was a major support level for the Dow.

In any given period, there are several support and resistance levels for the market averages and for individual stocks — levels based on past turning points in long-term, intermediate-term, and short-term price movements. When a stock (or market average) falls below a support level *on large trading volume*, technicians expect it to go lower; when it breaks through a resistance level on large trading volume, they expect it to go higher. Their rationale: if demand fails to exceed supply at a price that's previously attracted buyers, it's a sign of trouble. And if demand is greater than supply at a price that's previously triggered selling, it's a sign of new-found strength. The breaking of support and resistance levels on a small volume isn't significant; *the amount of buying or selling accompanying the breakthrough is the decisive factor.*

The price zone between a support and resistance level is called a channel or trading range. A stock that in recent months has fluctuated within a channel of 24 to 30 may, over the past 12 months, have had a trading range of 18 to 35. If the stock drops below 24, its next support level will be 18, and if it rises above 30, its next resistance level will be 35. If it declines to 24 two or three times *without dropping below that level*, it's said to have "successfully tested" its support; technicians generally consider that an indication that, in due course, the price will start moving upward. On the other hand, if the stock rises to 30 two or three times, but fails to break through that resistance level, technicians would conclude that its price (at least temporarily) is likely to turn downward.

I should caution you that minor and highly questionable support and resistance levels are often used in so-called technical letters as the basis for near-term forecasts and recommendations that can only be described as drivel. For example, a technical letter will say that if a market average — I'll use a hypothetical one standing 1,000 — breaks through 1,018, the advance should "carry to" 1060; on the other hand, a drop below 988 would give "a downside reading to 940–950." This is a nonforecast couched in mumbo-jumbo: all it's saying is that if the market doesn't go up, it will go down, and the probable swing will be about 60 points in either direction. Another standard gambit of some technicians is to tell you that a stock, currently selling at 24, should be bought if it penetrates minor resistance at 24¾ "for a move to 29," but if the stock drops to 22½ after you've bought it, cut your losses and sell. It's hard to believe, but many investors follow that kind of trading advice, presumably out of a neurotic need to enrich their brokers and impoverish themselves.

There are, however, situations in which significant support and resistance levels offer guidance that's worth heeding, if only because so many people playing the market piously believe in technical analysis and act accordingly. Here are four simple precepts that could improve your investment performance. The information you'll require about support and resistance levels and trading volume can usually be obtained from your broker; most brokers nowadays are technically oriented, and their firms supply them with reams of technical analysis.

1. If you are thinking of buying a stock or putting funds into the market, you'd be well advised to hold off if that stock or the entire market has just broken a major support level — *and trading volume was large.*

2. If you're thinking of selling, act promptly when a major support level has been broken (on large volume).

3. If you're considering buying a stock which, after a sharp runup, has risen to a significant resistance level and has repeatedly failed to penetrate it, the prudent policy is to wait and watch. The probabilities are that the stock has risen too much too soon and that it will pull back as more investors sell it to cash in their profits. (A retreat equal to roughly one-third of the advance would provide a good buying opportunity.) But if the stock, instead of retreating, bounces up again and finally breaks through its resistance level, buy it without delay. The chances are good that now it will continue to rise.

4. If you like a stock for fundamental reasons but want to check on your chances of buying it at a somewhat lower price, find out where it stands within its trading channel. If it's somewhere in the middle or below, buy it; if it's at the high end, there's a good chance it will backtrack — unless you know of a strong reason that could cause it to break through its resistance level or unless the market is rising sharply.

A final point about support and resistance levels. At any given moment, the only certainty about them is that sooner or later they'll be broken. In severe bear markets, stock prices crash relentlessly through a succession of descending support levels, and in bull markets they surmount resistance levels with the greatest of ease.

THOSE ELUSIVE CHART "FORMATIONS"

When the behavior of stock prices is recorded on charts, it assumes recurring patterns or formations, which technicians refer to as a head-and-shoulders, a flag, a pennant, a rounded top, a double bottom, and so on — one of the odder ones is known as a "Prussian helmet." It would be pointless to discuss them here, because interpreting chart formations is not a game that amateurs should play. Even professionals, looking at the same formations, often read divergent conclusions.

INDICATORS AND WHAT THEY INDICATE

Constant indicator-watching is neither practical nor necessary for the average investor. What he needs is to know which indicators to consult, and how to interpret them, when he's contemplating investment decisions or simply wants to sharpen his sense of the market's prospects. The technical indicators described below constitute a serviceable cross-section of the more than fifty tracked by market technicians. Although these indicators have been explained as simply as possible without lapsing into gross oversimplification, the pages that follow will be tough going for a novice. Rank beginners would be well advised to be guided by the fundamentals discussed in this book and not to try to decipher technical indicators, so I suggest that they skip the rest of this chapter. Investors who feel they could benefit from an elementary course in the use of technical indicators are urged to read on.

Moving Averages: A moving average (MA) of stock prices is a trend indicator; its function is to smooth out day-to-day fluctuations and reveal a trend that could otherwise be masked. A 10-day moving average smooths out ripples and reveals small waves; a 30-day average smooths out small waves and reveals large ones; a 200-day average smooths out all waves and reveals ebbs and flows in the tide. A change of trend is indicated when a moving average that was declining has flattened and is turning upward, which is bullish; or when a moving average that was rising has flattened and is turning downward, which of course is bearish.

A simple moving average is composed by first adding up the daily (or weekly) closing prices of a market index or a stock and dividing the total by the number of days (or weeks) in the period. Then — if the average is a 10-day one — you add the eleventh day's closing price and subtract the first day's, and you go on repeating the procedure daily. A simple 10-day moving average is a crude indicator. It exposes traders to the risk of being whipsawed — buying just before prices drop and selling just before they rise. Most traders therefore use a weighted or an "exponential" moving average; these give considerably more weight to the latest than to the earliest prices, so they are quicker to reflect a change of trend. Since short-term moving averages are designed to reveal minor trends, investors who are not traders are best served by 90-day or even 200-day moving averages. Charts that show moving averages often appear in brokerage house technical reports, but investors who use technical analysis systematically usually subscribe to one of the chart services. (The weeklies typically cost anywhere from $200 to $500 a year.) Leading chart services include Chartcraft (One West Avenue, Larchmont, NY 10538); R. W. Mansfield Co. (26 Journal Sq., Jersey City, NJ 07306); and Trendline Inc. (25 Broadway, New York, NY 10004).

Interpreting the behavior of a stock in relation to its moving average calls for considerable proficiency in technical analysis. In theory — to take a relatively simple example — when a stock rises above a declining moving average or drops below a rising moving average, its behavior indicates that the stock's trend may be reversing itself. The indication would be "confirmed" if the declining MA flattens and turns upward or if the rising MA flattens and turns downward. The former would be a signal to buy, the latter a signal to sell. It's advisable, however, to use moving average in conjunction with other indicators and with fundamental data.

The Advance/Decline Line — a moving average based on the ratio of stocks advancing to stocks declining — is a "breadth" indicator: it tells us whether the market is advancing or declining on a broad front or a narrow one. In its simplest form, the A/D Line is plotted by starting with an arbitrary number, say 10,000, and adding or subtracting the difference between the number of stocks advancing and declining; the difference is added to the base number if advances outnumber declines and subtracted if declines outnumber advances. (Advances and declines are reported on the next-to-last page of the *Wall Street Journal* and in other leading newspapers.)

A weighted market index such as the Dow often rises even when a majority of stocks are declining or falls when a majority are rising, because (as I explained in chapter 2) the Dow is strongly influenced by the behavior of its high-priced stocks. But the A/D Line, which reflects the cumulative difference between the number of stocks advancing and stocks declining, reveals whether the overall market is trending upward or downward. This indicator, which Joseph E. Granville has called "the single most important technical tool," has often been the first to show clearly a major change in the market's direction. For example, while the Dow Jones Industrials were soaring to their 1972 peak of 1052, the A/D Line was warning that the general market was in a menacing downturn — the downturn that eventually snowballed into the appalling crash of 1973–1974.

Volume Indicators: The volume of trading helps investors to identify trends in supply and demand, which price changes alone do not indicate reliably. The basic concepts are that it's bullish when volume tends to increase during price advances or decrease during declines; it's bearish when volume tends to decrease during advances or increase during declines. An important step forward in volume analysis was taken when Joseph E. Granville introduced the concept of "on balance volume" (OBV) in his book, *Granville's New Strategy of Daily Stock Market Timing for Maximum Profit* (Englewood Cliffs: Prentice-Hall, 1976). The essence of Granville's contribution can be easily explained, but you need to have studied his book thoroughly to use OBV as an indicator of precisely when to buy and sell. Granville defines trading volume as "demand volume" on days when a stock or the market (depending on which you're tracking) advances; on declining days, volume is "supply volume"; when there is no price change, volume is ignored. On balance volume is simply cumulative net supply or demand volume over a period of time. For example, XYZ stock rises on Monday on volume of 5,000 shares and declines Tuesday on volume of 20,000; OBV is 15,000 Down. Wednesday, XYZ rises on volume of 4,000; OBV is now 11,000 Down. XYZ's price may have risen one point on each of the up days and declined two points on the down day, ending the period unchanged. But the OBV reading of 11,000 down indicates that supply was stronger than demand. Thus OBV is a refined way of using price changes coupled with trading volume to detect whether money is moving into stocks or out of them. Volume figures are given in newspaper stock market tables, so tracking OBV for an individual stock or the New York Stock Exchange index is a matter of simple arithmetic.

Sentiment Indicators: These are indicators that reveal the expectations of different types of investors, in particular (1) the general public and the very small investors known as "odd lotters" who trade in units of less than 100 shares; (2) market insiders such as Specialists (market makers on the exchanges) and exchange members trading for their own accounts. When sentiment indicators show that the public is overwhelmingly bullish or bearish, they serve warning that it's time to take the contrary attitude. (The contrary opinion approach to investing is discussed in chapter 17.) And when sentiment indicators reveal a sharp divergence in the behavior of the general public and market insiders, it's sensible to take your cue from the insiders; the chances are they know more.

The Odd Lot Short-Sales Ratio is one of the most widely watched "contrary opinion" indicators. (A short sale is a sale of borrowed stock made in the expectation that its price will decline. For a full explanation, see Appendix D.) The rationale of the odd-lot short-sales ratio is that odd-lot *short-sellers* are the most unsophisticated of speculators. Indeed, the historical record shows them to have been *invariably* wrong: their selling has been greatest when bear markets were ending and smallest when bull markets were about to peak. (In contrast the ordinary odd-lotter, since the mid-1960s, has been among the savviest of investors; he has regularly been a buyer at market bottoms and has sold when prices were high.) The odd-lot short-sales ratio is generally computed by dividing odd-lot short sales by the average of odd-lot purchases and total sales (purchases and total sales divided by two). Over the past few decades the ratio has averaged 1.2 percent. Whenever it has soared above 4 percent — indicating that odd-lot short selling was exceptionally large — it has signaled a market advance; when it has dropped to 0.5 percent, it has signaled a market decline. Over more than half a century, the odd-lot short-sales ratio has proved to be one of the best indicators for forecasting major turning points in the market.

The Specialists' Short-Sales Ratio is the ratio of short sales made by Specialists to total short sales, calculated on a weekly basis. (The figures are published on Mondays in the *Wall Street Journal* and they appear in *Barron*'s on the "Market Laboratory" page.) As market makers, Specialists are forced to do a lot of short selling to help bridge the gaps that occur when buyers outnumber sellers. Since they make their living in part by short selling — and Specialists' earnings are so high that critics describe their function as "a license to steal" — it's almost axiomatic that Specialists as a group are the most knowledgeable of short-sellers. Consequently, the greater the volume of their shorting in relation to total short sales, the likelier it is that prices will decline; the smaller their share of total short selling, the likelier it is that prices will rise. When the Specialists' short-sale ratio rises above 60 percent, it's giving a bearish signal; when it falls below 45 percent, it's giving a bullish one. If it drops below 35 percent, the probability that stock prices will be higher a year later is 100 percent.

The Advisory Sentiment Indicator, which shows the percentage of advisory services that are bullish and bearish, is a contrary opinion indicator. It was explained in chapter 14 in the profile of the service that originated it, *Investors Intelligence.*

The Speculation Index compares the volume of trading on the American Stock Exchange with that on the New York Stock Exchange. Since there's a vastly larger proportion of speculative issues on the Amex than on the Big Board, the ratio of Amex volume to Big Board volume is a measure of speculative sentiment. Historically the ratio has ranged between 10 percent and 60 percent and has averaged about 30 percent. When it rises above 40 percent, it's warning us that the speculative temperature is dangerously high, and a reading of 60 percent is a strong sell signal. A reading of 20 percent is bullish and one of 15 percent or less is a strong buy signal. This indicator has correctly foretold major peaks and bottoms in the market for more than 50 years.

Seasonal Indicators: One of them merits attention because, though its rationale is vague, its predictive record has been phenomenally good. Its originator, Yale Hirsch, publisher of the *Stock Trader's Almanac,* calls it "the January Barometer." And what it indicates is that "as January goes, so goes the year as a whole." January was an up month for the S&P index in 19 of the 31 years from 1950 through 1981, and in all but one (1966) of those 19 years the index registered a gain. In 9 of the 13 years in which the market declined in January, the S&P index ended the year with a loss. On the basis of that record, the probabilities are 95 percent that a rise in January portends a rise for the year, and they are 69 percent that a decline in January portends a decline for the year. Overall, the January Barometer has proved prophetic 27 times out of 32, or 84 percent of the time.

Advisory services that track and interpret the leading indicators include five that were profiled in chapter 14: *Indicator Digest, Market Logic, The Professional Tape Reader, Systems and Forecasts,* and *The Zweig Forecast.*

17. The Psychological Approach: Profiting from Contrariness

When asked how he founded his great fortune, the nineteenth-century financier Russell Sage replied: "By buying straw hats in January." Buying summer hats in winter, when nobody wants them, is an example of the "contrary opinion" theory of investing, which holds that success comes from acting contrary to the herd. When panic prevails and the outlook for the stock market couldn't be darker, the theory says prices are close to a bottom and it's time to buy; when euphoria reigns, the market is approaching a peak and the time has come to sell.

But contrary opinion theory is much more than a psychological tool for anticipating market tops and bottoms. It's a mental discipline — a systematic way of thinking about investments — that can help investors to avoid the mistakes most commonly made by professionals as well as amateurs. Bernard Baruch said he saved himself millions of dollars by studying Charles Mackay's *Extraordinary Popular Delusions and the Madness of Crowds* (1841), one of the source books of contrary opinion theory.

The theory's modern formulator was Humphrey B. Neill, a successful stock-market trader who died in 1977. After retiring on his profits to Vermont, Neill wrote essays and newspaper columns, which first appeared in book form in 1954 as *The Art of Contrary Thinking* (Caxton Printers, P.O. Box 700, Caldwell, ID 83605; $3.95 paperback). This small, chatty volume has become the Bible of his disciples, who call themselves contrarians.

Neill credited the origin of his ideas to numerous writers on social psychology, but especially to Charles Mackay and Gustave Le Bon, whose classic, *The Crowd*, appeared in 1895. Neill's basic premise is that people acting as independent individuals are capable of rational thought and conduct, but people swayed by crowd psychology become totally irrational, succumbing to extremes of greed, fear, and gullibility. Said Neill, "A crowd thinks with its emotions, an individual thinks with his brain."

A celebrated example of mass folly in investing was the tulip mania that swept Holland from 1634 to 1636. When word got around that speculators were making fortunes in rare bulbs, ordinary people scrambled to sell their possessions, their land, even their houses, to invest in flowers, on the assumption that the boom would last indefinitely. At its peak, one rare bulb was paid for with 12 acres of choice building land. Another fetched a carriage and pair of horses. When tulip prices collapsed, the losses suffered were so great that the economy of Holland took years to recover.

Neill concluded that investors governed by crowd psychology cause the booms and busts, the fashions and fads of the stock market. "When everyone thinks alike, everyone is likely to be wrong" was his summation of his theory. It has a twofold rationale.

Since the future is largely unpredictable, an overwhelming consensus on where stock prices are heading usually ignores numerous uncertainties. Typically, consensus forecasts extrapolate current trends into the future and fail to take into account forces at work that could bring about change. Such consensus forecasts are therefore likely to be wrong. In addition, a market trend that nearly everyone expects isn't likely to occur, because investors act in anticipation of it, thereby changing the course of the market. By the time that an overwhelmingly bullish consensus (on the market or a stock) has taken shape most investors have already done their buying and there isn't enough purchasing power left to sustain a further advance. Similarly, by the time pessimism is ubiquitous, scared investors have dumped their stocks and the selling pressure that's driven prices down is abating.

Contrary opinion theory teaches investors to be nonconformists. Its defensive function is to keep them from being led astray by popular sentiment; its positive function is to help them profit from the follies of the crowd. The principles are easy to grasp, but putting them into practice calls for discipline and guts — because for most people it's second nature to think and act as others do. *Contrary opinion theory requires investors to do what does not come naturally.*

For example, the natural impulse of investors is to buy stocks that are being widely recommended by leading analysts; contrarians argue that it's generally best to avoid such stocks and dig, instead, for unrecognized values among issues that are neglected or downright unpopular. Their reasoning: the highly touted stocks have already been widely bought and are usually up in price, so they're liable to decline on any disappointing news, or as investors who got into them ahead of the pack cash in their profits. But the neglected stocks of sound companies with improving earnings will rise in price as investors gradually perceive their merits.

A leading exponent of contrary opinion theory is Humphrey Neill's former associate, James L. Fraser. An alumnus of Dartmouth College who served in army counterintelligence during the Korean War, Fraser worked at First National City Bank in New York and then at a Wall Street brokerage house before entering the investment counseling field in 1962. His firm, Fraser Management Associates (309 S. Willard, Burlington, VT 05401), publishes two fortnightlies, *Contrary Investor* ($70 a year) and the *Fraser Opinion Letter* ($45), and it manages investment accounts for individuals and small corporations. Fraser thinks it's easier to be a contrarian if you're far removed from the swirling emotions of Wall Street; his combined home and business headquarters is an old New England stone house overlooking Lake Champlain. The following excerpts from an interview I had with him there provide a concise guide to using the contrarian approach.

What's the first step in applying contrary opinion theory to the stock market?

Find out whether a powerful consensus exists — on the outlook for the market or certain types of stocks. You can learn this from the financial press and brokerage house reports; a shortcut is to subscribe to an investment advisory service that specializes in contrary opinion or keeps track of other services. For example, *Investors Intelligence* (see chapter 14) publishes a chart showing the percentage of services that are bullish and bearish.

When a powerful consensus exists, a contrarian acts on the opposite view. But it's only in the late stages of bull and bear markets that investors are overwhelmingly bullish or bearish. Most of the time you find a variety of conflicting views.

So what does a contrarian do then?

He starts out by trying to determine what is the majority view. Mind you, contrary opinion theory does not — as many people mistakenly believe — assert that the majority is always wrong. Unlike a powerful consensus, which is the product of crowd psychology, a simple majority view may be rationally founded. [For example, a majority of investment strategists were extremely bullish on energy issues in 1978 for reasons that were entirely rational and proved to be correct. But two years later, the valuations of these issues had in many cases doubled, and to contrarians the continuing enthusiasm for them smacked of irrationality. Indeed, in the course of 1981, the prices of most energy issues peaked and turned sharply downward.]

What does a contrarian do when he encounters a view that's held by a majority of analysts but is not an overwhelming consensus?

He scans that view with rigorous scepticism to determine as best he can whether it's supported by reason and fact. Then he takes the antithetical view and subjects it to the same scrutiny. Suppose, for example, that a majority of year-end forecasters are predicting a market decline in the first half of the coming year and a rise in the second half. A contrarian would critically examine the pros and cons of that projection and also those of its opposite — that the market will rise in the first half and fall in the second. After then considering other possibilities — one being that throughout the year the market could trend upward or downward — a contrarian will finally reach his own conclusion. I should emphasize that contrary opinion's greatest value is to investors willing to take a longer-term view. Since a contrarian isn't a trend follower, he will nearly always do his buying and selling too early and have to wait some time before being proved right. But, as Neill said, "If you're not early, you'll probably be late."

What types of stock do contrarians tend to favor?

It's risky to generalize. As a contrarian, I recommend stocks that fall into one of two main categories: (1) unpopular stocks of large well-known companies that I consider turnaround situations — that is, I find the prevailing assessment of their problems overly pessimistic; (2) stocks of little-known companies whose merits and potenti-alities aren't recognized because few if any analysts follow them.

What guidelines do you, as a contrarian, follow for selling stocks?

When I buy a stock, I project a price it will reach when it achieves popularity, which is my signal to sell. Since market psychology changes, I may have to readjust the stock's "popularity price." However, if something happens that spells sudden popularity for a stock, I sell it regardless of price. For example, my clients owned MCA stock when *Time* did a cover story in 1975 on the huge success of *Jaws*, an MCA movie. This prompted a surge of buying in MCA shares, which to me was a signal to sell. With all of the good news out, it was hard to see what could make the stock more popular. It was two years, in fact, before MCA again reached its $33.75 high of that week.

What would you do if the cover of a popular financial magazine featured a story on, say, the bright prospects for the aluminum industry?

If I owned any aluminum stocks, I'd sell them.

What's the toughest problem that faces investors who use contrary opinion theory?

To persevere in a course you consider right when months go by and it continues to look wrong. It's awfully tough to hang on to a stock that's acting like a tortoise when the market's full of sprinters.

How widely is contrary opinion theory practiced by money managers?

Its principles are widely accepted nowadays, but by its very nature the theory can never become popular — a crowd of money managers trying to act contrary to the crowd will simply become a different crowd. I would say, however, that every exceptionally successful money manager — and private investor — is a gifted contrarian. No one who has consistently beaten the market can possibly have done it by following the herd.

THE CASE OF THE CONTRARIAN HOG-RAISER

In the October 2, 1978, issue of *Forbes* magazine, John Train — president of a New York investment counseling firm and the author of two fine books on investing, *Dance of the Money Bees* and *The Money Masters* — recounted the beguiling saga of a Texas rice farmer and hog raiser who made a fortune in the stock market. This Mr. Womack had a simple system that he unswervingly followed for more than 40 years. Whenever a severe bear market had swept stock prices down to new lows, Womack would work his way through Standard & Poor's Stock Guide and pick about 30 stocks that had fallen below $10 a share — stocks of obscure, prosaic, profit-making companies in sound financial health and paying dividends. He would invest $25,000 in a package of these stocks and, if they declined much further, would buy another $25,000 worth. He would hold them — often for several years — until the next big boom in stocks was thundering along, and then sell all of his holdings. He would then stash away his gains until the bear was again clawing at the market. Mr. Womack, Train recounts, never seemed to buy a stock at its bottom or sell it at its top. But he never had a net loss on his round trips into and out of the market and he repeatedly made killings. Like Russell Sage, Mr. Womack bought straw hats in January, but his story reminds us to sell them in July. Train wrote this testimonial to Mr. Womack, who died in 1977: "He changed my investing lifestyle and I have made a profit ever since."

18. The Political Approach: "Election Cycle Investing"

In the August 1976 issue of *Money* magazine, an article of mine started with the following forecast: "The Stock market will end the year higher than it is on August 1. The Dow Jones industrial average will peak out early in 1977 and its subsequent decline will last about ten months. Then there will be a long and powerful recovery that should reach its high point after the 1980 elections." That forecast proved to be remarkably accurate. The Dow ended 1976 appreciably above its August 1 level. At the beginning of 1977, it went into a sustained downtrend that lasted 14 months. Then a long though erratic recovery got under way that lifted the Dow from its 1978 low of 742 to 1,000 on November 20, 1980. Regrettably, I can't claim credit for having displayed prophetic powers. The brilliant forecast wasn't made by me, nor did it come from Jeane Dixon, a supercomputer, or a wizard of Wall Street. It was based on an abstraction — the average behavior of the stock market over all of the 4-year presidential election cycles from 1948 through 1972.

Obviously, the market's behavior in any particular presidential election cycle has varied and will vary from the average pattern, to which it so closely conformed in the 1976–1980 cycle. Even so, the historical record clearly suggests which periods are apt to be the best for buying stocks, for selling them, and for staying out of the market. Tests have shown that since 1961 an investment strategy based on these timing pointers has significantly outperformed the market. And the beauty of this strategy is that it couldn't be simpler: you buy a diversified portfolio of stocks on November 30 of the *second* year *after* a presidential election and you hold them for exactly two years. Then you sell your entire portfolio and invest the proceeds in Treasury Bills or money-market funds. On November 30, two years after the subsequent election, you go back into the market. That's all there is to it. I'll give you specific figures showing the results of this strategy. But first let's look into the rationale of political cycle investing.

WHY WALL STREET DANCES TO WASHINGTON'S TUNE

The connection between the election cycle and recurring tendencies of the stock market is rooted in the interaction of politics and economics. Francis H. M. Kelly, a prominent investment strategist, has summed up this interplay as follows: "The government's management of economic affairs naturally looms large in the electorate's estimate of its worthiness. Therefore, a great deal of orchestration goes into the fine art of making the economy sing appropriate melodies to the score of the quadrennial elections."

Hard data on how the economy has been orchestrated are presented in Edward R. Tufte's book *Political Control of the Economy* (Princeton: Princeton University Press, 1978.) Tufte's figures show, among other things, that increases in federal spending, Social Security, and real disposable income have been either larger or more frequent — and sometimes both — in presidential election years than in others. Then, some time after a President takes office, the economy usually has to pay the price for policies designed before the election to woo voters, and for the neglect of problems that require unpalatable remedies.

All this tends to create a correlation between the presidential cycle and the business cycle. According to figures published by the National Bureau of Economic Research, the average duration of business cycles has been about 48 months — the same length as the election cycle. Since 1948 the economy, on average, has peaked out seven months after election day and has sunk to its low point eleven months later. This has left the administration an average of 30 months before the next election to put through policies that will increase the public's sense of well-being.

The stock market's recovery phases have therefore tended to start about 36 months before the next presidential election. The market usually anticipates future developments — it's one of the so-called leading economic indicators — and its average lead time is about 6 months. For similar reasons, the market has tended to top out in the early part of postelection years. It's anticipating the contraction that is apt to begin some months later. Says Yale Hirsch, editor of the *Stock Trader's Almanac:* "Paying the piper after the making of Presidents induces the 'post-presidential year syndrome.' These are the years in which most of the big bear markets began — 1929, 1937, 1957, 1969, 1973." In 1977, too, the Dow declined throughout the year and it wound up in 1981 with a 9 percent loss.

From the end of World War II to the Reagan era, the Dow advanced after eight of the nine presidential elections. The exception was Harry Truman's surprise victory over Thomas E. Dewey in 1948. Five of those advances topped out within two months after the election; one lasted for eight months (under Eisenhower), one for thirteen months (under Kennedy) and one for six months (under Reagan). Overall, the average length of the postelection advance was slightly more than four months. There's a warning in this for investors: after election day they should watch the market particularly closely for signs of an impending downturn.

The decline that has followed the market's postelection high has varied greatly in length — from six weeks under Lyndon Johnson to just over two years in Nixon's second term. On the average, this down phase has lasted ten to eleven months and the Dow has dropped about 22 percent. The ensuing recovery has almost invariably been long and substantial. It has averaged slightly more than three years for the period 1948 through 1980, with the Dow posting an average advance of nearly 60 percent.

The political-cycle timing strategy that I referred to earlier — buying stocks in November 30 of the second year after a presidential election and selling them on the November 30 following the next election — was formulated back in 1973 by David W. MacNeill, a senior investment officer of the First National Bank of Boston. (He uses November 30 rather than November 5 as his selling date, because the market usually continues to rise for a few weeks or months after election day.) MacNeill's research shows that between November 30, 1962, and November 30, 1980, Standard & Poor's 500-stock index had an average negative return or loss of 11.7 percent (taking into account dividends) in the two-year periods following a presidential election. In the two-year periods prior to a presidential election, the total return on the S&P index was a whopping 50 percent. Over the entire 18-year period, an investment in the S&P index managed in accordance with political cycle timing achieved a total return of 1,110 percent, or 14.6 percent compounded annually — more than three times the total return of 341 percent on an investment in the S&P index that was simply held throughout the period.

A study by Fred C. Allvine and Daniel E. O'Neill published in the *Financial Analysts Journal* (September–October 1980) amplifies Mac-Neill's findings by taking into account the brokerage commissions and capital gains taxes incurred in a political-cycle timing program. Allvine and O'Neill covered a slightly different period, 1961 to 1978, and they used the S&P 400-stock index rather than the 500-stock index as their stock portfolio. *They found that the political-cycle timing program outperformed a buy-and-hold strategy by a margin of 3½ to 1.*

There's an extraordinarily easy and economical way for the individual investor to use the political-cycle strategy. You simply put your money into a no-load, common stock mutual fund — preferably a growth fund — on November 30 two years before a presidential election; two years later, you switch into a money-market fund; and you continue to switch, back and forth, once every two years. It's that simple; you don't have to worry about stock selection and you don't pay any brokerage commissions.

If large numbers of investors were to adopt the political-cycle timing strategy, they would, of course, alter the quadrennial pattern of market behavior — and the strategy would cease to work. But it seems unlikely that political-cycle timing will achieve wide popularity. To date relatively few people know about it, and it's not something the brokerage houses will promote; it would be suicidal for them to tell their clients to stay totally out of stocks two years out of four. Second, for many people it goes against the grain to act like a rigidly programmed robot; following a formula takes the challenge and the fun out of investing. Third and most important, political-cycle investing isn't a strategy that institutions with billion-dollar portfolios can practice; they could not swing their huge assets into and out of stocks once every two years without altering the course of the market.

To anyone tempted to adopt a political-cycle timing strategy, let me proffer two *caveats:* (1) large market advances are not *invariably* confined to the two years preceding presidential elections, so you may find yourself out of stocks at a time when you'd dearly like to be in them; (2) if you tinker with the timetable or shoot for better results by, say, investing in a handful of speculative stocks instead of a mutual fund or a broadly diversified portfolio, then you are strictly on your own. When you invest according to the political-cycle timing formula, or any other formula, you must adhere to it faithfully.

A Postscript: The evidence that recurring tendencies in the stock market are related to the presidential election cycle refutes — or at least runs counter to — the Random Walk and Efficient Market hypotheses (discussed in chapter 12). The well-defined four-year pattern of market behavior that I've just described shows that, over the long term, stocks don't move randomly; they move in trends. And the discovery that, over an 18-year period, a political-cycle timing strategy achieved significantly higher returns than those on the S&P index punctures the Efficient Market doctrine that no investment strategy can consistently outperform the market.

V

MANAGING YOUR MONEY: STRATEGY AND TACTICS

19. Choosing a Portfolio Strategy That Fits Your Stance

Many of the mistakes that people make in managing their investments result from acting haphazardly. The top priority in investing is to develop and follow a coherent, reasoned approach—an overall battle plan or portfolio strategy. The main steps are these: (1) *select your investment objective*, which will hinge on the degree of risk you're willing to assume: (2) *decide on a timing policy;* will you hold stocks for the long pull or try to anticipate swings in the market? (3) *from time to time, evaluate the investment outlook*—the prospects for the economy, individual industries, and the stock and bond markets; (4) in light of the investment outlook, *decide on a portfolio "mix" that fits your investment objective* (the mix is the apportioning of your capital among different types of investments—stocks, corporate and municipal bonds, money market securities, precious metals and so on); (5) *select the specific securities for your portfolio;* (6) once a year, *review your performance.*

SETTING THE OBJECTIVE

Most people's definition of their investment objective will correspond, more or less, to one of the following designations, which in principle imply descending levels of risk: (1) maximum capital gains; (2) high growth with minimal concern for income; (3) average growth combined with income (for example, the growth and dividend yield of the S&P index); (4) income with some growth, but with the emphasis mainly on income; (5) the highest possible income compatible with safety of principal.

An investor's objective reflects the degree of risk he's willing to assume. And that—as you've probably heard all too often—should be determined by his age, family situation, current and prospective earning power, net worth, tax bracket, and temperament. A single person of thirty with excellent career prospects and expectations of a sizable inheritance can obviously take much larger risks than a middle-aged couple with young children, moderate earning power, and no hopes of inheriting a nest egg. It's obvious, too, that retired persons living on a modest pension and income from their savings must keep their exposure to risk low. What the homilies about risk-taking usually fail to mention is that *it's as foolish not to take risks that you can reasonably afford as it is to run risks that you can't afford.* In the long run, taking above average risks should bring larger than average rewards.

Risk can be measured, not with certainty but in terms of probabilities. And risk can be "managed." So let's take a closer look at the different types of risk and how to handle them.

Market Risk: The risk related to the overall behavior of any securities market. Nowadays, the standard yardstick of a stock's market risk is its volatility—the extent of its fluctuations in relation to the S&P index. The academics who developed Modern Portfolio Theory chose beta, the second letter of the Greek alphabet, to express the volatility of a stock (as shown by its price history). Since the S&P index was taken as representing "the market," it was assigned a beta of 1. Thus a stock whose beta is 1.5 can be expected to rise and fall one-and-a-half times as much as the index, and it's considered 50 percent riskier.

You can try to protect yourself against market risk in a variety of ways. One is to put a portion of your assets into gold investments—bullion, coins, and gold mining stocks—whose prices tend to move *counter* to the stock market, though not as consistently as they used to. (See chapter 24, "Gold Isn't Just for Goldbugs.") Another way is to use hedging tactics; you hedge your "long" positions, the stocks you own, by making short sales, picking stocks that you think are the likeliest to go down. (Short selling is explained in Appendix D.) If the market drops, you'll presumably make profits on your "shorts," which will offset, partially or wholly, the losses on your longs. The danger is that, if the market moves sideways, you may wind up making the worst of both worlds—your shorts go up and your longs go down. A vastly preferable way of hedging is through the use of options, which are discussed in chapter 25.

Brokerage house strategists still prescribe an old-fashioned way of reducing market risk when the outlook seems threatening; they tell you to switch out of stocks with above-average risks into so-called defensive ones—for example, food, tobacco, and cosmetics issues—whose earnings hold up well in recessions. This tactic may have made sense in bygone days when defensive stocks yielded substantially more than Treasury Bills, and there were no money-market funds. But nowadays switching into defensive issues will do no more for you in a market slump than add to your brokerage commissions; only 1 percent of all stocks move counter to a major bear (or bull) market, and that 1 percent includes the golds. In fact, a defensive issue might aptly be defined as a stock in which you'll lose less money than in other stocks when the market's in a slump. So if you're bearish, why settle for a probable loss when you can move into the safe haven of a high-yielding money-market fund? Defensive stocks certainly have a place in conservative, income-oriented portfolios. *But the best way to cope with mounting market risk is to decrease the proportion of your assets invested in the stock market.*

Unique or "Diversifiable" Risk: a stock's risk is, of course, only partly contingent on the behavior of the market — stock prices also rise and fall because of industry and company developments. This type of risk, which is not reflected in beta, is known as unique or diversifiable risk; it can be minimized by proper diversification, because price fluctuations caused by factors other than the market's behavior vary from industry to industry and company to company. For example, high beta stocks in the data processing industry will at times perform better and at times worse than high beta issues in the airline industry. Consequently, an efficiently diversified portfolio with an average beta of, say, 1.2 is considerably less risky than a couple of stocks with the same beta. Studies of the behavior of stock prices suggest that diversifiable risk accounts for anywhere from 30 percent to 70 percent of a stock's total risk (depending on the industry and the company).

How many stocks are needed to achieve good diversification? The answer provided by scholarly research is that, if you put an equal amount of money into ten stocks in different industries exposed to different types of risk, you will eliminate about 90 percent of the diversifiable risk involved in owning one stock; you can eliminate 80 percent of that risk by owning only five stocks, similarly chosen. So even small investors who don't choose to use mutual funds can easily achieve good diversification, provided they're willing to buy some stocks in less than hundred-share lots.

Remember, though, that diversification depends far less on the number of stocks you own than on choosing stocks whose risks are related to different economic, social, and political factors; without this qualitative diversification, a portfolio of 100 stocks can offer less protection against diversifiable risk than a 15-stock portfolio. Many brokers seem not to understand this. Their conventional "widows' and orphans' portfolio" — supposedly an ultraconservative portfolio designed to provide safety and high income — tends to be heavily invested in public utility stocks and bonds, all of which will decline simultaneously whenever interest rates rise. Even a portfolio of 50 or more stocks in the airline, auto, rubber, textile, and steel industries would offer very little diversification; all of those industries are highly cyclical, and most if not all of the stocks will take a beating whenever a serious recession is expected. A list of a dozen industries with differing types of risk might include airlines, banks, computers, cosmetics, drugs, electronics, energy exploration, fertilizers, financial printing and publishing, gold mining, hospital management, and telecommunications. But whether you're building a portfolio from scratch or tinkering with an existing one, your choice of industries must depend on the general outlook for the economy and the stock market.

Interest Rate Risk: the risk stemming from changes in interest rates applies primarily to bonds; precisely how it affects them will be shown in chapter 22, "Investing for Income." But it also applies to the stocks of companies whose earnings are significantly affected by the trend of interest rates — favorably by a downtrend and unfavorably by an uptrend. The groups that Wall Street categorizes as "interest-sensitive" include utilities, banks, savings and loans, finance companies, and housing and building materials. When interest rates rise, utilities incur higher costs for the heavy long-term borrowing they do to finance expansion; banks and finance companies pay more for lendable funds; S & Ls have a weaker mortgage market; and home building slackens because of the rising cost of mortgage money. Clearly, it's unwise to stay invested in these groups if you expect an upward spiral in interest rates. And you can make good profits in the interest-sensitive stocks when rates peak and start heading downward.

DECIDING ON A TIMING POLICY

Excluding in-and-out trading, a dumb policy for the average investor, there are three basic approaches to market timing. (1) You adopt a "buy-and-hold" strategy, which means that you invest for the long haul and ignore swings in the market. It doesn't mean, however, that you just "put away" the stocks you buy and plan to hold them indefinitely. Even issues bought as long-term holdings need to be watched, and a time may come when they should be sold — either because they've risen to levels at which they offer less potential than other stocks, or because they've been stagnating. (2) You adopt a "market timing" approach, which involves buying or selling when you anticipate major turning points in the market. (3) You use "dollar cost averaging," a timing system that eliminates timing decisions: you automatically invest a fixed amount monthly in the same selected stocks or mutual funds. Your money will buy fewer shares when prices are high and more shares when prices are low; so your average cost over a period of twelve months or longer will approximate the average price of the shares you've been buying. There's no reason why you can't combine two or all of these approaches except that it requires more time, effort, and discipline. You might, for example, invest part of your capital for the long term and manage some of your money in accordance with a market timing system. When you sell, you park the proceeds in a money fund until you get your next strong buy signal.

An important consideration in your choice of a timing strategy is income taxes. Gains taken on investments held for more than 12 months and a day are taxed at 40 percent of the rate on short-term gains, which count as ordinary income. So to maximize his returns in the stock market, an investor has to aim at long-term gains. Even people in the middle-income tax brackets should try to avoid taking substantial short-term profits; in addition to paying more than twice the long-term capital gains tax rate, they will push themselves into a higher bracket. However, to let your investment decisions be dictated at all times by tax considerations is a mistaken policy. For example, you may buy a stock that shoots up 50 percent or more in months because it's in a group that's become ultrafashionable. In such cases, it could be dangerously overpriced, and it might well be wise to grab your splendid profit, regardless of the tax bite. Stocks that skyrocket can drop sharply, either because of a change in investment fashions, a disappointing company development, or a sinking spell in the market. Paying 50 percent in income taxes on a short-term gain of $2,000 leaves you considerably better off than paying the lower long-term rate, in this case 20 percent, on a profit that's dwindled to $500; you come out $600 ahead. While there's no truth in the adage "you can't go wrong by taking a profit," it's sometimes true that you *can* go wrong by *not* taking a profit.

EVALUATING THE INVESTMENT OUTLOOK

The main factors to consider are whether the economy is in the early, middle, or late phase of an uptrend or a recession; the trend of corporate profits, of inflation, and of interest rates; and the policies of the Federal Reserve Board. How these factors affect stock prices was discussed in earlier chapters (6 through 8). Ideally, your evaluation would also include a scrutiny of the leading technical indicators discussed in chapter 16. And if there exists a strong consensus about the market outlook, you should give some thought to the contrary opinion view. A handy forecasting system that combines all of these approaches is described in the following chapter.

DECIDING ON THE PORTFOLIO "MIX"

Whether you are starting from scratch or reviewing your existing holdings, you have to ask yourself from time to time what types of investment you should be in and what proportion of your assets you should have in each of them. For most people, the main choices are common stocks — high-risk and medium-risk stocks and conservative stocks that pay high dividends — options; convertible issues; government, municipal, and corporate bonds; short-term fixed-income securities (which are highly liquid and essentially risk-free); and precious metals. The "mix" you choose at a given point reflects the overall degree of risk you're willing to assume; then you "manage" your risk by modifying the portfolio mix when there are significant changes in the investment outlook.

Let's consider the case of an investor with $40,000 whose goal is average growth combined with income. Assuming that he's on the whole positive about the investment outlook but not extremely bullish, he might distribute his assets as follows, using no-load mutual funds rather than individual securities: 50 percent in a common-stock fund (such as Fidelity Fund) whose goal is growth and income; 20 percent in a high-growth fund; 25 percent in a money-market fund; and 5 percent in a gold fund. If this investor later turns bearish, he should switch the assets in the high-growth fund and all or most of those in the growth-and-income fund into the money fund. If he becomes decidedly bullish, he might cut back to 15 percent in the money fund, and to 35 percent in the growth and income fund, and switch the proceeds into the high-growth fund. Switching between no-load mutual funds is discussed more fully in chapter 23.

Whatever your investment objective, there are any number of possible portfolio mixes that will give you the desired *overall* level of risk — and it's the overall risk of the portfolio that counts, not the risk or safety of its individual components. An investor aggressively seeking very high growth might invest all of his funds in high-growth, high-risk issues, or he could choose medium-risk growth stocks and leverage his risk and potential return by buying on margin with funds borrowed from his brokers. In this way, he could invest twice as much money in the market. A leveraged portfolio of medium-risk growth stocks would have about the same beta as one invested in riskier growth stocks, but it might be preferable for an investor in a high tax bracket because the interest on the broker's loan would be deductible from ordinary income. Yet another possible portfolio strategy for this same high-risk investor would be to put most of his capital into medium-risk stocks and to shoot for large speculative gains with the balance by buying options.

An investor whose objective is income and some growth also has a variety of possible portfolio mixes. He might put 40 percent in high-yielding blue-chip stocks with low betas, 30 percent in convertible bonds, and 30 percent in a money-market fund. Or he might use a combination of blue-chip stocks, closed-end bond funds (which are traded on the New York Stock Exchange — see chapter 22), and money-market funds. Whether your portfolio is an aggressive or middle-of-the-road one, the principles of managing risk remain the same. *When you turn bearish you cut back on the securities that represent your tier of maximum risk (relative to the overall character of the portfolio) and switch the proceeds into your minimum-risk tier. When you turn bullish, you do the opposite.* For all but the more conservative investors, good judgment as to when to lessen exposure to risk and when to increase it and push for higher returns is possibly the most important single factor in investment success.

SELECTING THE SECURITIES

The selection of individual securities will be covered in two separate chapters. One will focus on methods of stock-picking that seek to beat the market. The other will discuss security selection for investors whose primary objective is income.

REVIEWING YOUR PERFORMANCE

Investors who are trying to beat, or at least match, the results of the S&P index should measure the total return on their stock portfolios at least once a year; the total return is dividends received plus capital gains (or minus losses) actually realized and those still on paper. Divide this figure by the market value of the portfolio at the beginning of the year and you will get your percentage return. If you've done significantly worse than the S&P index, try to find out where you went wrong; you can learn a lot from your mistakes. Some sources of error: acting on unreliable tips from friends or a broker; not keeping abreast of your investments, with the result that you're slow to act when one of them turns sour; buying "hot" stocks after they've already had a spectacular runup; or selling your winners too soon and hanging on to your losers in the vague hope they'll eventually recover. A Wall Street maxim says, "Cut your losses and let your profits run." And a savvy trader observes, "Never hesitate to quit while you're behind — you could be farther behind."

20. Predicting Major Market Movements

A buy-and-hold approach was hard to beat during the period of fairly stable economic expansion that followed World War II; from 1949 through 1959, there were only two significant market declines — one of 19 percent and one of 17 percent in the Dow Jones Industrial Average — and the Dow rose from 177 to 679, a gain of 284 percent. But between 1960 and 1981 investors were hit by five landslides in stock prices in which the average loss of the Dow Jones Industrials was about 33 percent. Staying fully invested throughout a market slump has become a brutally punishing experience. It's even worse, of course, if you finally panic, sell out near the bottom, and then fail to get in again until stock prices have had a big rebound.

To avoid such disasters, you don't need uncannily good foresight. You can substantially improve your investment results if your timing is only partially right — that is, if you sell some or all of your stocks within a few months of the peak of a bull market and then move back into stocks not too long before or after prices have hit bottom. This doesn't entail frequent trading and heavy commission expenses. In fact, if you invest in no-load mutual funds, the cost of making switches is negligible.

From 1960 through 1980, there were only five ideal occasions to buy stocks — in mid-1962, late 1966, mid-1970, late 1974, and early 1978. And there were five ideal occasions to sell — in December 1961, early 1966, late 1968, early January 1973, and the fall of 1976. *That averages out at one buy or sell decision every couple of years.* If your timing had been partially right on those occasions — if you had caught, say, 70 percent of each uptrend — you would have done better than twice as well as by following a buy-and-hold policy (assuming your portfolio matched the behavior of the Dow, your tax rate on capital gains was 20 percent and you did not reinvest dividends). However, haphazard attempts at market forecasting can do more harm than good. And buying or selling because you "feel" confident or nervous is almost certain to lead you astray, since your feelings are likely to reflect the predominant mood among investors. To use market timing with any hope of success, you need to develop a system that isn't too complex and time-consuming — and stick with it.

Possibly the best system devised for the layman — one that neatly combines the fundamental, technical, and psychological approaches — was presented in a book entitled *Stock Market Strategy* by Richard A. Crowell, president of The Boston Company Advisors Inc., an investment counseling firm. The market-timing strategy that's described in the rest of this chapter is a slightly modified version of Crowell's system; its main goal is to help investors to anticipate the turning points in *major market cycles*.

The system simply requires you to answer two parallel sets of questions on "time to buy" and "time to sell" checklists. Investors should keep their answers current by updating them, ideally once a month. If all or most of the answers on the "time to buy" questionnaire are "yes," then the chances are strong that it's an excellent time to buy, and similarly for the "time to sell" checklist.

THE TIME-TO-BUY CHECKLIST*

("Yes" answers are favorable.)

The Business Cycle

1. Is business activity nationally in a downtrend, and if so, do you foresee the end of that downtrend?
2. Is inflation decelerating?
3. Have corporate profits declined from their previous peak, and if so, do you expect them to start turning upward soon?
4. Is the economic news largely negative and are most forecasters pessimistic?

Monetary Policy and Interest Rates

5. Have short-term interest rates started to decline?
6. Has the Federal Reserve Board given indications that there will be an easing of monetary policy?

Stock Valuations

7. What is the P/E ratio of the S&P index or the Dow Jones Industrial Average? Is it approaching or below the P/E ratio at the last cyclical low point of the market?

Sentiment Indicators

8. Are the mutual funds heavily in cash? (Chapter 9 told you how to interpret the mutual funds' Cash/Assets Ratio.)
9. Is the odd-lot short sales ratio exceptionally high?
10. Is the Specialists' short sales ratio exceptionally low?
11. Are your friends and business associates pessimistic or apathetic about the market?

State of the Market

12. Has the market been declining for many months since its previous cyclical high?
13. Has the market registered a large drop from its previous cyclical high? (Since 1960, bear market declines have averaged about 33 percent, but a decline of 20 percent could be considered large.)
14. Has the market recently accelerated its rate of decline, which is typical of the final stages of bear markets?

---

*From *Stock Market Strategy* by Richard A. Crowell. Copyright © 1977 by McGraw Hill, Inc. Used with the permission of McGraw-Hill Book Company.

15. Does the market appear to have bottomed? Has it rebounded from its low point, then tested that low a couple of times without falling below it, and then started to advance?

THE TIME-TO-SELL CHECKLIST*
("Yes" answers are worrisome or bearish.)
The Business Cycle
1. Is there growing evidence of a business cycle peak?
2. Is inflation accelerating?
3. Has the rate of gain of corporate profits slowed or is the current rate too strong to last?
4. Are most of the economic forecasts optimistic?
Monetary Policy and Interest Rates
5. Are short-term interest rates rising and are they as high as they were at the corresponding stage of the previous business upturn?
6. Has the Federal Reserve Board started to tighten monetary policy?
Stock Valuations
7. What is the market's P/E ratio? Has it approached or risen above the P/E at the last cyclical peak of the market?
Sentiment Indicators
8. Are the cash reserves of the mutual funds low?
9. Is the odd-sales short sales ratio exceptionally low?
10. Is the Specialists' short sales ratio exceptionally high?
11. Are your friends and business associates talking about winners they've bought and feeling euphoric about the market?
State of the Market
12. Has the market been advancing for many months since its previous cyclical low?
13. Has the market registered a large percentage gain from its previous cyclical low?
14. Is the Advance/Decline line underperforming the popular averages? (This would be an indication that relatively fewer stocks are advancing and the market's condition is deteriorating even though the averages are still rising.)
15. Does the market appear to have peaked? Has the Dow dropped below its recent high and climbed back to it a couple of times or more, but only to retreat again?

You will notice that the questionnaires are designed to give you a sell signal when the economy is still booming, the market is still rising (or close to a peak), and public sentiment is optimistic. And they will give you a buy signal when the economy is in the doldrums, when the market seems to be in deep trouble, and public sentiment is pessimistic. But most of the time neither checklist will give a clear-cut go-ahead signal, since major market turning points occur infrequently. So what should an investor do who finds it impractical to wait for the ideal moment, which may be far distant? Crowell doesn't say so himself, but the questionnaires can be of considerable help even when they're not giving a decisive signal. If "yes" answers substantially outnumber "no" answers on the time-to-buy checklist, you might consider doing some buying and increasing your portfolio's exposure to risk. By the same token, if "yeses" substantially outnumber "noes" on the sell checklist, it might be prudent to lessen somewhat your exposure to risk. But what if you come up with a majority of "no" answers to *both* questionnaires, which can happen? That would be a strong indication that you should stay put until the answers provide a less ambiguous reading. If you're in the market, hang on to your stocks until you get a sell signal; if you're out of the market, stay out and wait for a buy signal.

21. Stock Strategies to Beat the Market

Most if not all of the mutual funds managers and investment advisers who have dazzling performance records owe their success to astute stock selection rather than to brilliant market timing. Each of these superpros has his own distinctive investment style. But their methods in most cases are based on one of four basic approaches to stock selection: (1) the asset-oriented, or Benjamin Graham, approach, whose progenitor was the founder of modern security analysis, (2) the "contrarian" strategy, which consists of buying unpopular stocks with low price/earnings ratios, (3) the "emerging growth company" approach, which surfaced in the early 1960s, though it had been pioneered more than two decades earlier by the great mutual fund manager T. Rowe Price, (4) the "wonderful business" approach, which John Train, in his admirable book *The Money Masters*, associates with the fabulously successful money manager Warren Buffett. A fifth strategy available to individuals might be called "the discount store approach": you invest in closed-end common-stock mutual funds, whose shares normally sell at appreciable discounts from their asset value. Each of these strategies has its special merits and its drawbacks. And I see no reason why an investor trying to beat the market should limit himself to one method of stock selection.

LOADED LAGGARDS

Benjamin Graham's asset-oriented methods of stock selection and his rules for when to sell were described in chapter 15. A disciple of Graham's, Mark Boyar—president of a Manhattan brokerage firm that bears his name—has developed an asset-oriented system of his own, which combines three complementary approaches. Boyar hunts for stocks whose market price is less than their "net net working capital" per share—current assets minus all long-term liabilities (including lease obligations and certain pension liabilities), divided by the number of shares outstanding. Boyar also probes for "hidden assets"—assets such as real estate or natural resources, which are carried on the balance sheet at less than their current value. For example, in 1975 Boyar concluded that Tiffany stock, then selling at $7.50 a share, was on the bargain counter; the jeweler's Fifth Avenue headquarters and the famous Tiffany Diamond were valued on the balance sheet at 'way below their real worth, and the stock's price seemingly put no value on the celebrated Tiffany name. The hidden assets that Boyar detected proved to be pearls of great price. Three years later, Avon Products acquired Tiffany for $43 a share.

Boyar's third approach is to look for what he calls "business value." Essentially, this is the value that a company would have to a knowledgeable acquirer, and it's based on the company's historical earning power, its product line and market penetration, and its financial condition. The stocks featured in Boyar's $6,000-a-year monthly advisory service, *Asset Focus Analysis*, have had an impressive performance record, partly because a substantial number of the bargain-priced issues that he discovers are eventually acquired by other companies at very much higher prices.

The virtue of rigorous, asset-oriented approaches like Boyar's and

Graham's is that they more or less ensure that the price you pay for a stock will represent bedrock value. One research study found that over a six-year period in the 1970s, several portfolios of stocks priced at less than their "net net" asset value per share (see chapter 15) outperformed the market by two to one (without exposure to above-average risk). The drawback of investing in net net asset "plays" is that you very seldom find one with the glamour of a Tiffany; typically, they're the stocks of drab-looking companies or troubled companies with depressed earnings, and it often takes a long time for their lode of value to win recognition.

Discovering asset-rich stocks on your own calls for an awful lot of statistical drudgery. But a list of them, which you can get from your broker, appears weekly in the *Value Line Investment Survey*, and once a year or so you'll find such stocks catalogued in *Forbes* under the heading "Loaded Laggards." Some loaded laggards may be losing money or may have such serious problems that you wouldn't want to own them, so you have to be carefully selective.

If an asset-oriented approach appeals to you but seems too tough to handle, you can let a mutual fund do the work for you. Fidelity Asset Investment Trust, a no-load fund in the Fidelity group, specializes in stocks selling below their book value.

LOW PRICE/EARNINGS RATIOS

The strategy that I referred to earlier as "contrarian" — actually, it's just one of several approaches to contrarian investing — focuses on large, well-known companies paying liberal dividends, whose stocks are selling at P/E ratios well below the average for the market. Such stocks are at the low end of the popularity spectrum. If stocks in general are valued at, say, 8 times earnings, a stock priced at 25 times earnings is obviously a popular favorite and one valued at 4 times earnings is in the doghouse.

Research studies carried out by Francis Nicholson, Paul F. Miller, Jr., William Avera, and others found that low P/E stocks — the unpopular ones — consistently produced larger long-term returns than high P/E stocks; indeed, a grouping of stocks into five categories based on their P/E ratios revealed that returns diminished as one proceeded up the scale of P/E ratios. Steven Leuthold updated these studies by tracking the performance of a list of stocks widely held by institutions. Over a 6-year period starting with the market lows of 1974, the average price gain for the high P/E group was 60.7 percent, for the medium P/E group 91.9 percent, and for the low P/E group 143.7 percent. Since low P/E stocks produce higher returns, Modern Portfolio Theory would lead one to conclude that they are riskier than high P/E issues. But insofar as market risk is concerned the contrary is true; the betas of stocks decline as one goes from the highest to the lowest P/E groupings. And the risks of low P/E stocks not reflected in their betas can be largely eliminated by proper diversification.

Why are unpopular stocks more rewarding in the long run than popular issues? The leading proponent of the large-company, low-P/E approach, David Dreman, proffers the following explanation in his book *The Contrarian Investment Strategy*. The "visibility" of companies' future earnings is much less clear than analysts and investors like to think; forecasts frequently go wrong because, among other things, they tend to assume that current trends will continue. Moreover, analysts and investors give too much credence to these fallible forecasts. They become overenthusiastic about companies whose future growth seems to be highly "visible," and overly pessimistic about companies whose prospects look murky or drab. The historical record, Dreman argues, shows that in the aggregate the companies for which the strongest growth is projected don't do as well as is expected, and the companies with supposedly the worst prospects don't do as badly as investors anticipate. Thus disappointments occur frequently enough in the universe of high P/E stocks to cause them to underperform the market. On the other hand, there are enough favorable surprises in the unpopular universe to cause low P/E stocks to outperform the market. Dreman wisely qualifies this argument with the following observation: "It is true, of course, that there are excellent companies that will continue to chalk up above average growth for many years or even decades . . . and there are especially talented investors who will find them at reasonable prices."

Investors who opt for the low P/E strategy that Dreman advocates should observe the following guidelines. (1) Select the stocks of large, well-established companies that provide liberal yields, and preferably have a good record of dividend growth. Large companies offer more stability than smaller ones, and a high yield lessens downside risk and increases your total return. (2) Make sure that the company's financial condition is strong. The ratios and other factors you should consider were discussed in the chapters on annual reports and fundamental stock analysis. (3) Look for companies with a respectable record of earnings growth. (4) If a company is highly cyclical, check into whether its current P/E ratio is low simply because earnings are at a cyclical peak. For example, when Ford was selling above 50 in 1978, it was valued at only about four times that year's earnings, which were the second highest in Ford's history; in 1980, Ford reported a loss of $12.83 a share and the stock fell to just above 18. For a cyclical company, a genuinely low P/E is one that's low on the basis of average earnings over the previous four or five years. (5) Sell when the stock's P/E rises to the same level as that of the S&P index. (6) Diversify widely. Your portfolio should contain at least a dozen stocks in eight or nine different industries. If you can't afford to do this, put your money into a no-load fund that takes the contrarian, low P/E approach. John Neff's Windsor Fund, which is part of the Wellington group, would be an excellent choice. It concentrates on stocks that Neff describes as "the downtrodden, the pummeled, the overlooked," and it has had a fine performance record.

In mid-1981, stocks that met the requirements mentioned in the guidelines above included half a dozen leading oil issues; several banks such as Chemical, Wells Fargo and Western Bancorp; Aetna and Travelers in the insurance group; Dart & Kraft and Reynolds Metals. A broker in the San Francisco office of Sutro & Co., Josef Ben-Porat, has long specialized in managing individual and pension fund accounts in accordance with the large-company, low P/E strategy; I have seen his fully documented performance record over the past ten years and it has been remarkably good. I have not done business with Mr. Ben-Porat, and this reference to his work should not be taken as a personal recommendation.

THINK SMALL; THE "EMERGING" GROWTH STOCK APPROACH

Dramatic evidence that small companies have significantly outperformed larger ones has emerged from scholarly research published in the early 1980s. These findings don't invalidate the Dreman approach as a strategy that can produce better than average long-term gains with below average risks. But they do indicate that to make it big investors should think small.

Small firms listed on the New York and American stock exchanges produced annual returns 20 percent greater than those of large firms during the period 1963 to 1977, according to a study published in the March-April 1981 issue of *The Financial Analysts Journal* by Marc Reinganum, a professor at the University of California. Computations made for *Fortune* by Rolf W. Banz, a finance professor at the University of Chicago, also show that portfolios of the smallest stocks — those with market capitalizations of $50 million or less — outperformed portfolios of larger stocks. From 1975 to 1979, the total return on the midgets was more than double that of the S&P index; moreover, the little stocks have beaten the market fairly consistently for at least 50 years, even on a risk-adjusted basis. As *Fortune* commented, "The implication is obvious: 'buy little.' " But if you buy "little," you must diversify much. Small companies have greater chances both of going down the drain and of soaring into the stratosphere. So you have to own a lot of them to avoid getting massacred by the failures or missing the wild successes. The best way for most investors to get sufficient diversification is, of course, through a mutual fund. And the most diversified of the small company funds is Over-the-Counter Securities, which is sold through brokers; it owns more than 350 stocks and has had a first-rate performance record. Other funds that concentrate on small stocks include Acorn, American General Venture, and Evergreen.

There are a number of things that explain the superior performance of little stocks. The earnings of small companies grow faster than those of larger ones, because they're starting from a vastly smaller base. Small companies, too, have far greater flexibility, so they can quickly exploit the opportunities created by social and economic change. They are not hobbled by obsolescent facilities, and the small scale of their operations makes it easier for them to introduce new techniques than it is for the giants of industry. Most important of all, they are run by owner-entrepreneurs whose investment in the company gives them a significant stake in the success of their own efforts.

The stars that shine brightest in the small company universe are generally known as "emerging" or "junior" growth companies. A growth company — senior as well as junior — might be defined as one that's in a growth market and has a leading position in it or in a rapidly growing subsector of that market. For example, hospital management is a dynamic sector of the health care industry, and a company like Comprehensive Care is the leader in a subsector, in-hospital treatment of alcoholism. Different analysts have different criteria for a growth company in regard to earnings and profitability, but the following would be widely acceptable: (1) the company should have shown an increase in earnings in each of the past five years and an annually compounded growth rate over the period of at least 15 percent; (2) it should have strong prospects of maintaining or increasing its established growth rate; (3) it should have a high return on equity — preferably 20 percent or more — in order to be able to finance future growth without often having to borrow heavily or else issue new stock.

One of the leading proponents of investing in "junior" growth companies is John Westergaard, president of Equity Research Associates. The companies he focuses on typically have sales of less than $100 million (when he first recommends them); an established and prospective growth rate that is twice the nominal growth rate of the Gross National Product; and a return on equity of more than 25 percent. Westergaard favors a portfolio mix composed of three conceptual categories of stocks. The category that he calls the "Business Frontier" embraces two kinds of companies: (1) those that are developing a *primary new technology* — for example, Sci-Tex Corporation Ltd., which manufactures computed-based color image processing systems used for commercial graphics reproduction; (2) companies engaged in the *application or distribution of new technologies* or companies that have developed *new techniques for doing business* — for example, Quotron Systems, which operates a network of video terminals that provide price quotations and other information to the investment community.

The companies in Westergaard's second category, "American Lifestyles," are companies that are exploiting the opportunities created by social change and changes in American spending patterns. An illustration: the boom in the demand for children's day-care services that resulted from the growing number of women entering the labor force. The third conceptual category, "Special Situations," applies to companies in which there's an element of unrecognized value or which stand to benefit greatly if a particular event occurs. For example, the CRS Group, an architectural and construction firm, had the earmarks of a special situation in 1981; if its already substantial business in Saudi Arabia progressed favorably, the company would provide investors with participation in the enormous economic development under way in that country.

Historically, the average price/earnings ratio of junior growth stocks has been about the same as the P/E of the S&P index at the bottom of bear markets, and twice the P/E of the index at the peak of bull markets. Thus, in principle, junior growth stocks tend to be relatively undervalued when their average P/E is appreciably less than 1.5 times that of the index and relatively overvalued when their average P/E is appreciably more than 1.5 times the S&P multiple. Westergaard's strategy is to aim for large gains over a three-to-five-year period, and he insistently warns investors in junior growth stocks that they must have the fortitude to hang on through severe market declines. At the end of 1980, the recommendations he had made since 1976 showed an average gain of 140 percent.

Westergaard doesn't shrink from recommending stocks in the business frontier category that have lofty price/earnings ratios. In contrast, Charles Allmon, a money manager based in Bethesda, Maryland, tends to avoid glamorous high-tech companies because he believes their valuations are usually excessive. His policy is to ferret out small growth companies that have not yet achieved recognition and are selling at relatively low price/earnings ratios. He requires a five-year growth record of 15 percent to 20 percent compounded annually and a strong balance sheet. He also attaches great importance to the man who runs the company, and he especially likes the inner-directed entrepreneurial type who doggedly hews to his own course. Allmon has displayed an astonishing flair for discovering successful small companies, often in prosaic industries. From January 1976 to January 1982, his advisory service recommended 69 issues; only seven of them were losers and 37 of them more than doubled in price.

In the portfolios he manages, Allmon does some selling when he thinks the market is dangerously high, and he parks the proceeds in money-market securities until he sees a buying opportunity. He also cuts his losses, as a rule, in stocks that perform poorly; he tends to sell a Big Board stock if it drops 10 percent to 15 percent, an Amex stock (they are usually more volatile) if it drops 15 percent to 20 percent, and an OTC stock (they are still more volatile) if it drops 25 percent.

He has no hard-and-fast rules for selling stocks that have made big gains. But he is generally reluctant to stay in a stock when its valuation has climbed to 30 times earnings. Allmon is one of the relatively few successful money managers who will accept an account of less than $200,000; his minimum requirement is $100,000, and his annual fee is 1.65 percent of the assets under management.

Several mutual funds invest wholly or largely in emerging growth companies. Two of the outstanding ones are T. Rowe Price New Horizons Fund and Scudder Development Fund, both no-loads. Four others were mentioned earlier in this chapter.

THE "WONDERFUL BUSINESS" APPROACH

The achievement of Warren Buffett, writes John Train in *The Money Masters*, "stands alone in modern portfolio management." An investment of $10,000 in the partnership that Buffett founded in 1956 was worth $300,000 when the partnership was dissolved in 1969, and its portfolio never had a down year in spite of the bear markets of 1957, 1962, 1966, and 1969. Buffett has continued his brilliant investment career as president of a holding company, Berkshire-Hathaway, whose earnings increased from $16.47 per share in 1976 to $42.07 in 1980. Buffett's philosophy has been to invest only in the stocks of companies that he considers "wonderful businesses" and to buy them when they are out of favor. The key to a "wonderful business" is that it has a privileged or oligopolistic position — for example, that of broadcasters and newspapers (particularly newspaper chains such as Harte-Hanks and Gannett operating largely in single-paper towns). Other examples of companies with virtually unassailable business "franchises" would include Dun & Bradstreet, Phibro Corp. (formerly a part of Engelhard Minerals & Chemicals), which dominates worldwide metals trading, and American Express (which has a premier position in the credit card and traveler's check businesses). Another kind of wonderful business in the Buffett sense is a major advertising agency, because its profit growth stems from the investments of others. Corporations invest to increase their sales; and as their sales grow, so do their advertising expenditures and hence the profits of the ad agencies.

Some of the other characteristics of "wonderful businesses" are that they have a good return on equity; they are "cash-generating machines" — that is, they don't have to keep plowing back their profits in new plant and equipment or in research and development; they are easy to understand; and their earnings are fairly predictable.

The companies that Buffett is drawn to are for the most part large and well known; to practice his style of investing successfully you have to buy the stocks when they're out of favor or the market is weak. You can own a piece of Buffett's portfolio by investing in his holding company, Berkshire-Hathaway, which is traded over the counter; in early 1982, the stock was selling at $545 a share. There's a no-load mutual fund whose investment philosophy is similar to Buffett's; it's called the Sequoia Fund (540 Madison Avenue, New York, NY 10022).

THE "DISCOUNT STORE" APPROACH: BUYING CLOSED-END FUNDS

Unlike open-end mutual funds, closed-end funds don't issue shares after the original offering, nor do they redeem them. Closed-end fund shares are traded, in most cases on the New York Stock Exchange, in the same way as stocks. In other words, the price of the shares depends on what investors are willing to pay for them, which may be more or less than their net asset value per share (the market value of all stocks in the portfolio divided by the number of shares outstanding). Throughout most of the 1970s and early 1980s, the shares of closed-end common-stock funds sold at substantial discounts from their net asset values. Discounts provide leverage. When you buy $100 worth of stock at a 20 percent discount, you have the profit potential of $100 working for you, and you have put up only $80. Second, discounts mean higher yields; if for $80 you get $100 worth of stock paying $8 in dividends, your yield is not 8 percent but 10 percent. Third, discounts can improve capital gains potential and provide protection in declining markets; a large discount often narrows when stock prices are rising and — surprisingly — it often narrows, too, when prices decline sharply. In sum, if you can buy closed-end fund shares at a discount from their asset value, you will be getting a diversified portfolio of stocks at less than their current market price, and that, of course, improves your chances of beating the market.

Why do the discounts exist? Many explanations have been put forward. The one I find most plausible is given by Burton Malkiel in *The Inflation-Beater's Investment Guide* (New York: W. W. Norton Co.,

1980). The closed-end funds, Malkiel argues, are not supported by an active marketing campaign. Once the fund has been brought out, there's no payoff for the investment manager in promoting it, and brokers generally prefer to sell open-end load funds, on which they earn much larger commissions. The major closed-end stock funds, including specialized funds, are listed in the table below.

CLOSED-END STOCK FUNDS
(Source: *The Superyield Reporter*, April 1981)

CLOSED-END EQUITY FUNDS	PRICE[a]	DISCOUNT (percentage)	YIELD (percentage)	1980–1981[b]	1974–1981[c]
Quality Funds					
Adams Express	14	−18.0	6.4	+44.4	+252.3
Carriers & General	14	−13.6	5.6	+46.3	+195.8
Central Securities	8⅞	−26.0	6.6	+80.8	+482.2
Energy & Utility Shares	16⅝	−5.4	10.2	+28.6	+134.9
Lehman Corp.	14⅜	−14.7	4.6	+70.8	+299.9
Petroleum & Resources	37⅞	−7.7	3.9	+62.4	+383.2
Tri-Continental	22	−22.9	6.9	+49.1	+195.8
U.S. & Foreign Securities	21⅜	−26.6	4.7	+50.9	+260.6
Growth Funds					
Baker, Fentress	73	−27.6	3.7	+57.6	+382.7
General Am. Investors	19¾	−4.1	2.3	+106.6	+438.7
Madison Fund	22⅛	−16.5	4.0	+57.7	+653.9
Niagara Share	21⅝	−0.8	2.3	+84.3	+287.4
Source Capital	22¾	−16.2	5.5	+55.2	+780.4
Aggressive Funds					
ASA Ltd.	53⅛	−20.5	12.2	+67.4	+450.1[d]
Claremont Capital	20¾	−25.8	3.2	+69.6	+1416.6
Japan Fund	10	−22.5	1.5	+64.0	+387.3
Precious Metals Holdings	18	−6.7	7.6	+98.6	+586.0[d]

[a]4/7/81
[b]March-April 1980 lows to 4/7/81
[c]1974 low to 4/7/81
[d]1976 low to 4/7/81

WHAT TO AVOID: WHEN TO SELL

Many people prefer not to commit themselves to a single style of investing; they look for undervalued stocks of different types that could outperform the market. They might, for example, own some junior growth companies, some low P/E stocks selling below book value, some stocks in the "wonderful business" category and so on. To prevent an eclectic approach from becoming disorderly, you need to develop certain principles of your own in regard to stock selection and the timing of sales. Here — stated without elaboration — are some precepts that I favor.

Stay away from certain types of companies as long-term investments, if you're trying to beat the market. My list of undesirables includes: (1) companies that are labor-intensive and employ blue-collar, strongly unionized labor; they have relatively little control over a large portion of their costs, and wage increases often outstrip gains in productivity; (2) companies that are capital-intensive and are handicapped by obsolescent plant and equipment — some giants of the steel industry, for example; (3) companies whose sales growth has been coming more from price increases than from growth in unit sales — the number of cars, books, or refrigerators they sell (such companies are either losing market share to competitors or are operating in markets where there is little or no growth); (4) companies whose fortunes are significantly affected by government regulation — for example, public utilities. (Some utilities in high-growth regions, if their stocks are modestly valued, could be attractive to growth-oriented investors.) There are, to be sure, times when large trading profits can be made in the stocks of companies in the above categories; for example, U.S. Steel bounced from its 1980 low of 16¼ to 35⅛ in April 1981. But from a long-term standpoint, the stocks I've described are fundamentally unattractive.

Be careful not to overpay for expectations of high growth. As I've pointed out earlier, future earnings growth is not nearly as "visible" as analysts like to think it is. And stratospheric valuations make stocks highly vulnerable to any disappointment. As a rule, it's advisable to stay away from stocks whose price/earnings ratios — based on their estimated earnings for the current year — are more than four-fifths of their projected growth rate; if earnings are expected to grow 25 percent annually, a P/E of more than 20 would be on the high side for a value-conscious investor. And a P/E of 30 or more for any stock might reasonably be considered prohibitive.

Stay away from fashionable "concept" stocks with no earnings and no prospects of showing appreciable earnings for some time. Genetic engineering is "such stuff as dreams are made on," but even dreams can be overvalued; when Genentech went public in 1980, the prices that starry-eyed investors initially paid for its stock discounted the hereafter.

Decide on certain yardsticks that will tell you when to sell and do your best to act on them. The yardsticks will be different for different investors, but one injunction applies to all: forget about buying at the bottom and selling at the top. Some investors who try to get good returns by minimizing losses make it a practice to sell automatically when a stock has declined a certain amount from their purchase price — the amount might be 10 percent, 15 percent, or 20 percent. If you buy a stock in the expectation of a specific development — for example, huge success for a new product — and the development doesn't occur, sell promptly. When to sell your winners is always a tough decision. Here are some rules worth considering. (1) Unless you have an overwhelming aversion to taking short-term gains, sell a stock whose price has quickly shot up 50 percent. (This rule would not apply if some development has dramatically improved the company's prospects.) (2) Sell a stock when its price/earnings ratio — based on estimated earnings for the current year — is one-and-a-half times the P/E ratio at which you bought it. (3) Ben Graham's rule — sell if the stock hasn't risen 50 percent in three years — may be overexacting, but it's a sound principle not to stay wedded to stocks that aren't producing respectable returns. (4) Sell any stock that appears to offer substantially less potential than other stocks that you could buy if you had funds available.

22. Investing for Income

There are many people who firmly believe that, for them, the risks of investing for growth are too high and the rewards too uncertain: their attitude is summed up in the remark an investor made to his stockbroker, "I want income, not if-come." But the conventional wisdom that investing for income is a "safe" policy that brings assured returns has been shot full of holes. Two of the staples of income-oriented portfolios — bonds and public utility stocks — were rotten investments to own throughout most of the 1970s and the first eighteen months of the 1980s. Indeed, in an inflationary era, the only certainty about investing strictly for income is that you'll be a loser in the battle against inflation. If, for example, you put your savings into risk-free short-term investments such as money funds, the yield you'll get will normally be not much above the rate of inflation, and it will be taxed as ordinary income; meanwhile, the purchasing power of your capital will be shrinking each year by an amount equal to the rise in the Consumer Price Index. So most if not all income-oriented investors should include in their portfolios securities that provide some possibility of capital appreciation — for example, high yielding common stocks, convertible securities, and "deep discount" bonds (which are discussed later in this chapter).

Income-oriented investors should also get a firm handle on the four main types of risk that apply to fixed-income securities. And they should familiarize themselves with timing tactics that can significantly improve the returns on their investments. By selecting the proper portfolio "mix" and using timing tactics that reduce risk and exploit opportunities, income-oriented investors can do much to protect themselves against the ravages of inflation.

THE FOUR TYPES OF RISK

Credit Risk: the risk of default by the bond issuer on interest payments or repayment of principal when the bond reaches maturity. The bond quality ratings issued by Standard & Poor's and Moody's evaluate credit risk. Bonds rated AAA or AA by Standard & Poor's (Aaa or Aa by Moody's) are of the highest quality. An A rating stands for upper-medium quality; interest and principal are regarded as safe. The BBB, or medium-grade, category represents "adequate" quality; it's the lowest category in which commercial banks are allowed to invest. A BB rating signifies "lower medium grade," and B, CCC, and CC are speculative ratings that reflect increasing degrees of risk. Remember that bond ratings are relative yardsticks; a B-rated bond is riskier than an A-rated one, but that doesn't mean its chances of default are high. Even in the lower grades, the historical rate of default in this country has been low. During the Great Depression of the 1930s, only ½ percent of all bond issues defaulted on repayment of principal.

Market Risk: the risk that bonds will decline in price; it hinges mainly on changes in interest rates. When interest rates rise, bond prices fall, and vice versa. A bond's price can also decline because investors expect its rating to be lowered or because the supply of new bond offerings is abnormally large.

A bond's rate of interest, known as its coupon rate, is a fixed percentage of its face, or "par," value of $1,000; for example, the American Telephone bond maturing in 2005 with an 8.80 percent rate offers a fixed annual return of $88. Clearly nobody would pay the same price for a bond already on the market as for a newly issued bond of comparable quality with a higher return. So when interest rates rise, the prices of bonds with coupon rates below the prevailing rates fall sufficiently to make their yields competitive with those of newly issued bonds.

There is, however, a minor complication that needs to be explained. A bond's yield is measured in two ways. Its *current yield* is its interest rate divided by its market price; if the rate is 9 percent and the bond is selling at $900,* the current yield is 10 percent. But when that bond reaches maturity, its owner will receive not $900 but $1,000. *So the proper measure of a bond's return is its annual yield to maturity,* a figure that takes into account the gain or loss on the bond's current price when the bond is eventually redeemed. For example, if a bond with a 9 percent coupon selling at $900 matures in 10 years, the bondholder's total return to maturity will be 10 times $90 plus $100, or $1,000. The easiest way to get a bond's annual yield to maturity is to ask your broker to look it up for you in a yield table. But there's a rough-and-ready way of calculating yield to maturity: you simply divide the average annual return by the average price of the bond (the midpoint between its current price and its redemption value). Thus for a bond with a 10-year maturity, a 9 percent coupon, and a current price of $900, the arithmetic is as follows:

---

*Bond prices are quoted as a percentage of par. A price of "85" means that the bond is selling at $850.

$900 (interest) + $100 (gain) divided by 10 years

$900 + $1,000 divided by two (average price of the bond).

That equals $100/950$, or 10.53 percent. (This calculation doesn't take into account income tax considerations. The $100 gain will be taxed at less than half the rate on ordinary income, because it's a long-term capital gain.)

Since the true measure of a bond's return is its yield to maturity, bond prices tend to rise or fall to the extent necessary to make their yields to maturity competitive with those of newly issued bonds. A theoretical illustration: if long-term interest rates were to rise overnight from 10 percent to 11 percent (which, of course, couldn't happen), the price of a bond with a 10 percent coupon, selling at $1,000 and maturing in 10 years, would drop to around $936; at that price its annual yield to maturity (taking into account the eventual $64 gain) would be 11 percent.

In the fairly recent past, recurrent sharp swings in interest rates have resulted in unprecedented volatility in the bond market. In 1980, for example, drops or rises of more than 20 percent in bond prices occurred within periods of a few months. Moreover, since the underlying trend of long-term interest rates was upward in the 1970s and beyond, many bondholders have suffered severe losses. From January 1977 to October 1981, long-term Treasury bonds plunged in price nearly 54 percent, top-quality bonds 53.6 percent, and muncipals 54.4 percent.

Investors who intend to hold a bond to maturity sometimes argue that a drop in the bond's price is "only a paper loss" because eventually they'll receive $1,000. This reasoning is specious. Consider the case of an investor who bought at par the AT&T bond mentioned above and owned it in the spring of 1981, when top-quality corporate bonds offered yields to maturity of 13½ percent. By holding the bond—then quoted at around $695—for redemption in 2005, he would lose for 24 years the difference between his annual return of $88 and the available return of $135, a total of $1,128. And if he sold the bond at $695 (less commission) and reinvested the proceeds in a bond yielding 13½ percent, his annual return would still be only about $92. Either way, he suffers a very real loss.

These figures underscore a vital point; the old concept of bonds as a relatively "safe" long-term investment is thoroughly obsolete. One disconsolate bondholder dourly observed when I was writing this chapter, "Bonds have been my hedge against prosperity." Nowadays, interest rate risk is large, and the longer the bond's maturity, the greater is the risk. If long-term rates rise, a bond maturing in 30 years will have to drop much more than one maturing in 12 years for its yield to maturity to make it competitive with newly issued bonds. Because of their greater risk, long-term bonds normally offer higher yields than bonds with shorter maturities. But if you think that interest rates may rise and you still wish to own bonds because of the assured high yields that they provide, you should switch out of long-term bonds into intermediate bonds—preferably those with maturities of not more than 10 years. Another way of lessening somewhat your exposure to interest rate risk is to shun long-term bonds at all times and stick with intermediate maturities.

There is, of course, a case for owning long-term bonds; it hinges on the possibility that inflation will lessen and long-term interest rates will decline and not climb back to (or above) the peak levels they reached in the early 1980s. If that were to happen, owners of long-term bonds would profit in one of two ways: (1) holders of bonds issued when interest rates were at or close to peak levels will have assured themselves of much higher yields than those available in the future; (2) investors who own "deep discount" bonds—old bonds with low coupon rates, purchased when they were selling at large discounts from their par value—would make hefty capital gains, because the prices of such bonds rise sharply when interest rates fall. In mid-November 1981, an A.T.&T. bond with an interest rate of 7⅛ percent maturing in 2003 was selling at $580. If long-term rates were to drop back to 7⅛ percent—which, to be sure, seems improbable— a buyer of that bond at $580 might well make a profit of about $420 (before commissions), or 72 percent.

Call Risk: a bond selling above par (because interest rates have dropped) may be called away from you by the issuer and redeemed at below its market price. Most industrial bonds are protected against call for 10 years; utility bonds, for 5 years. But there are loopholes in call protection. So before buying a bond, don't forget to ask your broker to check out its call provisions.

Purchasing Power Risk: this has to do with the amount of *purchasing power* you will lose through inflation. Since the prospects of actual *deflation* appear to be virtually nil, loss of purchasing power in fixed-income securities that offer no possibility of capital gains is a near certainty. And the longer a bond's maturity, the greater the prospective loss, because your real capital will be shrinking each year. The bond you buy today for $1,000 will return $1,000 when it comes due. If inflation averages 7 percent annually, the $1,000 you receive 10 years hence will be worth only $508 in today's purchasing power; if inflation averages 6 percent and a bond matures in 15 years, the $1,000 you receive then will be worth, in today's money, $417.

TIMING MATTERS

Timing tactics are just about as important for income-oriented investors as they are for those seeking growth. If you stay in a money market fund when interest rates are declining, you will (1) get diminishing yields, (2) miss out on opportunities for profit in bonds or interest-sensitive stocks. Conversely, if you sit tight in bonds and interest-sensitive stocks throughout an upward spiral in interest rates, you'll suffer punishing losses and miss out on the high returns available from short-term securities. Ideally, you would buy long-term bonds or interest-sensitive stocks when an upward cycle in interest rates is close to its peak, hold them throughout the downward cycle, and switch into short-term securities before the next upward spiral begins. Calling the turns in interest rates that accurately is an impossible dream, but being partially right can make a big difference in your investment results. Chapter 8 explained how watching the weekly changes in the money supply and the actions of the Federal Reserve can help you to anticipate the trend of interest rates. In addition, the behavior of the Dow Jones Utility Average reflects investors' expectations about long-term interest rates; since utilities are heavy borrowers, the Utility Average tends to rise when long-term rates are expected to decline and it drops when there are fears that rates will move upward.

SHOPPING IN A SUPERMARKET

Investing for income has been made easier and more economic for the average investor by the emergence of no-load mutual funds that specialize in various types of income investments (see Appendix B). In addition, there are brokerage-house "unit trusts" that invest in bonds and then simply hold them to their maturity, thereby eliminating management fees. Indeed, so many choices are now readily available to income-oriented investors that investing for income has changed from shopping in a delicatessen to shopping in a supermarket. Here's a closer look at the main types of income investments.

U.S. GOVERNMENT SECURITIES

Treasury securities — bills, notes, and bonds — are guaranteed by the U.S. government and have the world's highest credit rating; there has never ever been a default. Treasury Bills are short-term securities with maturities of up to 1 year, but most commonly 13 and 26 weeks. The interest is paid up front — that is, the bills are issued at a discount and redeemed at their par value; their minimum denomination is $10,000. Treasury notes have maturities of 1 to 10 years and bond maturities range from 10 to 30 years; both are available in denominations of $1,000, and they pay interest semiannually. Treasury securities can be bought and sold through commercial banks and brokerage houses. The income from them is exempt from state and local but not from federal taxes. Because they have the highest credit rating, Treasury Bills, notes, and bonds normally offer somewhat lower yields than those provided by other fixed-income securities with comparable maturities.

Of the numerous other government securities, the most interesting to individual investors are Government National Mortgage Association certificates, familiarly known as "Ginnie Maes." These certificates, whose average life span is 9 to 12 years, represent shares in a government-guaranteed pool of home mortgages. Holders of Ginnie Maes receive monthly checks that include, in addition to interest, repayment of principal on their shares of the mortgages in the pool. The minimum denomination for Ginnie Maes is $25,000, but investors can own them through brokerage house unit trusts or through a specialized no-load mutual fund such as Lexington GNMA Income Fund (see Appendix B). Ginnie Maes are unique in that they offer complete safety, high yields, and gradual return of principal. Their interest payments, however, are subject to state and local as well as federal income taxes.

TAX-EXEMPT BONDS

State and local authority bonds — generically known as "municipals" or tax-exempts — have long ceased to be an investment only for the very rich. Nowadays, you don't have to be earning megabucks to find yourself in a tax bracket of 40 percent or higher, and if you're taxed 40 percent on every dollar of incremental income, a 9 percent yield on a municipal bond is equivalent to a taxable yield of 15 percent. Moreover, *the interest on municipals is exempt from state and city taxes in the state in which the bond is issued,* an important consideration to residents of California, Massachusetts, New York, and other states where the tax bite is large.

There are three ways of investing in tax-exempt bonds: (1) you can buy them individually through brokers or commercial banks; (2) you can buy "units" in one of the unit investment trusts that are regularly marketed by major brokerage firms and by bond houses such as John Nuveen & Co. in Manhattan; (3) you can buy shares in a no-load tax-exempt bond fund — a dozen of them are listed in Appendix B. You will have to decide for yourself which of these ways suits you best. Here's what you need to know about them.

Tax-exempt mutual funds have the following points in their favor. The minimum investment required can be as low as $1,000, and the funds offer professional management, diversification, and other benefits — you can have your dividends automatically reinvested; you can make additional investments of as little as $100; and you can switch at little or no cost into another type of fund within the same fund group.

The chief liability of tax-exempt bond funds is that management fees and operating expenses together reduce the portfolio's annual yield by about 0.8 percent; if the yield earned is 12 percent, bond shareholders receive 11.2 percent. For some investors a 0.8 percent loss of interest is a reasonable price to pay for the benefits the funds offer; for others, it's an undue sacrifice of income, since the fund managers haven't been sufficiently adept at risk management to mitigate appreciably the portfolio losses caused by upward spirals in interest rates.

Unit investment trusts are unmanaged portfolios of bonds; the bonds are assembled and then simply held to maturity. Some trusts require an investment of at least $5,000, others accept $1,000. The initial sales charge is 3½ percent to 4½ percent, but subsequent administrative expenses are small — they reduce the portfolio's yield by only 0.2 percent a year. If an investor wants out, his broker can usually arrange for his units to be redeemed by the trust at their current net asset value, or he can deal directly with the trust himself. The annual return to investors remains more or less fixed throughout the life of the trust. For people who live in states where income taxes are high, unit trusts have one clear-cut advantage over mutual funds: you can buy units in trusts composed entirely of bonds that are issued in your state and are therefore exempt from all taxes.

Conventional wisdom has it that small investors should not buy municipal bonds individually. The reasons: first, most municipals come in denominations of $5,000 and up, so an investor who has earmarked $10,000 or less for tax-exempts can't obtain diversification. Second, when you buy only one or two bonds, you usually pay more than the quoted price, and you get less than the quoted price when you sell.

These drawbacks aren't quite as bad as they may sound. The price differentials when you buy and sell, plus brokerage commissions, can amount to less than the management fees of a mutual fund or the sales charge on a unit trust. And if you buy a bond rated A or better, the risk you run by not diversifying is small. Moreover, buyers of individual bonds can choose bonds with special provisions designed by marketing strategists to make long-term bonds more inviting. One is the "super sinker" provision in some municipal bonds issued to raise mortgage money for single-family home buyers; certain bonds in the offering, designed as super sinkers, are redeemed ahead of the others with funds received from mortgage prepayments. The big attraction of super sinkers is that they are in effect short-term bonds with the higher yields of long-term maturities; their average life expectancy in 1981 was two to four years, according to research done by Joseph F. Coleman of Prescott Ball & Turben. Another sweetener available in a few long-term municipals is the "put" or tender option. It permits investors to cash in a bond at face value at the end of five years or on each anniversary of the issue date thereafter. Put bonds are the first bonds in financial history that give market protection to the buyer rather than to the issuer; if interest rates rise, an investor can tender his bond at no loss. Anyone interested in put bonds or super sinkers should ask their broker to alert him when offerings are announced.

CORPORATE BONDS

If you're buying bonds individually, it's prudent to stick to issues rated A or better. But with the diversification that a mutual fund provides, the risk of owning so-called junk bonds—those rated no higher than BB—is small; contrary to what you might imagine, defaults on low-grade bonds have been extremely rare, and studies show that their long-term returns have been much larger than those on high-grade issues. Funds that specialize in low-grade bonds include American Investors Income and Fidelity Aggressive Income (see Appendix B).

In the recent past, bond prices have taken such a drubbing during upward spirals in interest rates that there's a good case for trading bonds rather than buying them as a long-term investment. You buy when you think interest rates are close to a peak and you sell when you think they won't go much lower—or else when you've made a satisfactory profit and consider other investments more attractive. For investors of limited means, the simplest and most economical way of trading bonds is through a closed-end bond fund. These funds offer little-known advantages over buying bonds individually. They frequently sell at discounts of 5 percent to 15 percent or more from their net asset value; and when bond prices have rallied, investors have usually made an extra profit from a narrowing of the discount. Moreover, you can invest small amounts in the closed-end funds; in early 1982, most of them were selling at less than $15 a share. Twenty-one closed-end bond funds are traded on the New York Stock Exchange. Among them are CNA Income Shares, Drexel Bond Debenture, Excelsior Income Shares, J. Hancock Securities, INA Investment Securities, and Transamerica Income.

IT'S A BOND, IT'S A STOCK, IT'S A CONVERTIBLE

Convertible bonds and convertible preferred stocks are hybrids. Like bonds, they offer fixed returns; but they are also equities, since they can be swapped for a specified number of shares of the issuing company's stock. *The value of a convertible is therefore a composite of its value as a fixed-income security and as a stock.* Let's consider, first, the equity value of a hypothetical bond issued with a 10 percent coupon and convertible into 40 shares of common stock; the bond is currently priced at $900 and the common is selling at $18. The bond's *conversion value* is 40 times $18, or $720, so it's selling at a premium of 25 percent over its conversion value. Its *conversion parity* — the price at which an investor who bought at $900 would break even by converting into the common — is $22.50. Any rise in the stock above $22.50 would be accompanied by at least an equal percentage rise in the price of the convertible. If, for example, the stock were to go to $25, the bond would be worth $1,000 and would probably sell for more than that because of the value of the conversion feature.

Now let's look at what the same convertible might be worth as a straight bond. This is known as its *investment value;* it's the price at which the convertible's yield to maturity equals the yield to maturity offered by straight bonds of similar quality with comparable maturities. If our hypothetical convertible bond matures in 10 years, and if yields to maturity on comparable straight bonds are 13.5 percent, a glance at the bond yield tables will tell us that the convertible would have an investment value of about $800.

A convertible's investment value limits its downside risk; regardless of how much the common stock drops, the convertible won't decline below its investment value unless interest rates rise. On the other hand, the conversion feature, or "equity kicker," endows well-chosen convertibles with large profit potential. That's why it's sometimes said that there is a "floor," but no ceiling, on the price of convertibles. There is, however, a danger that the bondholder will be, so to speak, evicted; since most convertibles are callable, the company may force you to convert — at a price somewhat above par — by calling the issue. Moreover, the convertibility of some bonds diminishes or even vanishes after a time. Consequently, a convertible buyer should get his broker to look up the call and conversion provisions.

The dual character of convertibles makes them complicated to evaluate. The "ideal" convertible would have the following characteristics: (1) the common stock appears to have excellent prospects of advancing; (2) the current price of the common is not more than 15 percent to 20 percent below the conversion parity price; (3) the convertible provides a higher yield than the common stock; (4) the convertible's value as a straight bond is not more than 15 percent to 20 percent below its current price; (5) the price of the bond is not more than 20 percent above the current call price — this minimizes the risk of forced conversion.

It's unlikely that you'll find a convertible that meets all of those requirements. Although convertibles are, in principle, a middle-of-the-road species, there are some that will act more like stocks than bonds and some that will act more like bonds than stocks. The former are selling 'way above their investment value, the latter 'way above their conversion value. Your choice must depend on how much risk you're willing to assume. If you're seeking some growth, make sure you pick a convertible that stands a decent chance of getting a kick upward from its equity kicker.

For inexperienced investors, the best way of investing in convertibles is to buy shares in one of the four closed-end convertible bond funds. Two of them are traded on the New York Stock Exchange: American General Convertible Securities and Chase Convertible Fund of Boston. The other two — Bancroft Convertible Fund and Castle Convertible Fund — are traded on the Amex. In mid-1981, these funds were selling at discounts of 10 percent to 20 percent from their net asset values, largely because the merits of closed-end funds were not widely recognized. At that time, the four funds' total returns — dividends, capital gains distributions, and price increases — had averaged 21 percent a year since 1975. (Their total returns were nearly 35 percent annually in 1979 and 1980, which were years of sharply rising stock prices.)

LOVE THAT DISCOUNT

Deep discount bonds are old bonds with low coupon rates that are selling substantially below their face value; they may be Treasury bonds, municipals, corporates, or convertibles. When you buy a deep discount bond, your current yield is a lot lower than the prevailing rate, but the big advantage is that your profit when the bond matures will be taxed as a capital gain. A sound strategy is to buy deep discount bonds maturing within five years or less. For example, at this writing there's a low coupon A.T.&T. bond due in 1986 that is selling at $660. A buyer is assured of a $340 profit — 51.5 percent — in about four-and-a-half years and he doesn't have to worry about rising interest rates; as bonds approach maturity they become relatively insensitive to interest rate changes. To be sure, a buyer of the A.T.&T. bond sacrifices current income. But if he's in the 40 percent tax

bracket, his *annual return to maturity*—I'll spare you the arithmetic
—will amount to nearly 9 percent *after taxes*. (It could be greater if
the taxes on capital gains are reduced before 1986.) To sum up,
properly selected deep discount bonds often offer a virtually riskless
way of keeping up with or staying slightly ahead of a moderately high
rate of inflation.

PREFERRED STOCKS

Preferred stocks, like bonds, are fixed-income securities; they pay a
fixed dividend that must be met before any dividends may be paid on
the common. Preferred stocks that aren't convertible have little
appeal for the individual investor. They don't have the growth
potential of common stocks and, if a company gets into a financial
bind, the interest due to its bondholders takes precedence over the
dividend claims of the holders of preferred stock.

COMMON STOCKS

Even income-oriented investors should have a portion of their assets
in common stocks in order to give their portfolios some possibility of
growth. The equities traditionally favored for such investors have
been public utilities. The trouble is that anyone who allocates most of
his resources to bonds and utility stocks will have virtually no real
diversification; when interest rates rise, both his bonds and his
utilities will come tumbling down.

A stock selection strategy suitable for income-oriented investors
was described in chapter 21—investing in large, well-established
companies whose stocks are out of favor, are selling at low price/
earnings ratios, and pay liberal dividends. Another sound strategy is
to invest in a diversified package of companies whose dividend
growth has outpaced inflation. When this chapter was written,
companies that had increased their dividends more than 150 percent
over the previous ten years and whose stocks currently yielded more
than 6 percent included the following: American Brands, Avon Products, Bank America, Coca-Cola, Colgate-Palmolive, Cone Mills,
DeBeers Consolidated Mining, Emhart, Equitable of Iowa Companies,
Exxon, Florida Power & Light, International Telephone & Telegraph,
Liberty National Life Insurance, Kellogg, Lucky Stores, Mobil, Ne-
vada Power, Ohio Sealy Mattress Mfg., Rochester Telephone, Travelers Insurance, and U.S. Tobacco. A list of more than 200 companies

with the top records for dividend growth is published annually in the December issue of *Dun's Review*. It's an excellent source of leads for income-oriented investors. Another is the New York Stock Exchange's free pamphlet, *Dividend Leaders on the Big Board*. Since people investing for income are highly vulnerable to the inroads of inflation, they should try to include in their portfolios issues that are inflation-proof and still offer high yields — oil stocks such as Exxon, Mobil, or Texaco and (unless one considers them morally taboo) South African gold mining shares.

As a rule, the risks and potential rewards of investing for income are smaller than those of investing for growth. But you'd be wrong to conclude that the approach you take doesn't much matter. Far too many income-oriented investors simply reach out for the highest obtainable current yields. Except for elderly retired people, that's a shortsighted strategy; over the years, it will ensure that the purchasing power of your capital is seriously eroded by inflation. In an inflationary age, you can't afford to give up on growth or to be a passive investor. You have to try, as best you can, to "manage" your portfolio. That means staying alert to changes in interest rates and in the relative attraction of different types of securities. It also means remembering that, by the grace of our tax laws, one dollar of capital gains is worth more than two dollars of taxable interest or dividends.

23. The Manifold Merits of Mutual Funds

There is virtually no type of investment mentioned in this book that can't be made through mutual funds, and nearly always more economically than if you were to buy the securities individually. The existing types of funds include money-market, tax-exempt money-market, corporate bond, "junk" bond and municipal bond funds; income funds that invest mainly in high-yielding stocks; so-called balanced funds that maintain a balance between stocks and bonds; growth-and-income funds; "quality" growth, aggressive growth, and "maximum gains" funds; and gold funds. Funds with sales charges (usually 8½ percent) can be bought through brokers, who will help you to choose among those that fit your objectives. No-load funds sell directly to investors; you have to write (or telephone) the fund for a prospectus and order form. You'll find a classified directory of no-load funds, with a description of each fund's investment policy, in Appendix B.

If you see more no-load than load funds on a list of the top performers, it's simply because there are more of the former among the growth funds; there's no evidence that either type outperforms the other. For some investors, the convenience of buying through a broker and the guidance he provides may be well worth the commission. Or you may be so dazzled by a particular load fund's record that you feel you have to be in it, and the sales charge be damned. The big argument in favor of the no-loads is that when you invest $1,000, you get $1,000 of stock; in a load fund, you typically start out with $915, and its net asset value has to rise nearly 11 percent before you break even.

Here's a fast rundown of other basic facts that you need to know about mutual funds. The minimum initial investment is commonly $500 or $1,000, but a number of funds accept as little as $200 and a few (usually bond funds) require $2,500 or more. Subsequently, minimum purchases are typically $25 or $50, though a minority of funds won't take less than $100 or even $250. Most funds offer automatic reinvestment of dividends and capital gains, and most accept Keogh Plan Accounts and Individual Retirement Accounts. The money-market funds usually allow you to write checks (provided by the fund) for amounts not less than $500; to do this — or to make withdrawals by telephone — you must first have filed an authorization form with the fund. When a withdrawal request is made in writing, many funds require a stamped guarantee of your signature by a bank or a brokerage firm.

SWITCHING TO BEAT THE MARKET

In addition to eliminating the problems of security selection and diversification, investing through mutual funds provides fantastic flexibility: you can switch from one type of fund to another within the same family of funds — in most cases, by telephone — and save yourself the brokerage commissions you'd have to pay if you bought and sold individual securities. Some fund groups have even eliminated the need for a telephone call. Holders of shares in their growth fund can place "Stop Loss" orders at a specific price; if the shares decline to that level, they are sold automatically and the proceeds are transferred to the money fund. Investors can also specify the price at which they want to get back into the growth fund, and when it's reached, their order will be executed automatically. A switch or "exchange," as it's known, either costs nothing or a trifling $5. Most fund families set no limit on the number of switches a shareholder may make, but some do restrict the frequency — to four a year, for example. Fund-switching has caught on in a big way among individual investors. In 1975, the amount of money involved in exchanges was $700 million; in 1981, it was $14 billion and rising.

There are two basic approaches to fund-switching. Most aggressive investors take the all-or-nothing approach; they keep all of their assets in high-growth or maximum-gains funds when they're bullish and move completely into a money-market fund when they anticipate a market decline. The second, or "risk adjustment," approach, which consists in modifying the portfolio mix, was illustrated in chapter 19. In the example I used there, an investor with $40,000 seeking growth and income and feeling moderately bullish starts out with 50 percent of his assets in a growth-and-income fund, 20 percent in a high-growth fund, 25 percent in a money fund, and 5 percent in a gold fund. If he turns bearish, he would switch the assets in the stock funds into the money fund, or, if inflation is on the rise, he might use 5 percent of these assets to increase his investment in gold. If he becomes decidedly bullish, he could take a more aggressive stance by reducing his investment in the money fund or the growth-and-income fund or both and funneling the proceeds into the high-growth fund. A different investor might prefer simply to keep a portion of his assets in a growth fund and the balance in a money fund, and modify the percentages in accordance with his state of confidence.

Investors who take the "risk modification" approach can get the timing guidance they need from the system described in chapter 20. A preponderance of "yes" answers to the "time to buy" or "time to sell" checklists will indicate whether they should become more aggressive or more defensive. All-or-nothing fund-switchers, too, can use that system, provided their goal is simply to try to anticipate major turning points in the market and they're willing to ignore secondary swings. But they should switch only when the system gives a decisive buy or sell signal.

A great many all-or-nothing fund-switchers are market timing buffs who are out to catch secondary and even minor swings in stock prices. They usually get their signals from a weighted or exponential moving average (see page 123) of the price behavior of the growth fund they're using. The evidence I've seen suggests that short-term fund-switching doesn't produce alluring results even when it's done by pros. The all-or-nothing approach works best when it's used to avoid getting pummeled by major market declines and to make the most of major advances. That's the objective of a fund-switching mutual fund operated by Lowry Reports Inc., whose timing program was described in chapter 16; the minimum initial investment is $10,000.

FINDING THE RIGHT FAMILY

Investors who plan to use the switch privilege can choose among no fewer than 90 fund families, plus independent stock funds that have exchange arrangements with a money-market fund. If you're an aggressive investor you should look for a family with a growth fund that has an outstanding performance record or else select a top-performing independent with a tieup to a money fund. Don't pick a fund simply because it's been the number one over the past one-year, five-year, or ten-year period. Pick one that has a consistently excellent record; you'll find at the end of this chapter a list of funds that have been outstanding performers. Anyone who plans to buy and hold fund shares should check the fund's yearly record to find out how much it has dropped in bear markets. Some of the best-performing funds over the past decade were down 60 percent to 70 percent from 1973 through 1974. A shareholder losing that much might understandably get so nervous that he'd sell at a tremendous loss and be discouraged from going back in again.

Investors whose objective calls for a balanced portfolio will want to be in a fund group that offers a wide variety of funds; but they, too, should select a group that has a high-performance growth fund that they could switch into when they're bullish. Some of the families that meet these criteria are American General, Dreyfus Corp., Fidelity Group, Investors Group, Kemper, Massachusetts Financial Services, Oppenheimer, Putnam, T. Rowe Price, Stein Roe & Farnham, and Vanguard.

The mutual fund industry is constantly broadening the range of funds and services offered to investors. Here's a sampling of innovative "products" introduced in recent years. Spectrum — originated by Massachusetts Financial Services — is an annuity sold without commission through Nationwide Life Insurance Co. of Columbus, Ohio. As with traditional annuities, taxes on the earnings of an investment in Spectrum are deferred until you begin using the money, usually after retirement. Spectrum's advantage is that it enables you to invest in any of the numerous funds managed by Massachusetts Financial Services and to switch from one type to another as market conditions change. Massachusetts Financial Services is the sponsor of another innovation: a fund that invests in foreign bonds, which can be attractive to bond-buyers when the U.S. market looks endangered. And a growth-oriented fund that invests in small foreign companies was introduced by John Templeton in 1981.

ADVICE FOR FUND-SWITCHERS

Two advisory services that give timing advice to fund-switchers were profiled in chapter 13 — James Schabacker's *Switch Fund Advisory* and Gerald Appel's *Systems and Forecasts*. Dick Fabian's *Telephone Switch Newsletter* (P.O. Box 2538, Huntington Beach, CA 92647; $89 a year) offers an intermediate-term timing system that has yielded good results. Services that track fund performance include *Switch Fund Advisory*, *Growth Fund Guide* (see chapter 13), and Burton Berry's NoLoad Fund*X (DAL Investment Co., 235 Montgomery Street, San Francisco, CA 94104; $70 a year).

A dozen or more money managers specialize in handling fund-switching accounts. Some have already been mentioned (their addresses are given in chapter 14 or above): Gerald Appel, Burton Berry, Dick Fabian, Lowry Reports, Inc., and James Schabacker. Among the others are Charlesworth & Rugg (201 South Lake Ave., Pasadena, CA 91101), Amnivest Corporation (550 Park Avenue, New York, NY 10022), Growth Investment Counsel (6 Faneuil Hall Marketplace, Boston, MA 02110), and Roebuck & Co. (575 Lexington Avenue, New York, NY 10022). Annual fees are either 1 percent or 2 percent of the amount under management, and some managers accept as little as $10,000; others require $50,000 and up. Anyone thinking of entrusting his money to a switch-fund manager should write to several of them for information about their investment strategy, performance record, and fee schedule; inclusion in the list I've given should not be construed as an endorsement.

THE TWENTY-FIVE TOP PERFORMING MUTUAL FUNDS
OVER THREE TIME PERIODS
Percentage* increase in net asset value assuming reinvestment
of dividends and capital gains
(Source: *Lipper Analytical Distributors Inc.*)

20 YEARS: 9/30/61 TO 9/30/81

1.	Templeton Growth	1607
2.	International Investors	1506
3.	Over-the-Counter Securities	999
4.	Twentieth Century Growth	991
5.	American General Enterprise	826
6.	Twentieth Century Select	799
7.	Mutual Shares Corporation	775
8.	Plitrend Fund	769
9.	Pioneer Fund	676
10.	Value Line	665
11.	Financial Industrial Income	651
12.	T. Rowe Price New Horizons	615
13.	Decatur Income	571
14.	Guardian Mutual	560
15.	Investors Research	560
16.	Istel Fund	549
17.	American General Harbor	543
18.	American National Growth	534
19.	Axe-Houghton Stock	531
20.	Security Investment Fund	529
21.	Value Line Income	526
22.	Windsor Fund	516
23.	American Mutual	512
24.	American Growth	496
25.	Investment Company of America	494

5 YEARS: 9/30/76 TO 9/30/81

1.	Strategic Investments	621
2.	United Services Fund	595
3.	International Investors	534
4.	Research Capital Fund	527
5.	Twentieth Century Growth	376

---

*Rounded to the closest percentage figure.

6.	Fidelity Magellan Fund	331
7.	American General Pace	303
8.	Lindner Fund	288
9.	Twentieth Century Select	283
10.	Evergreen Fund	282
11.	Golconda Investors Limited	274
12.	Quasar Associates	269
13.	American General Venture	257
14.	Value Line Leverage Growth	252
15.	American General Growth	244
16.	Scudder Development	228
17.	IDS Growth	224
18.	Over-the-Counter Securities	224
19.	Sigma Venture Shares	221
20.	Weingarten Equity	221
21.	Massachusetts Capital Development	216
22.	Hartwell Leverage Fund	214
23.	Growth Fund of America	210
24.	Explorer Fund	207
25.	44 Wall Street	204

1 YEAR: 9/30/80 TO 9/30/81

1.	Lindner Fund	33
2.	Mutual Qualified Income	24
3.	FH&Z Tax-managed Fund	21
4.	Lindner Fund for Income	21
5.	American General Pace	21
6.	Fidelity Magellan Fund	19
7.	Bank Stock Fund	19
8.	Quest for Value Fund	18
9.	IDS Growth Fund	18
10.	Merrill Lynch Pacific	18
11.	Value Line Leverage Growth	17
12.	Delta Trend Fund	17
13.	NEL Growth Fund	17
14.	Loomis-Sayles Capital	15
15.	Lowry Fund	15
16.	United Vanguard Fund	15
17.	United Continental Growth	15

---

*Rounded to the closest percentage figure.

18. Tudor Fund	14
19. Oppenheimer Option†	14
20. First Investors Option Fund†	13
21. Janus Fund	13
22. Qualified Dividend Portfolio I	13
23. Franklin Utilities	12
24. Smith, Barney Income & Growth	12
25. Windsor Fund	12

*Rounded to the closest percentage figure.
†The fund "writes" options (see chapter 25).

24. Gold Isn't Just for Goldbugs

To John Maynard Keynes, gold was "the barbarous relic"; for Charles de Gaulle, it remained "the fiduciary value *par excellence.*" Embracing Lord Keynes's view, the U.S. Treasury — under Presidents Nixon and Carter — campaigned to downgrade gold's role in the international monetary sphere. And the Treasury conducted a series of gold auctions, which, it hoped, would be a depressant on the market — a curiously perverse policy for a nation that is by far the world's largest holder of gold; with every $10 swing in the gold price, the U.S. Treasury gains or loses more than two-and-a-half billion dollars. Fortunately for the United States, its antigold crusade flopped. The barbarous relic retained its "fiduciary value"; gold accounts for an overwhelming portion of the reserves of the world's central banks. And in the private sector, loss of faith in paper currencies has greatly enlarged the constituency whose motto is "In gold we trust."

Some members of the global gold Mafia are certainly not a lovable lot — the money men whose only allegiance is to their wealth, the primitive oil sheikhs, and the American doomsayers promoting fear and paranoia for profit. But investors in gold now also include large numbers of Main Street Americans, who are simply looking for a trustworthy hedge against inflation. Ownership of gold bullion was made legal again for U.S. citizens at the close of 1974. And from that time to 1980, gold was indeed a good inflation hedge; its price rose 2½ times as much as the Consumer Price Index. But it didn't rise steadily. Like any other investment, gold has had severe setbacks. It declined from $187.50 an ounce at the end of 1974 to $103 in the fall of 1976, and at the close of 1978 its average annual gain over the previous 4 years was a puny 5 percent. Gold then soared in 1979 and early 1980, but in November 1981 its price was back to where it stood about 2 years earlier, $399. In short, gold is an inflation hedge only if you buy it when the price is right. So let's take a closer look at the anatomy and dynamics of the gold price.

Gold has a dual personality. It's a "store of value" and it's an industrial commodity used mainly in jewelry but also in dentistry and electronics. The industrial use of gold declines whenever the price rises; it was much lower in 1980 than in 1970. On the basis of an index of the price history of other nonferrous metals, gold, valued strictly as an industrial commodity, was probably worth about $325 an ounce in 1981. At that time, several leading gold analysts estimated that a likely "floor" for the gold price was about $350. Their principal reasons: (1) a price below $350 would probably induce strong buying from the central banks; (2) *new production is shrinking:* the non-Communist world's gold output of 943 metric tons in 1980 was 26 percent lower than in 1970. Nearly three-quarters of this output comes from South Africa,* where most of the mines have a remaining life expectancy of less than 25 years. So by the end of this century, gold in the ground may be in short supply.

While there's a basis for estimating that $350, or thereabouts, is a floor for the gold price, there's no telling what might be its ceiling. Some goldbugs have predicted that we'll see a price of $3,000 before 1990. And we may — if some of the things that could go wrong for mankind, do go wrong. The gold price, at least in the short run, is a barometer of world anxiety. For example, fears triggered by the cutoff of Iranian oil, the taking of American hostages, and the Russian invasion of Afghanistan sent the gold price rocketing from below $400 to a peak of $850 on January 21, 1981. And when tension lessened, the gold price nosedived back to around $480. Bad news for humanity is good news for gold, and the converse holds true. An outbreak of peace and goodwill on this planet would cause a crash in the gold price.

Aside from the ebb and flow of political anxiety, the major determinant of the gold price is inflation — more specifically, the extent to which inflation prompts a flight from paper money (and investments

*The Soviet Union is the world's second largest producer of gold, with an estimated annual output of 280 to 350 tons.

such as bonds). Gold performs best when inflationary expectations are rising but interest rates are not yet in the stratosphere. Extremely high interest rates tend to depress gold because borrowing costs then become a deterrent to speculators who buy gold futures on margin. Moreover, gold, which produces no income, becomes less attractive to some investors when the yields on money-market securities are exceptionally high.

Since the inflation rate is strongly influenced by increases in energy costs, there exists a correlation between the price of gold and the cost of a barrel of oil. In the second half of the 1970s and the early 1980s, gold sold most of the time at 12 to 20 times the oil price; about 15 times is generally considered "normal." That ratio can be helpful in judging whether, at a given moment, gold seems to be significantly overpriced or underpriced.

BULLION vs. STOCKS

The conventional wisdom is that most investors should consider putting 5 percent of their assets into gold and 15 percent or more when inflation looks particularly threatening. In addition to being a hedge against high inflation, gold investments usually hold up or rise in price when there is a big slump in the stock market; they are, in effect, a form of "disaster insurance." The types of gold investment that best serve the purpose are the metal itself and bullion coins (which sell for only slightly more than the value of their gold content), gold mining stocks, certain U.S. mutual funds, and South African investment trusts. That list leaves out gold futures and collectors' coins. Trading futures is a fast-track game, suitable only for experienced speculators with plenty of money. The leverage is tremendous; initial margin requirements for the standard 100-ounce contract are not more than 10 percent and may be as low as $2,500. Anyone speculating with less than $10,000 has sharply increased chances of loss, because he won't have sufficient reserves to ride out short-term fluctuations in the market. Collectors' coins — which have been one of the strongest hedges against inflation — have an altogether different drawback: they're valued for their rarity and condition more than for their gold content, so buying them calls for a high degree of expertise. If you don't have it, you should let yourself be guided by a reputable firm that specializes in numismatics. (Some are listed later in this chapter.) Commissions on rare coins are rather high; one of the leading dealers charges a combined buying-and-selling commission of 20 percent. And if the commission rate is abnormally small, the firm is probably making an extra large profit on the price of the coins.

The pros and cons of investing in gold through the metal or through mining stocks can be summed up as follows. Bullion and bullion coins produce no income, and their safekeeping may involve you in storage or insurance costs. The Western Hemisphere mining stocks pay only trifling dividends, but most of the South African issues have provided annual yields of 12 percent to 20 percent. These payments are in effect a taxable "return of capital," since a gold mine is a depleting asset. Nonetheless, in five years the *after-tax* income received from a high-yielding mining stock can add up to 40 percent of your original investment. In spite of this, a conservative investor might prefer to own bullion or coins, because the risks in the stocks are significantly larger. So, too, are their potential rewards, which makes them much more attractive than bullion to an aggressive investor. The mutual funds and investment trusts have most or all of their assets in stocks. Like other investment companies, they provide diversification and professional management — significant benefits for an inexperienced person investing in gold. Here are the specifics you need to know about each of these forms of gold investment.

"WAFERS" AND BULLION COINS

The standard gold bar is one kilogram, 32.15 troy ounces. But bullion can be bought in small amounts in "wafers" that come in a variety of sizes; those of one ounce and upward are better value than the smaller ones. Alternatively, for as little as $2,500, investors can own a gold "certificate" issued by Deak-Perera, Dreyfus Gold Deposits Inc., or Citibank (whose minimum is only $1,000). The certificate is a receipt for a specific amount of gold which the issuer buys for you at the best available price; the commission is typically 3 percent or less, and there's an annual storage charge of half of one percent.

Bullion coins are official coins that typically sell for about 4 percent to 5 percent more than the current value of their gold content. The most widely owned is the South African Krugerrand, which contains one troy ounce of gold. Other bullion coins include the Canadian Maple Leaf (1 oz.), the Mexican 50-peso (1.2056 oz.), and the Austrian 100-corona (.9886 oz.). Bullion coins are traded by dealers all over the country and on the American Gold Coin Exchange, a subsidiary of the

American Stock Exchange. Reputable dealers include Deak-Perera, which has offices in 14 places (for information call the Washington, D.C., office, 1-800-424-1186), Numisco (1423 Fullerton Avenue, Chicago, IL 60614), Sinclair de Marinis (90 Broad Street, New York, NY 10004), and Dreyfus Gold Deposits Inc. (600 Madison Avenue, New York, NY 10022), an affiliate of Dreyfus Corp. Some major brokerage houses, including Bache and Merrill Lynch, do a limited business in gold. The commission rates on bullion and coins depend on the size of the order and vary somewhat from firm to firm; they range from slightly less to slightly more than commissions on stock trades.

Deak-Perera, Numisco, and Sinclair de Marinis are also specialists in numismatics. So, too, is New England Rare Coin Galleries (89 Devonshire Street, Boston, MA 02109; toll-free number 1-800-225-6794). From time to time, this firm has made public offerings (registered with the SEC) of limited partnerships in professionally managed portfolios of rare coins.

THE "KAFFIRS"

The South African gold mining stocks — traditionally known as Kaffirs — are traded in the over-the-counter market through American Depository Receipts (ADRs), which are claims to shares deposited in a foreign bank; their prices are quoted in the *Wall Street Journal*. A South African withholding tax of 15 percent is deducted from the semiannual dividend, but U.S. residents can subtract the full amount of the tax from their U.S. income taxes. Because of the political risks in South Africa, the Kaffirs sell at much lower valuations than the North American gold stocks; they were priced at 4 to 6 times earnings in mid-1981 as against 11 to 15 times earnings for the Western Hemisphere golds. Analysts who know South Africa have long insisted that the political risks there have been greatly exaggerated. If they're right, the Kaffirs are extremely undervalued in relation to the western gold issues. To some Americans, understandably, that's totally irrevelant; they won't buy anything South African because of their abhorrence for that country's racial policy.

The Kaffirs are generally grouped in three categories on the basis of the life expectancy of their proven reserves, their ore grade, and their extraction costs. A top analyst of South African gold stocks, John Crowley of Shearson/American Express, classifies the Kaffirs as follows:

The Top-Quality Group: long-life (20 years and over) or medium-life (10 to 20 years) mines with low to moderate extraction costs; life expectancy is indicated in parentheses, and an asterisk signifies substantial production of uranium: Driefontein Consolidated (L), Hartebeestfontein (M*), Kloof (L), President Brand (M*), President Steyn (M), Vaal Reefs (L*), Western Deep Levels (L). Dr. Joseph Collender, a leading mining geologist, has called Vaal Reefs "without doubt the world's best mine."

The Medium-Quality Group: mines with a medium life expectancy and low to moderate costs, unless otherwise indicated. Buffelsfontein,* Doornfontein, Free State Geduld, St. Helena, Harmony* (high cost), Kinross, Libanon, Randfontein (high cost), Winkelhaak.

The Speculative Group: "marginal" mines with a short life expectancy (less than 10 years) and high extraction costs, unless otherwise indicated: Blyvooruitzicht (medium cost), Bracken, Grootvlei, Leslie, Stilfontein (medium cost), Western Areas (M).

Long-term investors should stick to the quality group. The medium-quality issues tend to be somewhat more volatile and therefore offer larger profit potential in a bull market for gold. The earnings of the marginal mines are so leveraged that you make a killing in their stocks when gold stages a large advance and you'll be killed in them when gold settles into a downtrend. Here's an example of how a stock in each of these groups performed in a strong up market — their gains are measured from their 1979 lows to late January 1980: West Driefontein — 177 percent; Harmony — 367 percent; Grootvlei — 598 percent.

THE NORTH AMERICAN GOLDS

Campbell Red Lake operates a mine in Ontario, Canada, which is the only long-life, low-cost gold mine with major production in North America. The company (whose stock is traded on the New York Stock Exchange) also has a 25 percent interest in a property at Detour Lake, which may become Canada's largest gold mine. Production there is expected to begin in late 1983. Dome Mines (traded on the New York Stock Exchange) is a Canadian company that owns 57 percent of Campbell Red Lake and 26 percent of Dome Petroleum, and it operates a high-cost gold mine in Ontario. A large part of Dome's earnings come from oil and gas, so as a gold investment Campbell Red Lake is a more logical choice. Homestake Mining (New York Stock Exchange) operates a large high-cost mine in South Dakota, and it has discovered major gold reserves in California; production there is scheduled to begin in 1984. Homestake is not a "pure play" in gold; a sizable chunk of its earnings comes from silver, lead, zinc, and uranium.

MUTUAL FUNDS AND INVESTMENT COMPANIES

When you're investing in gold mining, there's an added need for diversification; a mine's earnings can be affected by natural disasters — fires, floods, cave-ins. But even a not-so-small investor putting 10 percent of his assets into gold stocks may not have enough money to diversify. So for many people the best way of owning these stocks is through a U.S. mutual fund or a South African investment company. Three gold funds can be bought through brokers for a sales charge of 8½ percent or slightly less: International Investors (the oldest and largest), Franklin Research Capital, and Strategic Investments. There are also two no-load gold funds: Golconda (11 Hanover Square, New York, NY 10005), which invests up to 50 percent of its assets in bullion, and United Services (110 East Byrd Boulevard, Universal City, TX 78148). In the five-year period ending March 31, 1981, Strategic Investments, United Services, International Investors, and Franklin Research Capital were among the five top performers of all mutual funds.

Shares in the South African closed-end investment companies are traded in the same way as stocks. For an investor who wants to own gold stocks and likes to keep things simple, ASA Ltd. is an unbeatable choice. It's listed on the New York Stock Exchange; it has an excellent portfolio, which includes large holdings in Driefontein Consolidated and Vaal Reefs; it often sells at a discount from asset value; it pays hefty dividends when the gold price is high; and in 1981 it was the only gold stock on which both put and call options were traded. (Calls but no puts were traded on Homestake Mining.) Anglo-American Gold Investment Company, known as "Amgold," has all the investment merits of ASA, except that it's traded over the counter and has no options. Both Amgold and ASA have been terrific performers when there's a bull market in gold. So if you want to speculate on a big advance in gold, just buy a call or two on ASA. (The use of puts and calls is discussed in chapter 25.)

A SIDE GLANCE AT SILVER

Buying silver rather than gold as an inflation hedge makes sense only when silver is sharply undervalued. There's a rough-and-ready way of determining this, according to Glen Kirsch, a vice-president of Deak-Perera in Washington. In the recent past, the "normal" ratio of gold's price to silver's has been 32 to 1. When the ratio climbs to 37 to 1, silver is probably the better buy; when the ratio sinks to 24 to 1, silver is overpriced in relation to gold.

A popular though cumbersome silver investment has been bags of U.S. coins minted before 1965 that have a face value of $1,000. These bags are available from bullion dealers and they usually sell at a 25 percent premium over the market price of their silver content because the coins have some scarcity value. When silver was priced at $10 an ounce, a bag containing 720 ounces sold for $9,000, plus a 4 percent dealer's commission. A more convenient way of investing in silver is through bullion certificates, which are similar to the gold certificates described earlier; they are issued by Citibank, Deak-Perera, and others.

All silver mines also produce zinc, lead, and copper, so there are no "pure" silver investments in mining stocks. Three North American mining companies with a major stake in silver are Callahan Mining Corp. (New York Stock Exchange), Hecla Mining Co. (New York Stock Exchange), and Coeur d'Alene Mines (traded over the counter).

PRECIOUS METALS OPTIONS

Gold, silver, and platinum options are issued by a worldwide metals dealer, Mocatta Metals, and a smaller Chicago firm, Dowdex; they can be bought and sold (at roughly 10 percent commissions) through a dozen brokers, including Bache Halsey Stuart Shields and Shearson /American Express. Metals options are as complex as stock options and even more alluring to speculators prepared to blow their stake, because wide price swings have multiplied the potential for profit. *As with stock options (but not commodity futures), you can't lose more than your initial investment. But you can occasionally double or even triple your money in a short time.* A brochure on metals options is available from Bache and other leading brokers who handle this business.

25. The Uses and Abuses of Options

Option buying is a game in which incredible profits have been made; a Conoco option contract, in 1981, soared in value 5000 percent in the space of a few months as a result of the bidding war for Conoco, eventually won by Du Pont. It's a near certainty, however, that any option buyer reckless enough to keep all of his money in play all of the time will eventually wind up broke. But options are by no means simply an instrument for speculators shooting for maximum gains. They have a variety of uses in the portfolio strategy of prudent investors; in particular, they can be a versatile and economic tool for managing risk.

The options market is an arcane world. An uninitiated reader plunged into it without a map and a dictionary would soon find himself in a state of total confusion. So it's necessary to begin this chapter with a rundown of the basics — the terminology and mechanics of option trading.

An option is a contract, and there are just two kinds of option — a call and a put. A *call* gives its holder the right to *buy* — a *put* gives its holder the right to *sell* — exactly 100 shares of a particular stock at a specified price during the stated lifetime of the option. The stock named in the contract is referred to as the *underlying stock* — a term that will be used throughout this chapter. The price specified is known as the *exercise* or *striking* price. The life of an option is never more than nine months, but it may be a few weeks or even days. The price that an option buyer pays, and a seller receives, is called the *premium*, and it's quoted in newspaper option tables on a per-share basis; if the premium is $4, the cost of a contract is $400, plus the broker's commission, about $25. (The commission rates on option transactions vary greatly. They depend on the size of the premium, the number of contracts traded, and the tariff scale of the particular brokerage house.)

Every options contract bought is a contract sold by another investor, who is known as the option writer. An option writer profits when the option he has sold expires worthless or worth less than the premium he received. For example, the writer of a call with a striking price of $45 and a premium of $3 per share ($300 per contract) will pocket

$300 if the price of the underlying stock is $45 or less at the option's expiration date; if at that time the stock's price is $46, the option will be worth $1 per share, so the writer's profit will be $300 minus $100. The put writer makes his profit in the same way, except that a put becomes worthless when the price of the underlying stock is at or *above* the striking price at the expiration date. A call *buyer* is betting that the underlying stock will rise; if it does, he exercises his option by requiring the writer of an identical call to sell him the stock at the predetermined (lower) striking price. A put *buyer* is betting that the underlying stock will go down; if it does, he exercises his option by requiring a writer of that particular put to buy the stock from him at the predetermined (higher) striking price. *But in most options transactions nowadays, stock does not actually change hands.* Buyers (and often writers) simply trade their contracts — as explained below — on an options exchange.

Before 1973, options trading was a small-scale business, handled by over-the-counter dealers. This situation was revolutionized when on April 26, 1973, the Chicago Board Options Exchange opened the first formal public options market in history. Later, the American, Pacific, and Philadelphia exchanges introduced options trading. At the end of 1981, calls were available on more than 300 stocks and puts on about 250. The options exchanges bring together buyers and sellers in the same way as a stock exchange. An option buyer can, at any time before the expiration date, sell his contract to another investor on the exchange on which it's traded. Similarly, an option writer can "close out" or "extinguish" his contract — at a profit or a loss, depending on the price behavior of the underlying stock — by buying an identical contract at its current market price from another investor. (This process is similar to "covering" a short sale of stock. See the definition in Appendix D of "Short sale.") However, there's a fundamental difference between the stock and option markets. The stock market is not a finite universe; when stock prices rise, investors collectively get richer. In the options market, *gains made by buyers represent losses for writers, and vice versa.** In fact, option trading is not a "zero sum" but a "minus sum" game; out of every $100

*A call writer who owns the underlying stock may — even though he loses money on the options transaction — make a net profit if the stock rises sharply; his gain on the stock can be larger than his loss on the option.

that enters the market, $97 or less is returned to investors — the balance is siphoned off in commissions collected by the brokerage firms. In short, when you play the options game, you are pitting your judgment and your luck against those of the other participants.

An option is "a wasting asset" — the closer it approaches its expiration date, the lower is its "time value." On any given day, the options traded on a particular stock have three different expiration dates, each of them three months away from the next. Some stocks have options that expire January, April, July, and October; others have options expiring in February, May, August, and November; and for others, the cycle is March, June, September, and December. The longest possible expiration time is nine months. So in March, an investor buying an option with a January-April-July-October cycle has the choice of options expiring in April, July, and October. When an option expires — say, the April one — trading in a new option with a nine-month life begins; in this case, it would be the January one.

The actual day on which options expire is the Saturday following the third Friday of the month named in the contract. But the Friday (or, if it's a holiday, the day before) is the deadline for exercising your option — that is, using it to buy or sell the underlying stock. As I've already noted, the majority of options are not exercised. Except in cases where an investor owns the stock on which he's sold an option — such cases are discussed later in this chapter — exercising an option requires two transactions and costs the investor two brokerage commissions. To cash in his profit by exercising, a call buyer has to purchase the underlying stock from the option writer and then turn around and sell it on the stock market. And a put buyer has to purchase the underlying stock on the stock market and then sell it to the option writer. It's far more convenient, and usually more economical, for option buyers to take their profit simply by selling their contract on an options exchange. For option writers, too, it may be advantageous to close out a contract by buying the same contract (at its current market price) instead of waiting for its expiration date. A case in point: a call writer who is losing money because the underlying stock has risen substantially above the striking price. By closing out his contract on an options exchange, this writer can avoid the potentially greater loss he might suffer by waiting until just before the option expires, at which point it will be exercised against him.

However, an option writer cannot close out a contract once he has received notice from his broker that the option has been exercised by its holder; when that happens, a call writer is forced to deliver the stock itself and a put writer is forced to take delivery of the stock.

When you buy or write an option, you usually have the choice of several striking prices. The intervals between them are $5 for stocks selling below 50; for stocks selling above 50, they are usually $10, though $5 intervals have been authorized by the SEC. When trading in a new option is introduced, the initial striking prices will be somewhat above and below the price of the underlying stock; if the stock's price is 22, the striking prices will be 20 and 25. But if the stock is selling at or very close to a round multiple of 5 — say, 20 — there will be three striking prices: 15, 20, and 25. As the stock's price rises or falls, new striking prices are created by the options exchanges. Thus, on April 15, 1981, when Atlantic Richfield closed at 47⅝, there were Atlantic Richfield options with striking prices of $40, $45, $50, $60, and $70.* A call option whose exercise price is *below* the market price of the stock is said to be "in the money" because it has an intrinsic cash value; with Atlantic Richfield selling at 47⅝, the $40 call had a cash value of $7.62 and the $45 call a cash value of $2.62. Similarly a put option is "in the money" when its exercise price is *above* the market price of the stock. An "at-the-money" option is one whose striking price is the same as the price of the stock.

The principal factors that determine options premiums are four. *(1) The current price of the underlying stock in relation to the striking price of the option, together with the length of time remaining until the option expires.* The farther the striking price is "in the money," the greater is the option's cash value; in addition, the option has a "time value" which depends on the length of its remaining life span. If an option is "out of the money," it has no cash value, but it has a time value. For options with the same expiration date, the farther "out of the money" the striking price, the lower will be the premium; if a stock is selling at $42, you would obviously pay less for the right to buy it at $50 within the next six months than you would for the right to buy it at $45 within the same period. And for "out of the money" options with the same striking price, the closer the expiration date, the lower will

---

*A quoted striking price that isn't a round multiple of five is one that's been adjusted for a stock dividend.

be the premium. *(2) The volatility of the underlying stock.* The options of stocks with large price swings command high premiums because they offer greater profit potential within a given period than the options of more stable stocks. *(3) Crowd psychology.* When investors are predominantly bullish, the demand for calls increases, causing premiums to rise. When pessimism prevails, premiums on calls decline and those on puts rise. *(4) The level of interest rates.* In principle, high interest rates strengthen the incentive for buying options contracts rather than buying the stock itself, because the option ties up less money; consequently, premiums tend to be larger when interest rates are high.

There are complicated formulas for determining whether a particular option is overpriced, underpriced, or fairly priced, but fortunately amateur investors have no need to master them. The options departments of major brokerage houses provide option valuations, which are usually based on the "Black-Scholes Model" (developed by Fischer Black and Myron Scholes) or are read off a computer terminal of the Options Monitor Service, a $1,000-a-month service sold to brokers by Monchik-Weber Associates.

Now that you have a handle on the basics, you should have no trouble understanding the options tables in your daily newspaper. In the table below, the price under the name of the stock is its last closing price on the New York Stock Exchange; the several prices in the first column are the available striking prices; the headings "Calls-Last" and "Puts-Last" refer to the last closing prices of the options expiring in the months named in the next bank of headings. The letter *r* means that the option was not traded that day; *s* indicates that no option is available for that exercise price.

Chicago Board

Option & NY Close	Strike Price	Calls — Last			Puts — Last		
		Nov	Feb	May	Nov	Feb	May
Amdahl	20	s	r	r	s	½	r
28	25	3	5¼	6¼	r	1½	r
28	30	1-16	5⅝	r	2	3⅝	4¼
28	35	r	1¼	2¼	6½	r	r
A E P	...15	2⅛	2 9-16	2¾	s	r	r
17¼	...20	r	⅛	¼	s	r	r

Stock	Strike						
Am Hos	30	7½	r	r	s	r	r
37⅝	...35	2⅝	4	r	s	r	r
37⅝	...40	1-16	1 5-16	2¼	s	r	r
A M P	..50	1¼	3¼	r	s	r	r
51¼	...55	r	2	3¾	s	r	r
51¼	...60	r	9-16	s	s	r	s
Bally	...25	3¼	r	r	r	r	r
28¾	...30	1-16	r	r	r	r	r
Baxter	22½	10⅜	r	r	r	r	r
33¼	...25	8½	9	r	r	r	r
33¼	.27½	6	r	r	r	r	r
33¼	...30	3¼	4½	5⅜	r	⅞	r
33¼	.32½	s	r	4⅛	s	r	r
33¼	...35	s	1½	2¼	s	3	r
Blk Dk	..15	1-16	1 1-16	1¾	s	r	r
14⅞	...20	r	⅛	⅜	s	r	r
Boeing	..20	2⅝	3⅝	4⅞	r	⅝	1
22¾	...25	1-16	1 3-16	2⅛	2⅜	3	3⅜
22¾	...30	1-16	7-16	1	7⅜	7	7¼
22¾	...35	1-16	⅛	s	12⅛	12¼	s
Bois C	...35	r	1½	2⅛	s	r	r
34	45	r	⅜	s	s	r	s
C B S	..45	6	7¼	r	s	r	r
50⅝	...55	r	1	r	s	r	r
50⅝	...60	r	¼	r	s	r	r
Cessna	..15	s	3¾	r	s	⅝	1⅛
18½	...20	1-16	1⅜	2¾	1⅝	2⅝	2⅞
18½	...25	1-16	½	1 3-16	r	6⅞	r
18½	...30	r	¼	½	r	r	r
Coke	30	4¼	r	r	r	r	r
34⅜	...35	1-16	1 7-16	r	9-16	1¾	r
34⅜	...40	r	¼	r	r	r	r
Colgat	..10	5	r	r	r	r	r
15¼	...15	3-16	15-16	1 7-16	1-16	⅝	13-16
15¼	...20	r	¼	7-16	r	r	r
Cmw Ed	15	7⅛	r	r	r	r	r
22¼	...20	2⅛	2 5-16	2⅝	r	r	r
22¼	...25	r	¼	½	r	r	r

Source: Wall Street Journal, November 20, 1981

OPENING AN OPTIONS ACCOUNT

A prospectus of the Options Clearing Corporation, an excellent manual on options trading, cautions that "both the purchase and writing of options involve a high degree of risk and are not suitable for many investors." Brokerage firms are required by the SEC to send this prospectus to an investor who wishes to open an options account. With it the brokerage house must mail a "qualification form," on which the investor states his objectives, age, income, and net worth. To qualify for options trading you must not only be willing to take risks, you must also indicate that you are able to afford them. If you plan to write so-called uncovered or naked options — that is, to sell calls and puts without owning the underlying stock — you will be required to maintain at all times a minimum equity in a margin account; the amount typically ranges from $10,000 to $25,000, depending on the brokerage house. The reason for this is that, if a naked call is exercised, the writer has to buy the stock in order to sell it (at the striking price) to the call owner — and there's no telling how much the writer stands to lose. Suppose, for example, that you write two naked at-the-money calls on a stock selling at $40, the stock then soars to $60, and the option is exercised. You have to cough up 50 percent of $12,000 (plus a commission of $190) to buy the stock on margin, and your loss on your sale price of $8,000 is $4,190, minus the option premium of perhaps $900.

OPTIONS FOR OFFENSE AND DEFENSE

There are literally dozens of option strategies, some of them highly esoteric. I'll confine myself to relatively uncomplicated strategies that can help to improve the performance of an investor actively involved in managing his portfolio. The greatest value of options is their convenience and their versatility as a tool for increasing or decreasing your exposure to risk, in accordance with your state of confidence about the market. Here's a closer look at some of the ways in which options can be used aggressively and defensively.

BUYING CALLS

You usually buy a call when you expect a stock to rise sharply but wish to limit the amount you could lose if you're wrong. For example, instead of investing $5,850 (plus a commission of $140) in 300 shares of a stock selling at $19.50, you might buy 3 calls with a striking price of 20 for $900, plus a $50 commission. (In this example, the premium is $3, so the cost of one contract is $300.) If the stock rises from $19.50 to $29, your three options contracts with a striking price of 20 would be worth about $2,700,* whether you exercise them or sell them on the options exchange on which they're traded. Your profit (before

---

*I've assumed the options are about to expire. They would be worth more than $2,700 if they had some time remaining.

selling commissions) would be $1,750: 184 percent on your invest-
ment of $950. That's about four times the percentage gain you would
have made by owning the stock. Moreover, the most you could have
lost on the options was $950; had the stock dropped to $14.50, a
holder of 300 shares would have been losing $1,640 ($1,500 plus the
original $140 commission). The big drawback is that you lose all of
the money invested in an option premium unless the stock rises above
the striking price, and you don't break even until the stock rises above
the striking price plus the price per share of the option. In the example
above, that adds up to $23, a price at which an investor who has
bought 100 shares of the stock itself at $19.50 has a gain of more than
15 percent.

The lure of buying options is leverage; when the underlying stock
rises, the price of its calls goes up much faster in percentage terms. In
one seven-week period in which Texas Instruments stock rose 36
percent, the price of its April $90 call shot up 850 percent. While that
kind of gain is exceptional, it's not exceptional for a call on a stock
that goes up 30 percent to rise in value 200 percent. Nonetheless, you
should buy a call for speculative profit only when you strongly believe
the underlying stock will rise sharply in a short space of time. And
however confident you are, remind yourself before you act that the
odds are against call buyers. The average premium on at-the-money,
six-month calls has ranged from roughly 7 percent to 11 percent of the
prices of the underlying stocks. Since most of the time stock prices
don't rise that much in half a year or less, a large majority of calls
expire worthless or worth less than the buyer paid for them. However,
call buyers can significantly improve their chances of making money
by observing the following precepts.

(1) Buy when you think a market decline appears to have bottomed
or when there's been a setback in what you believe to be a genuine
bull market; in the latter case, pick stocks that have come down
sharply but were previously among the strongest performers.

(2) Don't pay exorbitant premiums; ask your broker whether his
valuation model shows the premium to be fairly priced.

(3) Don't place "at the market" orders, which will result in your
paying whatever premium is currently being asked. Place a "limit"
order; the limit you set might be the price of the last sale or else the
current bid price.

(4) Select a striking price that is the same as, or not more than slightly above, the market price of the stock. Buying calls that are far out of the money is like betting on rank outsiders at the racetrack; your losses are likely to be so frequent that they won't be offset by the occasional bonanza.

(5) Don't buy deep-in-the-money calls — for example, a call exercisable at 40 on a stock selling at 49. Deep-in-the-money options are expensive, because you're paying for the intrinsic cash value of the call, and they offer limited profit potential. *There's an exception to this rule:* deep-in-the-money calls make sense if your policy is to invest in large, well-established companies whose stocks are out of favor and are selling at low price/earnings ratios. Since such stocks tend to be relatively stable, the risk of losing all of the option premium is slight, and any rise in the price of the stock will be matched, dollar for dollar, in the value of the option. Buying deep-in-the-money calls on unpopular, low P/E stocks is a preferable alternative to buying those stocks on margin; the advantage is that you put up less money for an option contract than for 100 shares bought on margin and you don't incur the high interest charges on money borrowed from your broker.

There's a simple strategy involving the purchase of calls that might appeal to a conservative investor with upward of $25,000. Instead of putting, say 65 percent of his assets into a money-market fund and 35 percent into stocks, he would keep 90 percent of his assets in a money fund and use the balance to buy a diversified package of calls. This would provide him with a high degree of security at all times, plus the possibility of handsome profits in a rising market. According to one scholarly study covering a 12-year period ending December 1975, a hypothetical portfolio with 90 percent of its funds in money-market securities and 10 percent invested in calls on the 30 Dow Jones Industrials achieved a significantly higher total return than a portfolio fully invested in the Dow stocks.

Calls can also be used for protective reasons — for example, in the following situation: you have large gains in a stock and you're uncertain whether it's due for a fall or whether it could climb substantially higher. By selling the stock and simultaneously buying a call on it, you can realize your gain without sacrificing the possibility of further profit. If the stock continues to rise, you make money on the call; if the stock drops sharply, your loss — the call premium — is likely to be smaller than the loss you would have suffered by holding the stock.

BUYING PUTS

A put, let me remind you, is the opposite of a call; it gives you the right to *sell* 100 shares of a particular stock at a specified striking price within the life of the option. You buy a put for speculative profit when you're confident the price of the underlying stock will drop. As a bearish strategy, buying puts is generally preferable to selling short; the put buyer's risk is limited to the option premium, whereas a short seller's losses can be catastrophic (and he must pay dividends to the owner of the borrowed stock). Except when sentiment is emphatically bearish, puts are cheaper than calls for several reasons, one being that, historically, stock prices have risen about two-thirds of the time. Aside from the fact that you are seeking to anticipate declines instead of advances, the precepts for buying puts are the same as those for buying calls.

Puts have a variety of defensive uses. For example, puts can be helpful if you've become apprehensive but have reasons for being reluctant to sell: you may own stocks bought or inherited long ago at such low prices that the capital gains tax on your profits would be huge; or you may simply be holding stocks that you consider attractive for the long haul. In such situations, buying puts on your stocks can be a relatively inexpensive form of insurance. If the stocks take a tumble, your losses will be partially offset by the gains on your puts. And if the stocks rise, your portfolio gains are likely to be larger than your losses on the option premiums. Buying a put on a stock that you've owned for more than a year doesn't affect the stock's tax status as a long-term holding. However, if you've held the stock for less than twelve months, the purchase of a put wipes out your entire holding period from the standpoint of the Internal Revenue Service; your holding period goes back to zero in the eyes of the IRS and stays at zero until you no longer own the put.

You can avoid this problem by buying puts on stocks you don't own. This is another defensive strategy worth considering when you're turning bearish but are not bearish enough to want to sell. In addition to the holding period consideration, the big advantage of buying puts on stocks you don't own is that you can select issues you consider particularly vulnerable should the market decline.

SELLING "NAKED" OPTIONS

Since the odds are against option buyers, it follows that they are favorable to option writers. Nonetheless, writing options on stocks you don't own is a high-risk strategy, because it exposes you to potentially catastrophic losses. For example, on February 24, 1981, when Ford Motor stock was selling at 19½, the premium on the Ford March calls with a striking price of 20 was 62½ cents. A speculator who sold 50 naked calls for a total premium of $3,125 had to cover them at a cost of $25,000; at the expiration date Ford stock had jumped to $25 and the March contracts were worth $5 a share, or $500 each.

An option writer may at any time have the option exercised against him. Consequently, writers of naked options — in addition to maintaining a minimum equity of $10,000 to $25,000 in a margin account — must deposit in the account at least 30 percent of the price of the underlying stock, plus (if the option is "in the money") or minus (if the option is "out of the money") an amount based on the difference between the market price and the striking price. Any marginable security may be used to meet this requirement.

The risks of writing naked options can be substantially reduced by closing out a losing contract as soon as the premium goes to a predetermined price. But, all in all, the writing of naked options is a strategy best left to highly sophisticated traders. There is, however, one fairly common situation in which any investor might find it advantageous to write a naked put. You have decided to buy XYZ stock, selling at 63, if it drops to 60. Instead of just waiting, watching, and hoping, you sell for $200 a naked put exercisable at 60. If XYZ doesn't drop to 60, you pocket the $200, presumably with no regrets because 60 was the most you wanted to pay for the stock. On the other hand, if XYZ declines to, say, 58, the shares will be sold to you by the put buyer at 60, and your actual purchase price, taking into account the premium, will be only $58. Even if XYZ sinks as low as 54, the option ploy has been successful; it has saved you $200, since your original intention was to buy at 60. Selling a naked put is an effective way to bid on a stock that you want to buy at less than its current market price; its big limitation is that puts are not available yet on the majority of stocks.

SELLING "COVERED" CALLS

Writing calls on stocks you own is a conservative strategy widely used by institutions and also by income-oriented investors. Covered call writing is often wrongly touted as a strategy that both lessens risk *and* produces increased income. Clearly, the premium that a writer collects must be regarded *either* as a reduction in the cost of his investment, and therefore a protection against loss, *or* as an addition to income; it can't be both. The effect of writing covered calls is either to reduce risk *and* lessen potential reward, or to increase income and leave risk unchanged.

Amateurs who plan to write covered options should own or buy stable, blue-chip stocks with relatively low price/earnings ratios. The losses they could suffer on volatile, high P/E issues could greatly exceed the option premiums, and the possibility of large rewards has been forfeited by writing the call. Indeed, if the stock price soars, a covered-call writer finds himself in a distressing situation; either he must close out the contract at a substantial loss, or the call will be exercised and he will have to part with his stock at the striking price. With low-beta, blue-chip stocks, there's relatively little risk of a quick, dramatic runup in the price.

At times when stock prices are moving sideways or downward or are not advancing rapidly, a call writer can get an annual return (including dividends) of 18 percent to 20 percent and sometimes more on a portfolio of blue-chip stocks. And under those market conditions, he may not have to part with any of his holdings, because relatively few calls will be exercised. But those numbers tell only one side of the story; they focus on yields and ignore the overall long-term performance of the portfolio. While mutual funds that write covered calls have sometimes done relatively well when the market was sluggish, their records over the long haul have generally been uninspiring. One scholarly study of the results of writing covered calls over a twelve-year period found that the total return on the portfolio — income plus net gains or minus net losses — was 4 percent lower than the return the stocks would have provided had the options not been written, even without considering the commissions involved in the options transactions. That shouldn't be surprising; writing covered calls provides protection, which doesn't come free — the price you pay for it over the long term is diminished performance. For conservative investors who are strongly income-oriented, the writing of covered calls makes sense, though it should probably be avoided after stock prices have suffered a serious decline. It is not, however, the panacea that it's sometimes represented to be.

PLOYS FOR THE PROS

Expert players in the options game trade combinations of options in which they like to think the odds are in their favor whether the stock rises or falls. "Straps" and "strips" are combinations of puts and calls on the same stock with the same striking price and expiration date. A "straddle" combines a put and a call on the same stock, each exercisable or salable separately and both having the same striking price. A "spread" involves the purchase of one option and the sale of another on the same stock, each having a different striking price or expiration date. A certain type of spread is derisively known as an alligator spread, because the commissions involved will eat you alive. The same can be said for most options combinations, if they're used regularly. So leave these ploys to the options buffs, who play around with complex valuation formulas and enjoy doing things the hard way.

SOURCES OF INFORMATION

A neophyte who plans to engage in options trading would be well advised to do some further study before laying his money on the line. By far the best book on options for the amateur investor is *The New Options Market* (New York: Walker and Company, 1979, $15.95) by Max G. Ansbacher, a top authority on options and a vice-president of the brokerage house Bear, Stearns & Co. A beginner can also learn a lot from the literature on options trading that's available free of charge. Booklets issued by the Chicago Board Options Exchange include: *Are Call Options for You? Are Puts Options for You? Call Option Writing Strategies*, and *Tax Considerations in Using CBOE Options*. They are obtainable from brokers or from the Office of Public Information, Chicago Board Options Exchange, LaSalle at Jackson, Chicago, IL 60604. You can get a similar assortment of pamphlets published by the American Stock Exchange (86 Trinity Place, New York, NY 10006) either from the Amex or from your broker.

Some brokerage houses put out explanatory reports on options strategies with current trading recommendations. In addition, there are any number of options advisory services, some of them garbage but some of them excellent. You can get sample copies of 20 options advisory services for $18 from Select Information Exchange, 2095 Broadway, New York, NY 10023.

26. Playing the New Issues Game

The market in new issues — companies making their first public offering of stock — is the most speculative sector of the stock market. It booms when speculative fever rises, slumps when investors turn cautious, and collapses when bearishness prevails. In 1969 and again in 1972, runaway speculation in new issues culminated in crashes that inflicted murderous losses on investors and cast a pall on the underwriting business. The new-issues market became a wasteland, but it was reborn in 1978, and for the ensuing three-and-a-half years it was a speculator's paradise. Investors fortunate enough to have backed front-runners among the newcomers of 1980 made handsome profits literally overnight and gains of 50 percent or more in months. In the fall of that year, roughly 1 in 4 of the class of 1980 were trading in the over-the-counter market at more than double their original offering prices and winners outnumbered losers by 7 to 1. The new-issues boom that started in 1978 peaked in mid-1981. Even so, in November 1981, the 96 issues recommended by the advisory service New Issues over the previous 37 months showed an average gain of 67 percent, after taking into account the losses of the 26 that declined.

While the new-issues market will assuredly suffer periodic slumps, its prospects for the 1980s look promising. Regardless of which political party is in power, it seems unlikely that national policy will turn its back on the commitment made by President Reagan to foster a revival of American industry through tax incentives for business expansion and private investment. A policy that encourages entrepreneurship helps new ventures to survive their infancy and encourages people to invest in them when they're ready to go public. The forward sweep of technology, too, will continue to vitalize the new-issues market by providing a flow of offerings by enterprises that are trailblazers in the new technologies. Such firms offer the best hope of overcoming the U.S. economy's most crucial problem — lagging productivity — and they have the kind of dramatic growth potential that puts stars into investors' eyes.

But make no mistake about it: buying new issues is playing a speculative game. From time to time, the owners of a large and long-established private company finally decide to go public, as the owners of Ford Motor did in 1956. But the majority of newcomers to the public market are young firms with a relatively brief history of profitability. Indeed, some of them have not yet turned a profit and some never will. When new issues are booming, companies too questionable for blue-ribbon underwriters to touch have little trouble finding unexacting sponsors.

Even new issues that have genuine substance — an impressive record of business performance, a respectable balance sheet, and well-defined prospects — tend to be overvalued in relation to comparable companies in the same industry that have been publicly traded for some time. Remember, too, that about 10 percent of the offering price doesn't wind up in the company's coffers; it goes to the underwriters and the brokerage firms who join the syndicate formed to market the issue.

So much for the necessary caveats. Here, now, is a short guide to how to handle yourself in this treacherous, intriguing, and sometimes enormously profitable sector of the market.

When investors learn of a new issue that the Wall Street grapevine says is "hot" — typically a classy high-tech company — the demand for shares usually runs way ahead of supply. For most investors, getting stock in the original offering is considerably tougher than securing choice seats to a new Broadway hit at short notice. Even huge financial institutions have to be satisfied with a modest number of shares. If you do business regularly with a broker, he may be able to scrounge some shares for you provided that (1) he does enough business to have pull with his branch-office manager; (2) the branch is important enough to have pull with the firm's syndicate department, which allots new issues; (3) the firm is a member of the selling group that has teamed up to market the issue. If those provisos are not met, your chances of getting in on a ballyhooed offering are virtually nil.

When Genentech, the highly publicized genetic-engineering company, was marketed in October 1980, one medium-sized New York brokerage house was allotted just 100 shares; two customers, selected by lot, received 50 shares each. Offered at $35, Genentech started trading at $80, up 129 percent.

If you miss out on a sought-after offering, you can still buy it in the aftermarket — that is, when the shares start trading over the counter. And at times when the general market is weak, the price you pay may be no higher than when the stock first came out. Avantek, a high-growth electronics firm, hit the market at $14 a share during the market slump of October 1978 and traded at $14 for some time; two years later it was selling at $47 after a two-for-one split ($94 on the original basis).

But when the stock market is strong, stellar issues often start trading at 25 percent to 30 percent above their offering prices. Moreover their valuations at these prices are apt to be several times the average valuation of stocks in general. So buying a favorite issue that's off and running is putting your faith in the "greater fool" theory, which holds that there'll always be a bigger fool than you around who'll be willing to buy the stock at a higher price.

A much more prudent policy, one that has worked well for patient and vigilant investors, is to keep track of choice new issues that are trading over the counter in hope of catching them if and when they take a tumble. A slump in the market creates such opportunities. Or a new issue may dive because the company reports disappointing earnings. For example, Floating Point Systems, a maker of special-purpose computers, came out at $18 a share in September 1978 and dropped to $8.50 after the company reported a fourth-quarter loss; 33 months later the stock was selling at $59. Buying a previously hot issue that's turned cold works out well only if the earnings' disappointment proves temporary, but the risks involved are usually lower than when you reach for winners selling at their peaks.

While the hard-to-buy issues get all the hoopla, they represent only the slim top tier of the new-issues market. Offerings that have substance but don't put stars into investors' eyes make up the middle tier. Decent middle-tier offerings are usually not difficult to buy. A sharp-eyed stock picker can find good long-term investments among them, and they tend to be less risky than top-tier ones because of their much less elevated valuations. Occasionally, they become instant winners in the aftermarket. For example, Brock Hotel Corp., which runs 52 Holiday Inns, was marketed in June 1980 at $4.08 (adjusted for a subsequent 3-for-1 stock split) and was selling at $6.70 in October; in the same year, Tylan Corp., a maker of semiconductor parts, jumped from its offering price of $17 to $32 in about 90 days.

The third or bottom tier of the market is the habitat of the nickel-and-dime issues, typically energy or precious metals exploration ventures. Many bottom-tier issues are "Regulation A" or "best efforts" offerings. Regulation A of the SEC permits companies raising no more than $1.5 million to cut through much of the red tape normally required to package a new issue. Best-efforts offerings — usually made by companies desperate for cash — allow the underwriter to take stock on consignment and return any unsold shares to the company. The risks of investing in the third tier are extraordinarily high, even by new-issue standards. But euphoric speculators figure that it's easier for a 10-cent issue to go up to 40 cents than for a $10 issue to go to $40. And when a superboom in new issues is under way, they sometimes prove to be right.

BONING THE RED HERRING

Getting information about new issues isn't especially difficult. Some brokerage houses publish weekly calendars of forthcoming offerings, and most brokers subscribe to the *Investment Dealers' Digest*, a weekly that covers the new-issues market. One advisory service devotes itself exclusively to this market, New Issues (profiled in chapter 14).

For the available facts about a new issue, you need to study the preliminary prospectus or "red herring." Your broker will send you a prospectus if he's participating in the underwriting; if he isn't, he can tell you where to get one. The red herring, unfortunately, lives up to its name; it's so filled with caveats and disclaimers that it makes all issues sound almost equally scary. The red herrings of two companies selling retirement homes, one in heaven and one in hell, would in both cases state: "There is no established market for the company's products and services, and there can be no assurance of a market in the future."

However, the prospectus does contain most of the data an investor needs to form a rough opinion of what the issue might be worth — the company's sales and earnings record, profit margins, accounting methods, competitive position, and so on. Other information with an important bearing on the merits of new issues is discussed below.

The Principal Underwriter: even the best underwriters make errors of judgment, but they won't knowingly market the stock of a company that's likely to damage their reputation. A *Who's Who* of top-echelon underwriters of new issues would include Blyth Eastman Paine Webber, Dean Witter, Goldman Sachs, Kidder Peabody & Co., L. F. Rothschild Unterberg Towbin and Shearson/American Express, all of them in New York; Alex Brown & Sons in Baltimore, Hambrecht & Quist in San Francisco, and Rotan Mosle in Houston.

The Holdings of Top Officers: if they are unloading much of their stock, the issue should be shunned.

Financing by a Venture-Capital Firm: strong backing by venture-capital entrepreneurs suggests that the company has been well groomed to go public and probably has genuine promise.

The Balance Sheet: are the company's finances strong enough to keep it going if profits don't meet expectations, or, if profit growth is on target, to provide capital for continued expansion? If you don't trust your own judgment on this score, don't invest in new issues without reliable professional guidance.

For investors braving this market for the first time, here are a few basic precepts. If a broker makes a big effort to sell you a new issue, don't buy it without checking it out especially carefully; the good stuff nowadays doesn't need a hard sell. Beware of "copycat" companies — those that resemble last year's big winners; the success of those winners may well have been largely due to originality in their concept or a well-entrenched position in their field. Remember that companies usually plan several years in advance to go public and they "manage" their earnings — through legitimate accounting devices — so as to show strong growth in the year or two preceding the offering. Be prepared to do a good deal of homework and spread your risk over several issues even if it means buying a small number of shares.

A Final Point: if you can't get an alluring issue at its offering price, be a contrarian; instead of chasing after it when it's selling at more than

30 times earnings, have the courage to buy when the market has taken a nosedive.

27. Profiting from Corporate Marriages

In recent years, a boom in mergers and acquisitions has brought bonanzas to thousands of fortunate stockholders; typically, a would-be corporate buyer offers a price in cash or stock that's 25 percent to 50 percent or more above the current market value of the sought-after company's stock. It seems likely that acquisition fever will continue to run high. Nowadays, many expansion-minded corporate planners would rather buy than build; it's often cheaper and less risky. Moreover, the trend toward deregulation is prompting the Justice Department and the Federal Trade Commission to tolerate some mergers that they might once have blocked as "anticompetitive." (Strictly speaking, "merger" and "acquisition" are not synonymous. One big difference: an acquisition is a purchase of assets for cash, and the seller's gains are taxable; a merger usually involves a nontaxable exchange of stock. But in this chapter, as in common parlance, the two terms are used interchangeably.)

Holding stock in a company that's about to be merged or acquired is usually a matter of luck, but it can sometimes be the reward of foresight. You can increase your chances by including in your portfolio stocks that are worth buying on their own merits and also have some of the earmarks of a candidate for takeover.

Corporate buyers make acquisitions for any number of reasons — to broaden their product line, enter new markets, achieve the economies that come with greater size. Some acquisition hunters seek ably managed, well-positioned companies; others go after plodding or troubled companies, hoping to revamp them. So candidates for acquisition are of all shapes, sizes, and qualities. They have included small energy-exploration and high-technology companies and senior citizens like Kennecott Corp. and St. Joe Minerals. But despite the diversity of the acquisitions market, there are guidelines for an investor seeking to spot companies that might become takeover targets.

Look Where the Bargain Hunters May Shop: a type of company that's alluring to corporate acquirers is one whose cash holdings are large in relation to its market value (the total price of all its shares outstanding); the buyer can recoup part of the purchase price from the selling company's very own cash. Also tempting are companies whose stocks are selling appreciably below book value, and such companies abound. In November 1981, 103 of the 1,700 issues covered by *Value Line* were selling at discounts of 55 percent to 85 percent from their book values. Many of them were losing money, and others were probably uninviting to acquirers because large investments would be needed to modernize their obsolescent plants. But among the profitable companies, there were some that might appeal to a corporate buyer. When you've acquired sufficient experience to judge whether a company might be a candidate for takeover, the *Value Line* weekly list — "Widest Discounts from Book Value" — can be a useful source of leads. (The *Value Line Investment Survey* is available in several thousand libraries, including those of brokerage houses.)

Even if a stock is selling at or slightly above book value, it can look attractive in the merger market. Book value nowadays usually understates the real worth of a company's assets by pricing them at their original cost less depreciation; this is 'way below the inflated cost of replacing them. Companies can also be appealing to acquirers if the price/earnings ratio of their stock is relatively depressed. (Chapter 15, "The Fundamental Approach: Judging What a Stock Is Worth," explained how to find out whether a stock's current P/E relative to the market is higher or lower than its relative P/E over the previous five years.)

Look Where the Owners May Sell: deal makers often search for companies whose principal owners have reasons to court, or be responsive to, a merger or takeover. Many brokers are eager to name their pet "sellout candidates," *but you should consider only companies that look like intrinsically good investments, not just speculative weaklings waiting to be rescued.* One kind of attractive sellout candidate could be a flourishing company whose executives are elderly, own the controlling interest, and have most of their personal fortunes in that one corporate basket. A sale for cash would enable them to diversify their holdings, or a merger into a bigger company would give their estates a stock that's more readily marketable in large amounts.

Strong motives for merger may also catch up with the youthful founder of a fast-growing company. To surmount increased competition or simply to maximize the firm's development, he may find that he needs the marketing muscle and infusions of capital that a senior corporate partner could provide.

Look Where the Merger Action Is Hot: a way of narrowing down the search for acquisition candidates is to look for them in industries where merger activity is already strong. An even better way is to look for companies in which an acquisition-minded company has already made a sizable investment. Then there's a good chance that one of two things will happen: either the corporate acquirer will eventually bid for the remaining stock, or it will facilitate a takeover by agreeing to sell its shares — at a handsome profit, of course — to another suitor.

There were more than 400 companies in which other companies owned significant amounts of stock in mid-1981. Among these so-called partially owned companies were C. R. Bard, a hospital-supply company; Clorox; Chromalloy-American and Walter Kidde, both large conglomerates; Federal Paper Board; Lomas & Nettleton Financial, a savings and loan association; Morton-Norwich Products, a food and drug company; and Robertshaw Controls, a manufacturer of temperature-control devices and home appliances.

Using the guidelines suggested above, I selected nine takeover candidates for an article in the August 1977 issue of *Money* magazine. Within the next five years, five of the nine companies were merged or acquired. When you invest in a company that you consider a takeover candidate, you must be prepared to be patient. If the acquisition you're hoping for does materialize, it's far more likely to take several years than several months.

THERE'S MANY A SLIP 'TWIXT THE BID AND THE BUY
The path from takeover bid to consummated union is an obstacle course that only a minority of runners manage to complete. Says Alan Greenberg, chief executive of Bear Stearns, the New York City brokerage house: "A lot can still happen after a merger proposal is made, and most of it is bad."

When a few large shareholders — a family or members of management — own a controlling interest in a company, a buyer has to meet their terms. Many deals blow up because the controlling stockholders hold out for too high a price. There's a saying among deal makers: "All sellers think their geese are swans." When management owns little of its company's stock, a takeover is easy in theory but may still prove difficult. Since the managers don't stand to make much profit from selling, they're likely to resist offers if they think their jobs are endangered. A standard defensive tactic is to obtain a preliminary injunction barring the would-be acquirer from following up on his proposal. The grounds for such suits are alleged violation of the securities laws that require full disclosure of pertinent facts by parties involved in mergers. Assuming that he wins that round, a would-be buyer must then persuade the company's public shareholders to override management and vote for his offer. Thus a so-called hostile takeover requires a litigious and costly campaign that only fiercely combative acquirers are willing to undertake.

Finally, despite a more permissive attitude among federal agencies, some kinds of mergers will continue to encounter regulatory roadblocks. As antitrust policemen, the Justice Department and the Federal Trade Commission may now accept consolidations involving major corporations where once they would have balked. But they might still oppose mergers between large and thriving companies in the same industry. For example, Mobil's attempt in late 1981 to take over Ohio-based Marathon Oil was blocked on the grounds that it would lessen competition for gasoline sales in the Midwest.

If you own a stock that has soared following a merger or takeover offer, you may wonder whether to sell and cash in your windfall or wait for larger gains — typically an additional 12 percent to 15 percent — if the deal reaches the finish line. In the case of tender offers (firm cash offers with a set expiration date), the smart policy is not to tender your stock until the deadline is near, because another buyer may suddenly announce a higher bid. Merger proposals are harder for the stockholder to decide about, since they involve an exchange of stock, and either party to the deal could call it off. Every case is different, but the questions you must try to answer, preferably with your broker's help, are basically the same.

Is the acquiring company one you would normally invest in and, further, do you currently rate its stock a good buy? If either answer is no, sell.

How large is the risk that the merger won't go through? The stakes would be discouragingly high if either the suitor or the sought-after company had a poor record for completing mergers, or if the two companies were in an industry — broadcasting, for example — where regulatory authorities might oppose consolidations.

If the deal collapses, will your stock lose all or most of what it gained after the merger announcement? It probably will, unless the merger terms weren't particularly favorable to your company and the resulting publicity has made the merits of your stock better known — or unless the chances look good that your company will eventually find another suitor.

Holders of stock in an acquiring company are usually less likely to be affected, in the short run, by the outcome of merger negotiations. The announcement of a prospective merger may give the acquirer's stock a slight lift, but more often causes it to fall. For example, American Express shares dropped $2.37 to $40.75 after news of the merger proposal to Shearson Loeb Rhoades in April 1981, whereas Shearson stock rose $4 just before the announcement and a further $6.37 after it, to $48.62.

The reason the acquirer's stock often slips is that the buyer is usually paying a hefty premium over the seller's market price. So it's likely to be some time before the benefits of a takeover translate into higher earnings. In fact, when a company whose stock you own has made an important merger or acquisition, you should give it another checkup. You might decide that the deal was ill-advised and that it's time to sell your stock.

Investors sometimes wonder whether there are easy profits to be made by buying shares in companies just after they've received a merger offer. In many cases, the stock is still selling at a healthy discount from its estimated merger value. This is known as risk arbitrage, and it's a game best left to highly sophisticated investors with large amounts of money. According to Ellen Greenspan, an analyst in the Oppenheimer & Co. customer arbitrage department, you need to invest at least $100,000 in different merger situations in order to diversify your risks. Moreover, when a deal has soured, the professional arbitrageurs watching the Dow Jones ticker will know about it and unload their shares before an amateur investor reads the bad news in the newspaper; and by that time, his stock has probably been devastated.

Searching for merger and takeover candidates brings benefits even if you never succeed in picking a company that gets acquired. It will sharpen your nose for value, and will probably lead you to discover undervalued investments that you would otherwise have missed.

VI

CONCLUSIONS

28. A Portrait of the Ideal Investor

Will Rogers had a nifty formula for successful investing: "Don't gamble. Take all savings and buy some good stock and hold it till it goes up, then sell it. If it don't go up, don't buy it."

During my fifteen years on Wall Street, I observed that some investors have an uncanny knack for buying stocks that don't go up and not selling those that do go up until they've tumbled down. The chronic losers I knew could not be typed as dimwits: among them were doctors and dentists, successful businessmen, a magazine editor (who wrote a book about his losses), even brokers and security analysts.

After I myself had been battered by a long losing streak in the early 1970s, I began to wonder whether there was a syndrome that causes people to act self-destructively in the stock market. My own errors weren't hard to diagnose. I had drifted away from a consistent policy that for many years had brought me considerable success — investing for the long pull in growth companies I considered reasonably valued. Instead, I had slipped into buying stocks that were in fashion and not selling them when they turned sour. I had let myself be tugged this way and that by conflicting market forecasts and had become overeager to make quick profits but fearful of further losses.

Generalizing from my own mistakes, and those committed by some clients of mine who appeared to be bent on losing money, I came up with a composite portrait of the chronic loser. He is mentally lazy, gullible, apprehensive but greedy, overly impressed by authorities, and also easily infected by the emotions of the crowd. If he's not mired in indecision, he's swinging to extremes of optimism and pessimism. Consider this portrait, and you'll recognize in it Everyman with all of his human frailties hanging out. In other words, the traits that make for failure in investing are deeply rooted in human nature. An investor's worst enemy lurks within himself.

It follows that success in investing hinges on doing what does not come naturally. For example, an investor must condition himself not to sell stocks but to buy them when panic prevails, and not to buy but to sell when the market's booming and euphoria is everywhere. That's the surest way of buying low and selling high.

To do unfailingly what doesn't come naturally is not humanly possible; the ideal investor does not exist. But to set him up as a model is the best way I know to develop a winning style in the market. Here, then, is a portrait of the paragon that we can all profit by emulating.

The ideal investor has learned to be rigorously honest with himself; he knows his weaknesses and watches for signs that irrational impulses are clouding his judgment. He has also rid himself, through study and experience, of all innocence about the stock market. The ideal investor knows, for example, that the most widely recommended stocks are probably bad buys because too many people have already bought them; that the only reliable forecast of the market anyone can make was J. P. Morgan's: "It will fluctuate"; that acting on tips from the average broker is like buying hair-grower from a bald barber; that success lies not in making a bundle quickly but in making a fortune slowly.

The ideal investor knows, too, that supersuccessful investors — figures like Bernard Baruch and Joseph P. Kennedy — have been loners. So he does his homework, trusts his common sense, and charts a course of his own. He spares no effort to be well informed, because to profit from events you have to be one jump ahead of the headlines. An Irish proverb says, "Good luck beats early rising." But the men I've known who made fortunes in the market got lucky by getting places early.

There is one more ingredient, a crucial one, in the makeup of the ideal investor. It was suggested to me in an essay, "The Nature of Genius," by the late Ernest Jones, one of the pioneers of psychoanalysis. After studying the lives of Copernicus, Newton, and Freud, Jones detected in their characters a common singularity. Unlike most people, who tend to be either credulous or skeptical, each of these geniuses combined to an extraordinary degree credulity and skepticism. Jones shows how this fusion of opposite traits guided them on their journeys of discovery. His insight into the nature of genius applies to the world of investing, where great success is won by a process of discovery — the perception of future values not discounted in present market prices. Skepticism is the armor that protects investors against rumors and phony tips, à la mode "concepts," pipe dreams, or just exaggerated expectations. But chronic skepticism leads to chronic negativism and self-defeating inertia. Investors must have the credulity—I prefer to call it vision or faith in their judgment—to heed evidence that tells them a sweeping change is coming in the market or that a young company has the makings of a giant. The ideal investor maintains an interplay between skepticism and belief—an internal dialogue between his critical faculties and his creative imagination. That's something all of us can try to do. If we succeed even some of the time, we won't be chronic losers; if we succeed much of the time, we're certain to be winners.

29. Investment Vistas: Where Growth Will Be the Fastest in the Eighties

Futurology is an exercise doomed to error. Who, at the beginning of the 1970s, could have foreseen that the decade would bring a twelve-fold increase in the cost of oil and make cheap energy—historically a prime source of industrial growth—a thing of the past? But, clouded though our crystal ball may be, peering into the future is a mandatory exercise for investors. Generals, it's been said, are always fighting the last war. And the same is true of investors who act without a tentative outline of the shape of things to come. So, without further protestations of fallibility, I'll discuss the investment vistas of the 1980s as I see them, focusing on five major themes. These are the changed structure of the U.S. economy, the forward sweep of the technological revolution, the service industries, demographic and social changes, the prospects for common stocks.

THE FRAGMENTED ECONOMY

A special report in the June 1, 1981, issue of *Business Week* presented this important insight into the changed structure of the U.S. economy: "The economy has devolved into five separate economies that no longer act as one; these subeconomies do not grow together in periods of prosperity, nor do they decline in periods of recession. They have lives of their own because each is driven by unique forces." *Business*

Week defined the five subeconomies as "old line industry," energy, high technology, agriculture, and services.

Old-line industry consists of the basic manufacturing industries that once were the mainstay of this country's growth — autos, steel, heavy machinery, textiles, and the like. This subeconomy is what Wall Street analysts refer to as "Smokestack America," and it is strongly represented among the 30 companies of the Dow Jones Industrials. Smokestack America entered the 1980s beset with problems: deteriorating productivity, a worsened competitive position in world markets, an inadequate return on invested capital, and obsolescent facilities, which, because of the high cost of capital, will cost huge sums to modernize. No "revival" that this sector of the economy could experience in the 1980s is likely to make it a rewarding area for growth-oriented investors. Don't misunderstand me: there will be times when the "uglies" — the stocks of old-line industry companies — may be undervalued in relation to the glamour issues and may outperform them for 6 to 12 months or possibly somewhat longer. But for investors seeking high long-term growth, old-line industry will remain fundamentally unattractive. So, too, will the agricultural economy; the relatively few publicly owned companies involved in agriculture are basically cyclical. (The list of 160 small-growth companies listed in Appendix A includes only one whose business is agricultural: Alico.)

The energy economy — broadly defined — will in all probability remain an area of vigorous growth. In its drive to develop more sources of energy and to preserve capital, the U.S. government will make some compromises with the stricter dictates of environmentalism. There will be, because there must be, more production of nuclear power. And there will be, because there must be, more mining of coal; coal production may nearly double between 1981 and the end of the decade. The rate of growth of companies in the oil and gas industry, and its oilfield services sector, will depend on the future of petroleum prices. Despite the highly publicized "glut of oil" in early 1982, most forecasters still expected oil prices to go on rising, though probably at a very much slower pace than in the 1970s. That forecast doesn't allow for a possible cutoff of Middle Eastern oil by the Arab countries, a danger that can't be ruled out. The state of Arab-Israeli relations is one of the ticking time bombs that could explode in the 1980s; and if it were to explode, there's no telling what the repercussions would be.

Even if a Middle East disaster is averted, it seems likely that well-positioned companies in the energy economy should continue to enjoy superior growth.

TECHNOLOGY TRIUMPHANT

The application of technologies that came off the drawing board, or out of the laboratory, over the past three decades has assumed the force and breadth of a tidal wave. Throughout the rest of the 1980s and beyond, the technological revolution will have a dramatic impact on industry's methods of production, on our ways of doing business and on American life-styles. The universe of high-growth-technology companies is so large and so complex that only a full-length book written by a team of specialists could attempt to explore it. I must limit myself here to presenting a layman's catalogue of some of the sectors of technology that already are, or could become, the fastest-growing segments of industry in the 1980s. The names of some 90 companies in these sectors will be found among the 160 small-growth companies listed in Appendix A, and others are mentioned below.

Cable television: the number of CATV subscribers is expected to reach 30 million by 1985, more than double the 1980 figure. And within the foreseeable future, cable TV systems will offer "narrowcasting" — the linkage of a video screen with a computer in a two-way system that could make possible banking, information retrieval, and shopping from the home. The problem for investors is that there are no longer any sizable companies that offer a "pure play" in CATV; nearly all of the independent systems have been merged into giant companies such as Time Inc. and Warner Communications. A small operator, United Cable Television, is listed in Appendix A, but it may not be around long as an independent entity. Several publicly owned companies make cable television equipment. The glamour company in the field when this chapter was written was Scientific Atlanta, which was selling most of the saucer-shaped antennas that allow cable operators to pick up programs transmitted by satellite. Data on two smaller equipment makers, Microdyne Corp. and RMS Electronics, are tabulated in Appendix A.

Computer-assisted Design/Computer-aided Manufacturing: CAD/CAM systems are used to automate graphic and production processes, and their applications are almost unbounded. They are used, for example, in the design and production of calculators, engineering projects, gas turbines, microwave components, molds for plastics, motors, printing presses, semiconductor integrated circuits, and typewriters. The growth prospects of leaders in this technology such as Computervision Corp. quickly captured the imagination of investors, with the result that stock valuations in the early 1980s were exceptionally high.

Data Processing: this catch-all label applies to innumerable companies involved in computer technology — manufacturers of such equipment as memory systems; makers of "intelligent" data terminals linked to a central computer — for example, the cash registers used in supermarkets and other businesses; firms that use computers to gather, store, process, and distribute information; and firms that provide computer programming — the tremendous growth in the use of computers of all kinds is creating an almost unlimited demand for programming. See Appendix A for names of small-growth companies in the data processing business.

Instrumentation: this is a large and varied sector, which includes instruments used to automate temperature control, and industrial processes and quality control; those used in flight and navigational systems; and instruments used for scientific and medical research. Growth prospects seem particularly favorable for the companies that help to save energy and to improve industrial productivity through process and quality control. A sampler of instrument companies, large and small: Beckman Instruments, Hewlett-Packard, Johnson Controls, Kratos Inc., Measurex, Nicolet Instrument, Tektronix, Teradyne.

Laser Technology: growth in the use of lasers — in the aerospace and other industries, in communications, in medicine and surgery, and by the military Establishment — will be explosive in the 1980s. A pioneer in the laser field is Perkin-Elmer. Smaller companies are listed in Appendix A.

Other Medical Technology: this will be an area of stunning growth, powered by advances in radiology, ultrasonic diagnostic devices, improved systems for monitoring the vital functions, and other innovations. A mutual fund that invests only in companies contributing to medical progress, Medical Technology Fund, was started in 1979. It's listed in Appendix B.

Robotics: industrial robots bear no resemblance to the "droids" of *Star Wars*, but they can be programmed to manipulate tools, materials, and instruments. They can "see" and "feel" in a limited way and have some decision-making capabilities. Analysts have estimated that industry sales, which were only $60 million at the beginning of the eighties, could grow to at least $800 million or possibly as much as $2 billion by 1990. At this writing, three publicly owned companies that appear to be particularly well positioned to benefit from the growth of robotics are Unimation, Prab Robots, and Ransburg. Champion Spark Plug and Cincinnati Milacron also manufacture robots, but their other lines of business are so large that robots are not likely to have a major impact on their growth.

Small Computers, Home Computers, and Word Processors: the market for computers of less than standard size will continue to be a high-growth market — but competition will be fierce. Major producers of so-called minicomputers — which, paradoxically, are the biggest small computers — include Digital Equipment, Data General, and Prime Computer. The leader in really small business computers — systems costing as little as $9,000 to $11,000 — has been Wang Laboratories, which has also been an innovator in the development of word processors; these are essentially computerized typewriters that automate many of the secretarial functions. Sales of home or "personal" computers started to take off at the beginning of the 1980s and are expected to climb to $9 billion annually, worldwide, by 1990. The early leaders in the home computer field were Apple Computer, Commodore International, and Tandy. IBM and Xerox introduced their home computers in mid-1981.

Semiconductors/Microprocessors: American business is wedded to electronics, and semiconductors are the basic building blocks of electronics. The semiconductor industry is enormously competitive and is subject to cyclical downturns. But well-managed, innovative companies in the field should continue to enjoy dynamic growth in the eighties. Semiconductor technology took a great stride forward when Intel Corp. pioneered the microprocessor, which has been called "a computer on a chip." Other giants in the semiconductor industry are Motorola, National Semiconductor, and Texas Instruments. Smaller companies include Advanced Microdevices, Standard Microsystems, and Unitrode.

Solar Energy: the number of solar thermal systems installed in this country grew from fewer than 100 in 1973 to 200,000 at year-end 1980. In late 1981, the publicly owned companies whose principal business was thermal heating were still small enterprises, but some seemed to be on the verge of achieving profitable growth. Among them were American Solar King, Novan, Olympic Solar, and United Solar Associates. Solar heating, it would seem, is an idea whose time has come. More remote, when this book was completed, were the possible rewards of a more recent solar technology known as photovoltaics, a process employing solar cells to produce electricity from absorbed sunlight, and one that in the next century might provide the world with a mind-boggling source of power. Large companies in the forefront of solar cell technology include Atlantic Richfield, Mobil Oil, Texas Instruments, and Westinghouse. Some of the leading smaller companies in their field are Applied Solar Energy, Energy Conversion Devices, and Photovoltaics, Inc.

Telecommunications: the label applies to communications systems that use cable, microwave, or satellite to transmit large amounts of information over long distances at reasonable costs and also to so-called interconnect systems — privately owned telephone systems that interconnect with the regulated carriers (A.T.&T. and the independent telephone companies). Telecommunications is yet another segment of the technology economy with seemingly unlimited growth potential. Some emerging growth companies in the telecommunications field: Aydin Corp., California Microwave, Granger Associates, M/A-COM, MCI Communications, Plantronics, Rolm, and Telecom Equipment Corp.

Genetics: biotechnology, or "gene-splicing," is a new primary technology that can alter the genetic makeup of a cell to program it to perform a specific task such as the production of proteins. The potential applications of biotechnology go far beyond its proven uses, which include making insulin and interferon, a seemingly promising substance for the treatment of cancer. Given time and capital, this new technology may revolutionize medicine and agriculture; it could also be employed in the chemical industry, food processing, pollution control, and other areas. But if biotechnology's promise is realized, it will be in the fairly distant future — more distant than was imagined by investors who rushed to buy stock in the firms that were the first to go public: Enzo Biochem, Genentech, and Cetus. As of mid-1981, neither they — nor anybody else — had as yet sold a genetically engineered product, except to other researchers. And it seemed unlikely that these firms would show significant profits for quite some time to come.

The stocks of companies mentioned in this chapter (and in Appendix A) are not, it should be stressed, investment recommendations; they are simply some of many possible candidates for investigation by interested investors. Investing in high-tech stocks can be exhilarating — some stocks double in months, some more than triple in a few years. But a caveat issued earlier needs to be repeated: beware of overpaying for expectations of growth, however dazzling they may seem to be. When something goes wrong for a high-tech issue selling at a stratospheric valuation, its price comes tumbling down. You have to try to catch a high-tech stock either before it's on the hit parade, or when it's suffered a setback, or when the general market has slumped.

The Service Industries: the service economy is a growth economy. As an area for investment, it has two advantages for the layman over the universe of high technology: the companies are easy to understand and their stocks — even those with impressive growth records — tend to sell at significantly lower valuations than the favored high-tech issues. I can't tell what stock valuations will be when this book is in the hands of a particular reader. What I can do is to suggest where some of the many investment opportunities in the service industries may lie. (This text, I hope, will have equipped the reader to judge whether or not a stock seems reasonably valued.)

With crime ubiquitous and booming, companies that provide protection services appear to have plenty of growth in their future.

Hospital management, too, has been and could continue to be a high growth business. The brokerage industry — traditionally cyclical and precarious — seemed in the early 1980s to be running on a sounder track; the brokerage firms* are better capitalized and better managed, and the wider range of products that they offer has made their earning power somewhat less volatile. Other changes in the large, varied, and rapidly expanding world of financial services should make it a rewarding hunting ground for sharp-eyed investors. They should, in particular, be on the lookout for innovative companies in the financial sector that create their own base for growth by performing a specialized service. National Data Corporation, which consolidates the cash receipts of national chains such as McDonald's, is one example. Another is SafeCard Services, whose "Hotline" service provides credit card holders with a convenient way of reporting loss or theft to the card issuers. A third is Comdata Network, whose "better idea" is making money transfers via a computerized telecommunications network. How well these companies will do in the future is, of course, uncertain. But they had rewarded early-bird investors when this chapter was written, and they exemplify the innovativeness that generates superior growth. Other fields in which companies have won success by performing highly specialized services include insurance, pilot training (Flight Safety International), disposal of toxic wastes (Waste Management), and laboratory testing (Charles River Breeding Laboratories). Investing in the service industries, once you know the basics of stock valuation, simply requires common sense, plus a dash of prescience. The overall strategy: look for companies that have positioned themselves to exploit growing demands created by changes in American lifestyles and in business techniques. You will find them in many sectors in addition to those mentioned above. You may well run across them in your daily life.

The New Demographics: the makeup of the American population will be substantially altered in the 1980s, according to the projections of the Census Bureau. A rising tide of births will enlarge the under-5 group; annual births are expected to climb to more than four million by the mid-1980s, compared with 3.6 million in 1980. The over-65

---

*Three of the largest Wall Street firms — Bache Halsey Stuart Shields, Shearson Loeb Rhoades, and Dean Witter Reynolds — were acquired in 1981, by, respectively, Prudential Insurance, American Express, and Sears Roebuck.

group will grow about twice as fast as the overall population. And the biggest increase — about 25 percent in the course of the decade — will come in the 25-to-44-year-old segment, whose ranks will be swelled by 76 million Americans born in the baby-boom era, 1946 through 1964. The groups that will decline or show little growth are teenagers, young adults, and people of 45 to 65.

Some of the implications of these population shifts are clear. The demographics of the 1980s appear to be unfavorable for businesses with a large teenage clientele; in the major industries, these would include soft drinks, "junk" foods, and cosmetics and toiletries. The growth of the under-five-year-old group will benefit makers of food and pharmaceutical products for infants and small children, and of course makers of toys. It also spells growing demand for day-care services, since so many women are now part of the labor force. (The two leading publicly owned companies solely engaged in providing this service are Children's World and Kinder-Care.) The prime beneficiaries of the bulge in the elderly population will be the health-care industry — in particular hospital and nursing-home management companies and drug companies that are strong in geriatric products. Retirement communities will benefit, too, but at this writing no major publicly owned company has emerged as a promising investment in this field.

The largest surge in consumer demand will come from the 25-to-44-year-old population group, whose biggest segments will be affluent, two-income families — and have-nots. Specialists in marketing expect the spending of this huge group to be the strongest at the high end and the low end of the price spectrum. Its beneficiaries will be purveyors of luxury goods and services — and discounters. The "middle market" is likely to find the going tougher.

The demographics of the 1980s, coupled with a postponed demand for housing caused by sky-high mortgage rates, point to an eventual boom in home building. A. Gary Shilling, a leading economic consultant, has estimated that the average annual number of housing starts between 1983 and 1990 will, at worst, be 1.7 million and could be as high as 2.5 million; annual housing starts in 1980 and 1981 averaged 1.2 million. The prospects look even more favorable for mobile homes, which nowadays are really low-cost manufactured housing. Schilling expects mobile-home shipments to rise from

200,000 in 1982 to 300,000 annually from 1983 to 1986, and to 400,000 a year from 1987 through 1990. If these projections prove fairly accurate, the stocks of home builders and mobile home manufacturers should be strong performers in the 1980s.

An astute money manager, Martin D. Sass, predicted in 1981 that home entertainment would be "the Nirvana industry of the 1980s." In addition to companies involved in cable television, probable participants in the growth of home entertainment would include leading producers of television films and programs, makers of electronic games, companies that capture a large share of the market for video recorders, and companies that provide videotaping services. Two of Sass's favorite companies with large stakes in his "Nirvana industry" were Warner Communications and Matsushita of Japan, which he called "the smartest consumer electronics company in the world."

THE DECADE OF COMMON STOCKS

In an interview with this writer in 1980, Louis Rukeyser — host of the television program *Wall Street Week* — predicted that "the 1980s will be the decade of common stocks." John Templeton, the most successful fund manager of the past twenty-five years, subsequently revealed that he is no less optimistic than Rukeyser about the long-term prospects for the stock market. In a message conveyed to his fund shareholders on a phonograph record in 1981, Templeton said that stocks were "ridiculously cheap" and that the Dow Jones Industrials could rise to 3,000 before the end of the eighties.

The thesis that the 1980s will be a great decade for common stocks rests on two related arguments. The first is that a significant change has occurred in our political and economic beliefs — a so-called swing toward conservatism — which will bring a much improved climate for American business and stronger incentives for the individual to save and invest. The second argument is that — in light of this favorable change — common stocks are sharply undervalued in relation to other kinds of investments. Time alone will tell whether these arguments are valid, but my belief is that they probably are.

It seems incontestable that a reaction has set in against the ideology loosely defined as liberalism, which has been the dominant American ideology for roughly half a century. In its doctrinaire form, liberalism condemns the profit motive and is hostile to business. It favors tight government regulation of industry, and the use of tax and welfare policies to redistribute wealth. It holds that combating unemployment is more urgent than fighting inflation, and backs labor's demands for higher wages without regard to the effects on productivity. It contends that all social problems can and should be solved by government, if necessary by throwing at them increasing amounts of the taxpayers' money.

These beliefs, though they are still widely held, are no longer dominant. Jimmy Carter ran for reelection in 1981 essentially as a conservative — a conservative "with compassion." And Ronald Reagan won the presidency with a platform that assailed many of the tenets of liberalism. It stressed, for example, that job creation must be accomplished not through federal largesse, which would be inflationary, but by revitalizing American industry. It promised, among other things, to trim the size of government, slash federal spending, lessen regulation of industry, reduce taxes for all individuals — the rich included — and for business, too, and encourage capital formation by providing incentives for personal saving and investment. The endorsement of such a program by the voters certainly justifies the belief that doctrinaire liberalism is a weakened ideology, and that the social and political climate has become a more favorable one for American industry — or at the very least less hostile.

The "new conservatism" (which is not so new) is in principle bullish for common stocks. But if the 1980s are to be a golden era of the stock market, significant and durable progress will have to be made in holding down the level of inflation. Whether Reaganomics — otherwise known as "supply side" economics — will help to achieve a durable lessening of inflation will not be known until the mid-1980s. But in early 1982, there were reasons for believing that the inflation rate could drop substantially below its upper levels of the 1970s and early 1980s, assuming a reduction in the huge federal budget deficit before the middle of the decade. The Federal Reserve Board seemed to be committed to stick with inflation-fighting monetary policies. More importantly, perhaps, it appeared that the cycle of hyperinflation that began in the late 1960s might come to an end because the major forces that triggered it and fueled it were no longer at work. The first was the prodigious surge of "guns-and-butter" spending of the Lyndon Johnson era — the combined cost of financing the Great Society programs and fighting the Vietnam War. The second was the ballooning of that war's cost. The third was the twelvefold increase in oil prices between 1974 and 1981. Oil prices will continue to rise, but not at the incendiary rate of that seven-year period. And gains in productivity coming from technological advances should also contribute to a gradual easing of inflation.

If expectations of high inflation diminish, the tangible investments that lured funds away from stocks in the 1970s are likely to lose some of their appeal. In that decade — according to figures compiled by Robert S. Salomon, Jr., of Salomon Brothers — the investments that produced the highest annually compounded returns were: gold (31.6 percent annually), silver (23.7 percent), U.S. stamps (21.8 percent), Chinese ceramics (18.8 percent), rare books (16.1 percent), U.S. coins (16 percent), diamonds (15.1 percent), Old Master paintings (13.4 percent), U.S. farmland (12.6 percent), and residential housing (10.2 percent). The return on stocks was only 6.8 percent and on bonds 6.4 percent. Thus at the beginning of the 1980s stocks were deeply depressed in relation to tangible investments, whose prices, in many cases, had shot up spectacularly over the previous decade. In light of the seemingly improved outlook for American business and for some abatement of inflation, there was a good case for believing that stocks were, as John Templeton put it, "ridiculously cheap."

What would it take for the Dow to hit the 3,000 level that Templeton considered a possibility by 1990? A common forecast at this writing is that inflation will average 7½ percent or 8 percent annually in the years ahead, and that the real growth of the Dow's earnings could be about 3 percent. This would mean that the Dow's nominal earnings per share will grow at an annually compounded rate of 10½ percent or 11 percent, which would raise them to slightly more than $300 by 1990. On the basis of that guesstimate, a valuation of 10 times earnings would put the Dow at 3,000; a valuation of 9 times earnings — which seems to me more probable if the inflation rate doesn't go appreciably below 8 percent — would mean a level of 2,700. Since it's virtually certain that the growth sectors of the market will substantially outperform the Dow, the 1980s might very well turn out to be "the decade of common stocks." I suggest, therefore, that you follow Will Rogers's advice: "Buy some good stock and hold it till it goes up. . . . If it don't go up, don't buy it."

Appendixes

Appendix A
A Growth Hunter's Game Preserve: 160 Little Stocks with Large Potential

This appendix is NOT a recommended list. It's a list of companies worthy of investigation by investors seeking to find small growth companies that might be among the big winners of the 1980s. In the fall of 1980, Equity Research Associates, assisted by Wm. O'Neill & Co. of Los Angeles and the Media General organization, screened more than 6,000 small companies and selected from them 450 that met certain criteria that suggested they might some day qualify as Equity Research recommendations. In the spring of 1981, the author arbitrarily reduced this list to 160 companies, eliminating in most cases those having annual sales of less than $5 million or operating at a loss, and omitting others for a variety of reasons, one being apparent overvaluation.

In the tabulation that follows, the sales figure represents sales for the latest reported fiscal year available when the screening was made. The earnings per share (EPS) are for the latest reported 12-month period as of May 1981; an asterisk in this column means that EPS *declined* in that period. Stock prices and per share earnings have been adjusted for stock splits through September 1981. The growth rate is the annually compounded growth rate of earnings per share over a 5-year period starting 1975. The earnings base in most cases was small or minute, so the higher growth rates certainly do not indicate a sustainable trend; indeed, by 1982 or 1983 companies whose 5-year growth rate at that time has been 25 percent or better will have demonstrated exceptional dynamism. "N.A." in the growth-rate column indicates that a 5-year rate was not available. The seventh column, headed ROE, gives the percentage return on stockholders' equity for the latest year available at the time of the Equity Research screening. For reasons of space the description of company's "type of business" is a broad one that simply indicates the sector of industry in which the company operates.

A reader scanning this list in 1982 or thereafter will enjoy benefits of hindsight that should make up for the missed opportunities. With a Standard & Poor's monthly *Stock Guide* in hand, he will quickly see which of the companies have failed to fulfill their promise and can be scratched from the performance derby. He will know which ones have sustained a high rate of growth. In comparing their mid-1981 valua-

COMPANY AND LOCATION	SALES $ MILLIONS	EPS, MAY 1981 LATEST 12 MONTHS	PRICE MAY 1981
Acmat Corp. Hartford, CT	13.0	0.59	6
Air Wisconsin Appleton, WI	26.0	1.09	18½
Alico, Inc. Labelle, FL	17.0	2.27*	42
Alpha Industries Woburn, MA	23.0	1.08	31
American Recreation Centers Sacramento, CA	16.0	2.16	9
Anacomp Inc. Carmel, IN	67.0	1.03	20
Analogic Corp. Wakefield, MA	62.0	0.97	31
Andersen 2000 Atlanta, GA	5.0	0.30	13½
Anthem Electronics Inc. San Jose, CA	37.0	1.33	21
Applicon Inc. Burlington, MA	57.0	0.92	37
Applied Data Research Princeton, NJ	32.0	1.27	21½
Atlantic America Corp. Atlanta, GA	35.0	1.76	15
Atlas Hotels Inc. San Diego, CA	49.0	3.06	25
Avantek Inc. Santa Clara, CA	48.0	0.93	39

tions (price divided by EPS) with their current valuations, he will have a basis for judging whether or not they have climbed too high on the ladder of popularity. In short, with this list, an investor who does his homework should be able to assemble a winning portfolio of junior growth stocks.

EXCHANGE	GROWTH RATE (Annual percentage)	ROE (percent)	TYPE OF BUSINESS
OTC	100+	25.4	Building maintenance and services
OTC	47	31.0	Transportation, airline
OTC	72	45.3	Citrus fruit, cattle
ASE	60	24.7	Electronics, military systems
OTC	27	22.5	Leisure and recreation services
OTC	38	33.1	Computer services
OTC	95	40.2	Computer peripheral equipment
OTC	100+	22.3	Pollution control equipment and services
OTC	N.A.	N.A.	Electronic components, semiconductors
OTC	N.A.	10.7	Computerized graphic systems
ASE	N.A.	6.9	Computer services
OTC	52	N.A.	Insurance, property and casualty
OTC	27	22.3	Hotels and motels
OTC	41	29.8	Electronic communications equipment

COMPANY AND LOCATION	SALES $ MILLIONS	EPS, MAY 1981 LATEST 12 MONTHS	PRICE MAY 1981
Base Ten Systems Trenton, NJ	9.0	1.12	15
Bentley Laboratories Irvine, CA	46.0	2.13	39
Bolar Pharmaceutical Copiague, NY	10.0	0.56	18
Boston Digital Corp. Hopkinton, MA	16.0	0.59	13
Bowne & Co. New York, NY	95.0	3.32	37
CACI Inc. Arlington, VA	35.0	1.32	20
CPT Corp. Eden Prairie, MN	60.0	2.13	52
Cado Systems Torrance, CA	36.0	1.50	38
California Microwave Sunnyvale, CA	38.0	1.46	27
Cavco Industries Phoenix, AZ	16.0	0.36*	5
Charles River Breeding Wilmington, MA	34.0	1.72	37
Chattem Inc. Chattanooga, TN	72.0	1.43	14½
Chem-Nuclear Systems Kirkland, WA	46.0	1.69	34
Children's World Inc. Evergreen, CO	14.0	0.35	6
Cobe Labs Inc. Lakewood, CO	85.0	2.87	34
Coherent Inc. Palo Alto, CA	59.0	0.73*	25½
Comcast Corp. Bala Cynwyd, PA	24.0	0.77	25

EXCHANGE	GROWTH RATE (Annual percentage)	ROE (percent)	TYPE OF BUSINESS
OTC	55	28.5	Aerospace electronic equipment
OTC	26	13.8	Medical instruments
OTC	51	44.5	Drugs and medical products
OTC	95	30.3	Machine tools, automated
ASE	31	25.0	Printing, financial
OTC	52	47.4	Computer services
OTC	38	26.6	Office equipment, word processers
OTC	N.A.	62.0	Computer manufacturing
OTC	6	25.5	Telecommunications, avionics
OTC	31	43.7	Building, mobile/modular homes
OTC	19	15.4	Laboratory testing
OTC	27	17.8	Medical and beauty products
OTC	55	34.2	Pollution control equipment and services
OTC	62	28.1	Day-care centers
OTC	22	14.5	Medical instruments
OTC	78	23.8	Instruments, scientific
OTC	37	23.4	Cable TV

COMPANY AND LOCATION	SALES $ MILLIONS	EPS, MAY 1981 LATEST 12 MONTHS	PRICE MAY 1981
Comdata Network Inc. Nashville, TN	13.0	0.65	24
Communications Industries Dallas, TX	40.0	1.17	34
Community Psychiatric San Francisco. CA	47.0	1.35	30
Compact Video Systems Inc. Burbank, CA	36.0	1.20	20
Comprehensive Care Newport Beach, CA	39.0	1.13	31
Computer Consoles Rochester, NY	35.0	0.96	27
Computer Products Fort Lauderdale, FL	17.0	0.57	13½
Computer Task Group Buffalo, NY	20.0	1.15	18
Control Laser Corp. Pompano Beach, FL	13.0	0.47	18
Corcom Inc. Libertyville, IL	19.0	1.10	28½
Core Laboratories Dallas, TX	74.0	1.36	27
Cray Research Mendota Heights, MN	50.0	0.31	37
Cullinane Database Systems Wellesley, MA	22.0	1.27	59
Data Access Systems Blackwood, NJ	34.0	1.31	14
Data-Design Laboratories Cucamonga, CA	66.0	1.52	20
Dranetz Engineering Laboratories Plainfield, NJ	14.0	1.02	20
Drexler Technology Palo Alto, CA	17.0	0.48	13

EXCHANGE	GROWTH RATE (Annual percentage)	ROE (percent)	TYPE OF BUSINESS
OTC	42	72.7	Money transfer services
OTC	18	19.9	Radio communications
NYSE	35	26.3	Hospitals and nursing homes
OTC	38	18.4	Mobile videotape systems rentals
OTC	41	40.1	Hospital management
OTC	N.A.	42.5	Data management systems
OTC	47	21.9	Machine tools and related products
OTC	100+	42.0	Computer services
OTC	47	21.4	Lasers
OTC	47	31.4	Digital circuitry filters
ASE	20	14.3	Oil and gas field services
OTC	N.A.	31.7	Scientific computers and software
OTC	61	40.3	Computer program packages
ASE	23	29.7	Computer peripheral equipment
OTC	32	28.5	Engineering military systems
OTC	117	47.4	Electronic measuring instruments
OTC	42	27.4	Photo plates for electronics

COMPANY AND LOCATION	SALES $ MILLIONS	EPS, MAY 1981 LATEST 12 MONTHS	PRICE MAY 1981
Dunkin' Donuts Randolph, MA	60.0	1.61	15
Dunlap & Associates Darien, CT	30.0	1.10	17
Dynatech Corp. Burlington, MA	39.0	1.40	30½
EIP Microwave Newport Beach, CA	7.0	0.73	12
Electronics Corporation of America Cambridge, MA	39.0	3.40	41
Evans & Suterland Computer Salt Lake City, UT	28.0	2.38	92
Evans-Aristocrat Industries Newark, NJ	22.0	1.64	13
Flagg Industries Van Nuys, CA	22.0	0.76	11
Flight Safety International Flushing, NY	47.0	1.55	49
Floating Point Systems Portland, OR	39.0	0.64	22
Flow General McLean, VA	77.0	0.96	45
G & K Services Minneapolis, MN	36.0	1.41	14
General Employment Enterprises Chicago, IL	17.0	0.81	7
Gibson-Homans Co. Cleveland, OH	54.0	1.72	12
Haemonetics Corp. Braintree, MA	20.0	1.01	28
Hazleton Laboratories Vienna, VA	43.0	0.85	19

EXCHANGE	GROWTH RATE (Annual percentage)	ROE (percent)	TYPE OF BUSINESS
OTC	19	19.5	Retail food and restaurants
OTC	N.A.	28.0	Flight simulators
OTC	32	29.9	Medical instruments
OTC	N.A.	24.5	Microwave test equipment
ASE	42	26.1	Electronic controls
OTC	55	22.9	Computer graphics systems
ASE	30	24.4	Tools, hand-held
ASE	21	16.7	Hospitals and nursing homes
NYSE	30	25.1	Aircraft training
OTC	59	20.0	Computer manufacturing
ASE	31	19.5	Biomedical products, R & D services
OTC	19	15.1	Textile leasing and related activities
ASE	141	64.4	Personnel placement
OTC	23	38.8	Paints and allied products
OTC	32	26.0	Blood processing systems
OTC	14	12.4	Biological research, medical supplies

COMPANY AND LOCATION	SALES $ MILLIONS	EPS, MAY 1981 LATEST 12 MONTHS	PRICE MAY 1981
Hungry Tiger Van Nuys, CA	36.0	0.85	7
Hunt Mfg. Co. Philadelphia, PA	54.0	1.41	20
Hyatt International Chicago, IL	12.0	1.38	24
Impell Corp. San Francisco, CA	46.0	2.09	47
Interface Mechanisms Mount Lake Terr., WA	11.0	0.73	19
International Clinical Labs Inc. Nashville, TN	25.0	0.71	15
Ionics Inc. Watertown, MA	44.0	0.98	23
Kallestad Laboratories Minneapolis, MN	11.0	0.70	20
Kinder-Care Learning Centers Montgomery, AL	57.0	0.56	13
Kroy Inc. St. Paul, MN	25.0	0.93	23½
Kulicke & Soffa Industries Horsham, PA	47.0	2.15	20
La Quinta Motor Inns San Antonio, TX	62.0	0.86	20
Lawson Products Des Plaines, IL	85.0	1.59	23
Lazare Kaplan International New York, NY	49.0	(1.60)* loss	15½
Lumex, Inc. Bay Shore, NY	19.0	1.58	30
MTS Systems Corp. Eden Prairie, MN	65.0	2.75	31
Macrodyne Industries Los Angeles, CA	26.0	0.22	8

EXCHANGE	GROWTH RATE (Annual percentage)	ROE (percent)	TYPE OF BUSINESS
OTC	65	39.5	Retail food, restaurants
OTC	19	18.7	Office and art materials
OTC	11	N.A.	Hotels, motels
OTC	33	34.4	Service to nuclear industry
OTC	93	58.3	Computer peripheral equipment
OTC	37	14.6	Regional laboratory systems
ASE	23	14.7	Pollution control and equipment and services
ASE	58	27.6	Medical instruments
OTC	62	34.1	Day-care centers
OTC	N.A.	34.8	Graphics, printing
OTC	60	49.3	Electronic components, semiconductors
NYSE	37	24.8	Hotels, motels
OTC	17	23.2	Metal products distributor
ASE	N.A.	N.A.	Diamonds
OTC	27	N.A.	Hospital furniture, equipment
OTC	33	24.4	Electronic measuring instruments
ASE	N.A.	61.2	Aerospace/aircraft equipment

COMPANY AND LOCATION	SALES $ MILLIONS	EPS, MAY 1981 LATEST 12 MONTHS	PRICE MAY 1981
Magnetic Controls Minneapolis, MN	46.0	1.51*	25
Materials Research Orangeburg, NY	63.0	1.40	26
Matrix Corp. NJ Northvale, NJ	18.0	0.70	25
Micro Mask Sunnyvale, CA	22.0	1.12	13½
Microdyne Corp. Rockville, MD	17.0	0.83	32
Minnetonka Inc. Chanhassen, MN	42.0	0.83	17½
Mobile Communications Corporation of America Jackson, MS	12.0	0.18	5½
National Computer Systems Edina, MN	34.0	1.09	20
National Education Corp. Newport Beach, CA	78.0	1.98	15
Thomas Nelson Nashville, TN	38.0	0.73	13
New Penn Motor Express Lebanon, PA	42.6	3.44	16½
Nicolet Instrument Madison, WI	63.0	1.00	23
Norstan, Inc. Minneapolis, MN	19.0	0.74	15½
Nuclear Metals Inc. Concord, MA	22.0	0.90*	23
Oakwood Homes Corp. Greensboro, NC	43.0	2.32	18
Ohio-Sealy Mattress Cleveland, OH	52.0	0.95	8
Olsten Corp. Westbury, NY	83.0	1.23	18

EXCHANGE	GROWTH RATE (Annual percentage)	ROE (percent)	TYPE OF BUSINESS
OTC	50	35.9	Telecommunications equipment
ASE	67	31.1	Electronic products, miscellaneous
ASE	N.A.	69.6	Medical instruments, sound systems
OTC	49	24.9	Photomasks and photoplates
OTC	86	45.5	Telemetry, satellite CATV equipment
OTC	100+	24.8	Cosmetics and toiletries
OTC	66	27.8	Data communications services
OTC	37	26.2	Computer manufacturing
ASE	69	23.4	Vocational training
OTC	8	12.2	Publishing Bibles
OTC	26	21.1	Transportation, trucking
OTC	26	21.5	Electronic measuring instruments
OTC	43	39.4	Machinery, general industrial
OTC	32	19.9	Metal process and fabrication
ASE	34	19.1	Building mobile/modular homes
ASE	22	18.7	Mattresses and box springs
OTC	24	26.4	Financial/business services

COMPANY AND LOCATION	SALES $ MILLIONS	EPS, MAY 1981 LATEST 12 MONTHS	PRICE MAY 1981
Optical Radiation Corp. Azusa, CA	15.0	1.15	15
Pacesetter Corp. Omaha, NB	43.0	1.01	13
Pacific Scientific Anaheim, CA	54.0	1.29	17
Paradyne Corp. Largo, FL	56.0	0.84	45
Penn Engineering and Manufacturing Danboro, PA	29.0	2.50	30
Penril Corp. Rockville, MD	31.0	1.30	15
Pic'n'Save Corp. Carson, CO	99.0	2.95	52
Pioneer Group Boston, MA	9.0	1.59	16½
Plantronics Inc. San Jose, CA	98.0	1.27	23
Plenum Publishing New York, NY	24.0	1.86	14
Postal Instant Press Los Angeles, CA	14.0	0.82	15½
Prime Motor Inns Clifton, NJ	36.0	1.34	14
Printronix Inc. Irvine, CA	41.0	1.16	27
Quotron Systems Los Angeles, CA	55.0	1.38	41½
RLI Corp. Peoria, IL	23.0	1.45*	7½
RMS Electronics Bronx, NY	17.0	0.88	16
Radiation Systems McLean, VA	8.0	0.76	18

EXCHANGE	GROWTH RATE (Annual percentage)	ROE (percent)	TYPE OF BUSINESS
OTC	71	25.9	Electro-optical products
OTC	36	29.8	Building products, doors and trim
NYSE	66	24.7	Electronic control instruments
ASE	100	17.3	Data communication services
ASE	36	28.3	Metal products, fasteners
ASE	34	26.5	Electronic components, miscellaneous
OTC	37	30.7	Retail discount and variety stores
OTC	55	N.A.	Mutual funds
NYSE	18	21.6	Telecommunications equipment
OTC	36	32.9	Journals, books, tapes
OTC	40	27.9	While-you-wait printing
NYSE	66	39.2	Hotels, motels
OTC	100+	41.9	Minicomputer printers
OTC	70	40.0	Financial information services
OTC	29	30.4	Contact lens insurance
OTC	73	44.4	CATV equipment
OTC	34	23.7	Communications antennas

COMPANY AND LOCATION	SALES $ MILLIONS	EPS, MAY 1981 LATEST 12 MONTHS	PRICE MAY 1981
Redcor Corporation Common Concord, CA	25.0	1.11	20
Reeves Communications New York, NY	41.0	0.85	30
Research Inc. Minneapolis, MN	20.0	1.17	14
Reuter Inc. Hopkins, MN	12.0	1.27	13
SafeCard Services Ft. Lauderdale, FL	14.0	0.66	16
Safety-Kleen Corp. Elgin, IL	95.0	1.43	33
Save-Way Industries Hialeah, FL	45.0	1.23*	11
Scientific Computers Inc. Minneapolis, MN	13.0	0.95	11
Sealectro Corp. Mamaroneck, NY	40.0	0.95	13½
Sealed Air Corp. Saddle Brook, NJ	82.0	2.46	32
Semicon Inc. Burlington, MA	23.0	0.35	8
Sensormatic Electronics Hollywood, FL	39.0	1.24	38½
Shared Medical Systems King of Prussia, PA	93.0	1.17	32
Shopsmith, Inc. Vandalia, OH	33.0	1.29	11½
Showboat Inc. Las Vegas, NV	34.0	2.99	18½
Sierra Research Corp. Buffalo, NY	43.0	1.43	23
Sigmaform Corp. Menlo Park, CA	13.0	0.76	17

EXCHANGE	GROWTH RATE (Annual percentage)	ROE (percent)	TYPE OF BUSINESS
OTC	103	37.1	Electronic components, semiconductors
OTC	100+	59.0	TV programming and production
OTC	30	20.5	Heating, control instruments
OTC	N.A.	30.5	Precision-machined metal parts
OTC	86	27.3	Financial/business services
OTC	25	27.6	Chemical preparations, miscellaneous
OTC	66	53.9	Retail drugstores
OTC	82	26.0	Data processing services
ASE	69	22.6	Electronic component connectors
NYSE	23	18.7	Containers, paper/plastic
OTC	69	38.2	Electronic components, semiconductors
OTC	49	31.4	Protection and safety equipment and services
OTC	31	29.3	Hospital computer services
OTC	65	N.A.	Tools, hand-held
ASE	15	24.9	Las Vegas Hotel and Casino
OTC	19	22.9	Radar systems, military avionics
OTC	88	25.5	Heat-resistant tubing

COMPANY AND LOCATION	SALES $ MILLIONS	EPS, MAY 1981 LATEST 12 MONTHS	PRICE MAY 1981
Spectradyne Inc. Richardson, TX	11.0	0.74	16
Stocker & Yale Beverly, MA	7.0	1.45	14
Stryker Corp. Kalamazoo, MI	33.0	1.06	24
Sykes Datatronics Rochester, NY	14.0	0.32	17
Systems Engineering & Manufacturing Stoughton, MA	21.0	1.93	24
Tandem Computers Cupertino, CA	93.0	0.51	29
Telecom Equipment Corp. Long Island, NY	28.0	0.55	17
Telecredit Inc. Los Angeles, CA	40.0	1.01	31
Thousand Trails Seattle, WA	28.0	1.56	11
Topaz, Inc. San Diego, CA	24.0	0.65	18½
Triad Systems Sunnydale, CA	50.0	1.09	41
Trico Industries Gardena, CA	73.0	1.16	18
Trion Inc. Sanford, NC	9.0	0.77	8
Trus Joist Corp. Boise, ID	95.0	1.80*	27
Tucker Drilling San Angelo, TX	20.0	1.42	14½
U.S. Surgical Corp. Stamford, Ct	72.0	0.96	33
United Cable Television Tulsa, OK	45.0	0.81	25

EXCHANGE	GROWTH RATE (Annual percentage)	ROE (percent)	TYPE OF BUSINESS
OTC	63	35.0	Pay-per-view hotel movies
OTC	44	25.4	Machine tools/instruments
OTC	28	22.4	Specialty medical devices
OTC	100+	27.5	Computer peripheral equipment
OTC	40	24.1	Pollution control equipment and services
OTC	100+	20.9	Computer manufacturing
OTC	N.A.	N.A.	Private telephone systems
OTC	24	13.9	Financial services
OTC	100+	55.2	Campground resorts
OTC	73	N.A.	Electronic power conditioning equipment
OTC	100+	68.4	Computer systems
NYSE	15	20.1	Oil field machinery and equipment
OTC	22	22.8	Electronic air cleaners
OTC	52	32.9	Prefab construction materials
OTC	43	39.8	Contract drilling
OTC	48	26.7	Medical instruments
OTC	100+	23.1	Cable television

COMPANY AND LOCATION	SALES $ MILLIONS	EPS, MAY 1981 LATEST 12 MONTHS	PRICE MAY 1981
Unitrode Corp. Lexington, MA	97.0	1.67	23
Vagabond Hotels San Diego, CA	40.0	2.85	15½
Vallen Corp. Houston, TX	29.0	1.30	17½
Vermont Research Corp. North Springfield, VT	15.0	1.63	25
Vertipile Inc. Leominster, MA	23.0	0.86	4
Vicon Industries Inc. Huntington, NY	17.0	0.92	14
Vishay Intertechnology Malvern, PA	37.0	1.13*	12
Walbar Inc. Peabody, MA	56.0	3.02	41
Wespercorp Anaheim, CA	10.0	0.75	15
Xidex Corp. Sunnyvale, CA	59.0	1.52	27
Zero Corp. Burbank, CA	70.0	1.97	27

EXCHANGE	GROWTH RATE (Annual percentage)	ROE (percent)	TYPE OF BUSINESS
NYSE	44	18.1	Electronic components, semiconductors
OTC	32	24.6	Hotels and motels
OTC	48	N.A.	Protection and safety equipment and services
ASE	100+	51.9	Computer memories
ASE	60	20.5	Textile mill products
ASE	27	26.9	Protection and safety equipment and services
ASE	33	21.3	Electronic measuring instruments
ASE	55	40.1	Aerospace/aircraft equipment
OTC	95	45.8	Electronic control products
OTC	32	25.5	Duplicate microfilm
NYSE	26	21.7	Electronic packaging

Appendix B
A Guide to No-Load Mutual Funds

(REPRODUCED BY PERMISSION FROM THE 1981 NO-LOAD
MUTUAL FUND ASSOCIATION INC. DIRECTORY)

MONEY-MARKET FUNDS

Fund Name *(Advisor)* Address and Telephone Number	Investment Objective and Policy
CAPITAL PRESERVATION FUND, INC. *(Benham Management Corp.)* 755 Page Mill Rd. Palo Alto, CA 94304 800-227-8380/800-982-6150 (CA only)	Safety: U.S. Government securities backed by the full faith and credit of the U.S. Treasury and maturing within 1 year.
CAPITAL PRESERVATION FUND II *(Benham Management Corp.)* 755 Page Mill Road Palo Alto, CA 94304 800-227-8380/800-982-6150 (CA only)	Safety: U.S. Government securities backed by full faith and credit of the U.S. Treasury and maturing within 7 days.
DELAWARE CASH RESERVE *(Delaware Management Co.)* 7 Penn Center Plaza Philadelphia, PA 19003 800-523-4640/215-988-1333	As high a level of current income with preservation of principal and maintenance of liquidity.
DOLLAR RESERVES *(Bull & Bear Management Corp.)* 11 Hanover Square New York, NY 10005 800-431-6060/914-657-3300	Maximum current income consistent with preservation of capital and maintenance of liquidity; invests in high quality money market instruments.
DREYFUS LIQUID ASSETS *(The Dreyfus Corporation)* 600 Madison Ave. New York, NY 10022 800-223-5525/212-223-0303	Maximization of current income to extent consistent with preservation of capital by investing in money market instruments.

Fund Name
(Advisor)
Address and Telephone Number

Investment Objective
and
Policy

FINANCIAL DAILY INCOME SHARES
(Financial Programs, Inc.)
P.O. Box 2040
Denver, CO 80201
800-525-9831/303-779-1233

As high a level of current income as is
consistent with liquidity and safety of
capital.

FIRST VARIABLE RATE FUND
(Government Securities Management Co.)
1700 Pennsylvania Ave., NW
Washington, DC 20006
800-424-2444/202-328-4000

High yield, stability, liquidity. Invests
exclusively in short-term and variable
rate obligations backed by the U.S.
Government.

FLA. U.S. GOVT. MONEY MARKET
(Fla. Mutual Fund Group, Inc.)
Landmark Bank Building, Suite 1507
Ft. Lauderdale, FL 33394
305-522-0200/800-432-1592 (FL only)

Fund seeks to obtain as high a level of
current income as is consistent with the
preservation of principal and liquidity.

FOUNDERS MONEY MKT. FUND, INC.
(Founders Mutual Depositor Corp.)
1300 First of Denver Plaza
Denver, CO 80202
303-292-1820

Current income consistent with
preservation of capital and maintenance
of liquidity.

GOVERNMENT INVESTORS TRUST
(Bankers Finance Invest. Mgt. Corp.)
1800 N. Kent St.
Arlington, VA 22209
800-336-3063/703-528-6500

Highest possible current income
consistent with quality of government
securities having short maturities or
variable interest rates.

IDS CASH MANAGEMENT FUND, INC.
(Investors Diversified Services)
Box 369 IDS Tower
Minneapolis, MN 55472
800-IDS-Idea/800-437-4332

Maximum current income consistent
with liquidity and conservation of
capital by investing in money market
securities.

JOHNSTON CASH MGMT. FUND
(Douglas T. Johnston & Co., Inc.)
One Boston Place
Boston, MA 02106
800-343-6324/617-722-7250

As high a rate of current income as is
consistent with the preservation of
capital and liquidity by using money
market instruments.

LEHMAN CASH MGMT. FUND
(Lehman Mgmt. Co., Inc.)
55 Water Street
New York, NY 10041
800-221-5350/212-558-3288

Current income consistent with
preservation of capital and liquidity:
invests in high-quality short-term money
market instruments.

Fund Name *(Advisor)* Address and Telephone Number	Investment Objective and Policy
LEXINGTON MONEY MARKET TRUST *(Lexington Management Corp.)* Box 1515, 580 Sylvan Ave. Englewood Cliffs, NJ 07632 800-526-4791/800-932-0838 (NJ only)	High current income consistent with preservation of capital and liquidity.
LIQUID GREEN TRUST *(Unified Corporation)* Guaranty Building Indianapolis, IN 46204 800-428-4492/317-634-3300	Current income from diversified money mkt. instruments; U.S. Gov., 150 largest U.S. bank short term corp. debt and repurchase agreements.
MIDWEST INCOME SHORT/GOVT. *(Midwest Advisory Services, Inc.)* Dixie Terminal Building Cincinnati, OH 45202 800-543-0407/513-579-0414	High current income consistent with protection of capital; invests in U.S. Govt. obligations with average maturity of 120 days or less.
PRINCIPAL PROTECTION GOVT. FUND *(Principal Protection Advis. Serv. Inc.)* 327 S LaSalle St. Chicago, IL 60604 312-939-5575	Current income consistent with preservation of capital and maintenance of liquidity.
T. ROWE PRICE PRIME RESERVE *(T. Rowe Price Associates, Inc.)* 100 East Pratt St. Baltimore, MD 21202 800-638-5660/301-547-2308	Preservation of capital, liquidity, and high income through prime money market instruments.
SCUDDER CASH INVESTMENT TRUST *(Scudder, Stevens & Clark, Inv. Counsel)* 175 Federal St. Boston, MA 02110 800-225-2470/617-482-3990	Invests in debt securities with maturities of not more than one year. Constant net asset value.
SELECTED MONEY MKT FUND, INC. *(Lincoln Nat'l. Investment Mgt. Co.)* 111 W. Washington St. Chicago, IL 60602 800-621-7321/312-630-2762	Maximize current income to the extent consistent with preservation of capital by investing in money market instruments.
TEXAS MONEY FUND, INC. *(CMC Funding, Ltd.)* 6350 L.B.J. Freeway, Ste. 234 Dallas, TX 75240 214-239-3100/800-442-5103 (TX only)	Maximum current income consistent with safety and stability of principal.

Fund Name *(Advisor)* Address and Telephone Number	Investment Objective and Policy
UNION CASH MANAGEMENT FUND *(J. & W. Seligman & Co., Inc.)* One Bankers Trust Plaza New York, NY 10006 800-221-2450/800-522-6869 (NY only)	Preserve capital and maximize liquidity and current income by investing in high quality money market instruments.
USAA MUTUAL FUND/MONEY *(USAA Investment Mgmt. Co.)* P.O. Box 33277 San Antonio, TX 78233 800-531-8181/800-292-8181 (TX only)	Seeks the highest income consistent with preservation of capital and maintenance of liquidity.
VALUE LINE CASH FUND, INC. *(Arnold Bernhard & Co., Inc.)* 711 Third Ave. New York, NY 10017 800-223-0818/212-687-3965	Invests in high grade money market instruments.
VANGUARD MONEY MARKET TRUST *(Wellington Management Company)* The Vanguard Group/Drummer's Lane Valley Forge, PA 19482 800-523-7025/800-362-0530 (PA only)	Invests in domestic money market instruments of the highest quality.

TAX-EXEMPT MONEY-MARKET FUNDS
(Excluding funds requiring minimum investment of $10,000 and up)

LEXINGTON TAX FREE DAILY INCOME *(Lexington Management Corp.)* Box 1515, 580 Sylvan Ave. Englewood Cliffs, NJ 07632 800-526-4791/800-932-0838 (NJ only)	Current income, exempt from Federal income taxes while maintaining stability of principal, and liquidity.
T. ROWE PRICE TAX-EXEMPT MONEY FUND *(T. Rowe Price Assoc. Inc.)* 100 East Pratt St. Baltimore, MD 21202 800-638-5660/301-547-2308	Preservation of capital, liquidity, high income exempt from Fed. income taxes through short-term municipal securities.
SCUDDER TAX FREE MONEY FUND *(Scudder, Stevens & Clark, Inv. Counsel)* 175 Federal St. Boston, MA 02110 800-225-2470/617-482-3990	High grade portfolio of municipal notes and bonds with weighted maturity of not more than 1 year.

Fund Name *(Advisor)* Address and Telephone Number	Investment Objective and Policy

VANGUARD MUNI. MONEY MARKET
(Citibank, N. A.)
The Vanguard Group/Drummer's Lane
Valley Forge, PA 19482
800-523-7025/800-362-0530 (PA only)

Tax-free income, primarily from high quality municipal bonds with an average maturity of 120 days or less.

TAX-EXEMPT BOND FUNDS

ALPHA TAX-EXEMPT BOND FUND
(Montag & Caldwell, Inc.)
2 Piedmont Center, N.E., Suite 500
Atlanta, GA 30363
800-241-1662/404-262-3480

Highest interest income exempt from Federal taxes with preservation of principal by investing in diversified marketable municipal bonds.

DREYFUS TAX-EXEMPT BOND FUND
(The Dreyfus Corporation)
600 Madison Ave.
New York, NY 10022
800-223-5525/212-223-0303

Highest interest income exempt from Federal income taxes consistent with preservation of capital by investing in municipal securities

FIDELITY HIGH YIELD MUNICIPALS
(Fidelity Group.)
82 Devonshire St.
Boston, MA 02109
800-225-6190/617-523-1919

Carefully selected long-term municipal bonds of medium quality.

FIDELITY MUNICIPAL BOND FUND
(Fidelity Group)
82 Devonshire St.
Boston, MA 02109
800-225-6190/617-523-1919

Invests primarily in high grade or upper medium grade, long-term municipal bonds.

ROWE PRICE TAX-FREE INCOME
(T. Rowe Price Associates, Inc.)
100 East Pratt St.
Baltimore, MD 21202
800-638-5660/301-547-2308

High income exempt from Federal income taxes through investment grade municipal bonds.

SCUDDER MANAGED MUNI. BONDS
(Scudder, Stevens & Clark, Inv. Counsel)
175 Federal St.
Boston, MA 02110
800-225-2470/617-482-3990

Invests in a high grade portfolio consisting primarily of municipal bonds.

SELECTED TAX-EXEMPT BOND FUND
(Lincoln Nat'l. Investment Mgt. Co.)
111 W. Washington St.
Chicago, IL 60602
800-621-7321/312-630-2762

Invests primarily in a portfolio of "high grade" bonds and notes to earn current income exempt from Federal income tax.

Fund Name *(Advisor)* Address and Telephone Number	Investment Objective and Policy
STEINROE TAX-EXEMPT BOND FUND *(Stein Roe & Farnham)* 150 S. Wacker Dr. Chicago, IL 60606 800-621-0615/312-368-7826	High current income. Invests primarily in municipal bonds so that at least 80% of income is exempt from Federal income taxes.
VANGUARD HIGH-YIELD MUNI BOND *(Citibank, N. A.)* The Vanguard Group/Drummer's Lane Valley Forge, PA 19482 800-523-7025/800-362-0530 (PA only)	Tax-free income, primarily from medium and lower quality municipal bonds with an average maturity of more than 25 years.
VANG. INTERMED.-TERM MUNI BOND *(Citibank, N. A.)* The Vanguard Group/Drummer's Lane Valley Forge, PA 19482 800-523-7025/800-362-0530 (PA only)	Tax-free income, primarily from high quality municipal bonds with an average maturity of 7-12 years.

INCOME FUNDS—FOR HIGH CURRENT INCOME, LONG-TERM INVESTMENT

ALPHA INCOME FUND, INC. *(Montag & Caldwell, Inc.)* Suite 500, 2 Piedmont Center, N.E. Atlanta, GA 30363 800-241-1662/404-262-3480	Highest income consonant with preservation of principal. At least 70% in higher-rated debt securities.
AMERICAN INVESTORS INCOME *(American Investors Corp.)* 88 Field Point Rd. P.O. Box 2500 Greenwich, CT 06830 800-243-5353/203-622-1600	High current income. Capital appreciation secondary. Diversified investments in generous yielding lower rated bonds and pfd. stocks.
CAP. PRES. TREASURY NOTE TRUST *(Benham Management Corp.)* 755 Page Mill Rd. Palo Alto, CA 94304 800-227-8380/800-982-6150 (CA only)	Capital preservation. U.S. Treasury notes, bills and repurchase agreements. Maturities between 13 months and 4 years.
DREYFUS A BONDS PLUS, INC. *(The Dreyfus Corporation)* 600 Madison Ave. New York, NY 10022 800-223-5525/212-223-0303	Current income with preservation of capital and liquidity—80% in debt obligations rated "A" or better.
DREYFUS SPECIAL INCOME FUND *(The Dreyfus Corporation)* 600 Madison Ave. New York, NY 10022 800-223-5525/212-223-0303	Current income with capital appreciation secondary—invests in both bonds and stocks with high current dividend and appreciation potential.

Fund Name *(Advisor)* Address and Telephone Number	Investment Objective and Policy
FIDELITY CORPORATE BOND FUND *(Fidelity Group)* 82 Devonshire St. Boston, MA 02109 800-225-6190/617-523-1919	Income: At least 80% of assets in investment-grade (rated BBB or better) debt securities.
FIDELITY EQUITY-INCOME FUND *(Fidelity Group)* 82 Devonshire St. Boston, MA 02109 800-225-6190/617-523-1919	Growth and Income: at least 80% in income-producing equities with remainder generally in convertible securities.
FIDELITY GOV. SECURITIES LTD. (Fidelity Group) 82 Devonshire St. Boston, MA 02109 800-225-6190/617-523-1919	Income from obligations issued by U.S. Govt., its agencies, or instrumentalities; income is exempt from state and local income taxes.
FIDELITY HIGH INCOME *(Fidelity Group)* 82 Devonshire St. Boston, MA 02109 800-225-6190/617-523-1919	High current income through diversified portfolio of high-yielding, fixed-income corporate securities.
FIDELITY THRIFT TRUST *(Fidelity Group)* 82 Devonshire St. Boston, MA 02109 800-225-6190/617-523-1919	Income: Corporate obligations (AA or better). Govt. securities, and money market instruments; maturity not to exceed ten years.
FINANCIAL BOND SHARES *(Financial Programs, Inc.)* P.O. Box 2040 Denver, CO 80201 800-525-9831/303-779-1233	High level of current income through bonds and other debt securities. Potential capital appreciation is secondary.
FINANCIAL INDUSTRIAL INCOME *(Financial Programs, Inc.)* P.O. Box 2040 Denver, CO 80201 800-525-9831/303-779-1233	Current income with capital growth given additional consideration.
FLORIDA U.S. GOVT. INTERMEDIATE TERM *(Fla. Mutual Fund Group, Inc.)* Landmark Bank Building, Suite 1507 Ft. Lauderdale, FL 33394 800-432-1592/305-522-0200 (FL only)	Uses U.S. Treasury securities up to 5 yr. maturities. Seeks high current income consistent with preservation of principal and liquidity.

Fund Name *(Advisor)* Address and Telephone Number	Investment Objective and Policy
FOUNDERS INCOME FUND, INC. *(Founders Mutual Depositor Corp.)* 1300 First of Denver Plaza Denver, CO 80202 303-292-1820	Income consistent with investment quality. Purchases dividend paying stocks and other income securities. Also writes covered call options.
GATEWAY OPTION INCOME FUND *(Gateway Investment Advisers, Inc.)* 1120 Carew Tower Cincinnati, OH 45202 513-621-7774	High current income. Invests in diversified portfolio of common stocks and sells covered call options on those stocks.
JOHNSTON INCOME FUND *(Douglas T. Johnston & Co., Inc.)* One Boston Place Boston, MA 02106 800-343-6324/617-722-7250	High level of long term income consistent with preservation of principal using intermediate and long term government and corporate bonds.
LEXINGTON GNMA INCOME FUND *(Lexington Management Corp.)* Box 1515, 580 Sylvan Ave. Englewood Cliffs, NJ 07632 800-526-4791/800-932-0838 (NJ only)	High current income, liquidity, safety. Invests in mortgage-backed "Ginnie Mae" certificates, guaranteed by U.S. Govt.
LIBERTY FUND, INC. *(Neuberger & Berman Management Inc.)* 522 Fifth Ave. New York, NY 10036 212-790-9800	High level of current income through diversified portfolio of high yielding, lower rated fixed income securities.
LINDNER FUND FOR INCOME, INC. *(Lindner Management Corp.)* 200 South Bemiston St. Louis, MO 63105 314-727-5305	Income. Invests largely in common stocks with above-average yield and potential for future dividend increases.
MAIRS & POWER INCOME FUND *(Mairs And Power, Inc.)* W-2062 1st Nat'l Bank Bldg. St. Paul, MN 55101 612-222-8478	Income.
MIDWEST INCOME INTERMED/GOVT. *(Midwest Advisory Services, Inc.)* Dixie Terminal Building Cincinnati, OH 45202 800-543-0407/513-579-0414	High current income consistent with protection of capital; invests in U.S. Govt. obligations with average maturity of 5 yrs. or less.

Fund Name *(Advisor)* Address and Telephone Number	Investment Objective and Policy
NEWTON INCOME FUND, INC. *(Heritage Investment Advisors, Inc.)* 733 N. Van Buren St. Milwaukee, WI 53202 414-347-1141	Above-average current income consistent with preservation of capital.
NORTH STAR BOND FUND INC. *(Investment Advisers Inc.)* 600 Dain Tower Minneapolis, MN 55402 612-371-7780	Invests in corporate and government bonds.
T. ROWE PRICE NEW INCOME FUND *(T. Rowe Price Associates, Inc.)* 100 East Pratt St. Baltimore, MD 21202 800-638-5660/301-547-2308	High current income with reasonable stability through investment grade fixed income securities.
PRO INCOME FUND, INC *(PRO Services, Inc.)* 1107 Bethlehem Pike Flourtown, PA 19031 800-523-0864/800-822-3977 (PA only)	Seeks the highest investment income available consistent with preservation of principal.
SAFECO INCOME FUND, INC. *(Safeco Asset Management Co.)* Safeco Plaza T15 NL Seattle, WA 98185 800-426-6730	Seek high current income plus capital growth. Invests primarily in convertible and common securities of medium to large companies.
SAFECO SPECIAL BOND FUND, INC. *(Safeco Asset Management Co.)* Safeco Plaza T15 NL Seattle, WA 98185 800-426-6730	High level of income consistent with preservation of capital. Invests in BBB or higher rated debt securities with 10 yrs. or less to maturity.
SCUDDER INCOME FUND, INC. *(Scudder, Stevens & Clark, Inv. Counsel)* 175 Federal St. Boston, MA 02110 800-225-2470/617-482-3990.	To provide income with due consideration to prudent investment of the capital.
STEINROE BOND FUND, INC. *(Stein Roe & Farnham)* 150 S. Wacker Drive Chicago, IL 60606 800-621-0615/312-368-7826	High current income. Invests primarily in marketable debt securities.

Fund Name *(Advisor)* Address and Telephone Number	Investment Objective and Policy
UNIFIED INCOME FUND, INC. *(Unified Management Corporation)* Guaranty Bldg. Indianapolis, IN 46204 317-634-3300/800-428-4492	Current income and capital appreciation. Invests without quality restrictions. May buy stock and write options.
USAA MUTUAL INCOME FUND *(USAA Investment Mgmt. Co.)* *Box 33277* *San Antonio, TX 78233* *800-531-8181/800-292-8181 (TX only)*	Maximum current income without undue risk to principal. Flexible, diversified portfolio.
VANGUARD GNMA PORTFOLIO *(Wellington Management Company)* The Vanguard Group/Drummer's Lane Valley Forge, PA 19482 800-523-7025/800-362-0530 (PA only)	Current income, primarily from mortgage-backed securities, whose timely payment of interest and principal is guaranteed by the U.S. Government.
VANGUARD HIGH YIELD BOND *(Wellington Management Company)* The Vanguard Group/Drummer's Lane Valley Forge, PA 19482 800-523-7025/800-362-0530 (PA only)	Current income, primarily from high yielding medium and lower quality bonds.
VANGUARD INVSTMNT. GRADE BOND *(Wellington Management Company)* The Vanguard Group/Drummer's Lane Valley Forge, PA 19482 800-523-7025/800-362-0530 (PA only)	High current income, primarily from corporate bonds.
WISCONSIN INCOME FUND, INC. *(Nicholas Company, Inc.)* 312 East Wisconsin Ave. Milwaukee, WI 53202 414-272-6133	High current income consistent with conservation of capital.

BALANCED FUNDS — FOR LONG-TERM GROWTH OF CAPITAL AND INCOME THROUGH A BALANCED INVESTMENT OF STOCKS AND BONDS

DODGE & COX BALANCED FUND *(Dodge & Cox)* One Post St., 35th Fl. San Francisco, CA 94104 415-981-1710	Regular income, conservation of principal, long-term growth balanced between common stocks & fixed-income securities.

Fund Name *(Advisor)* Address and Telephone Number	Investment Objective and Policy
LOOMIS-SAYLES MUTUAL FUND *(Loomis. Sayles & Co.)* Box 449, Back Bay Annex Boston, MA 02117 617-267-6600	Reasonable long-term capital appreciation and current income return, without undue risk.
SELECTED AMERICAN SHARES, INC. *(Lincoln Nat'l. Investment Mgt. Co.)* 111 W. Washington St. Chicago, IL 60602 800-621-7321/312-630-2762	Combination of growth of capital and income. Invests in common and preferred stocks, and bonds.
STEIN ROE & FARNHAM BAL. FUND *(Stein Roe & Farnham)* 150 S. Wacker Dr. Chicago, IL 60606 800-621-0615/312-368-7826	Maintain and increase capital while providing income. Diversified investments: bonds, preferred and common stocks.
UNIFIED MUTUAL SHARES, INC. *(Unified Management Corporation)* Guaranty Bldg. Indianapolis, IN 46204 800-428-4492/317-634-3300	Capital growth and current income. Flexible with emphasis on high quality stocks and convertibles; uses covered option writing.
VANGUARD/WELLESLEY INCOME FUND *(Wellington Management Company)* The Vanguard Group/Drummer's Lane Valley Forge, PA 19482 800-523-7025/800-362-0530 (PA only)	Seeks as much current income as is consistent with reasonable risk: 65-75% fixed-income securities; balance in high yielding stocks.
VANGUARD/WELLINGTON FUND *(Wellington Management Company)* The Vanguard Group/Drummer's Lane Valley Forge, PA 19482 800-523-7025/800-362-0530 (PA only)	Conservation of principal; reasonable income; profits without undue risk. 60-70% in common stocks; balance in fixed-income securities.

GROWTH FUNDS SEEKING GROWTH-AND-INCOME, OR GROWTH PRIMARILY, OR "MAXIMUM GAINS"
(as indicated in "Fund Objective and Policy")

ABLE ASSOCIATES FUND *(Able Management Inc.)* 174 Birch Drive Manhasset Hills, NY 11040 201-288-6611	Capital growth. Invests up to 75% in oil and gas companies exploring mainly on the North American continent.

Fund Name *(Advisor)* Address and Telephone Number	Investment Objective and Policy
ACORN FUND *(Harris Associates, Inc.)* 120 S. La Salle St. Chicago, IL 60603 312-621-0630	Capital growth. Seeks smaller growth companies with financial strength whose investment qualities have not been widely recognized.
ADV FUND, INC. *(ADV Management Co., Inc.)* One New York Plaza New York, NY 10004 212-422-7216	To achieve a return consisting of capital appreciation and current income.
AFUTURE FUND, INC. *(Carlisle-Asher Management Co.)* Legal Arts Bldg. Front & Lemon Sts. Media, PA 19063 800-523-7594/215-565-3131	Growth—appreciation of capital.
ALPHA-FUND, INC. *(Montag & Caldwell, Inc.)* 2 Piedmont Center, N.E., Suite 500 Atlanta, GA 30363 800-241-1662/404-262-3480	Growth of capital. Invests primarily in common stocks or securities exchangeable for common stocks.
AMERICAN INVESTORS FUND, INC. *(American Investors Corp.)* 88 Field Point Rd. P.O. Box 2500 Greenwich, CT 06830 800-243-5353/203-622-1600	Growth of capital. Emphasis on timing as well as on selecting securities believed to have best potential for capital appreciation.
ANALYTIC OPTIONED EQUITY FUND *(Analytic Investment Mgt.)* 2222 Martin St., Suite 230 Irvine, CA 92715 714-833-0294	Seeks greater total return with less risk by writing covered call options on its diversified high quality stocks.
ARMSTRONG ASSOCIATES INC. *(Portfolios Inc.)* 2400 First International Bldg. Dallas, TX 75270 214-744-5558	Capital growth by investing primarily in common stocks and securities convertible into common stock.
BASIC GROWTH FUND, INC. *(Basic Money Mgmt. Corp.)* 505 Northern Blvd. Great Neck, NY 11021 516-466-9571	Growth of capital through long-term investment.

Fund Name *(Advisor)* Address and Telephone Number	Investment Objective and Policy
BEACON HILL MUTUAL FUND, INC. *(Beacon Hill Management, Inc.)* 75 Federal St. Boston, MA 02110 617-482-0795	Growth—specializes in quality growth stocks but is flexible.
CAPAMERICA FUND, INC. *(Bull & Bear Mgmt. Corp.)* 11 Hanover Square New York, NY 10005 800-431-6060/914-657-3300	Invests for current income and long-term growth of capital and income.
CAPITAL SHARES, INC. *(Bull & Bear Mgmt. Corp.)* 11 Hanover Square New York, NY 10005 800-431-6060/914-657-3300	Invests in emerging growth companies and special situations for long-term capital appreciation.
DE VEGH MUTUAL FUND, INC. *(Wood Struthers & Winthrop Mgt.)* 120 Broadway New York, NY 10005 800-221-7780/212-635-3551	Long term capital appreciation
DIRECTORS CAPITAL, INC. *(Directors Management Corp.)* 30 Broad St. New York, NY 10004 212-635-0616	Seeks appreciation through buying options, writing options, leveraging and short sales.
THE DIVIDEND/GROWTH FUND, INC. *(AIM Management Co.)* 11400 Rockville Pike, Suite 300 Rockville, MD. 20852 301-770-1600	Primary income orientation with growth secondary. Emphasis on fundamentally sound stocks, income tax-sheltered.
DODGE & COX STOCK FUND *(Dodge & Cox)* One Post St., 35th Fl. San Francisco, CA 94104 415-981-1710	Long term growth of principal and income with current income secondary. Primarily in a diversified list of high-grade common stocks.
THE DREXEL BURNHAM FUND *(Drexel Burnham Lambert Mgt. Corp.)* 60 Broad St. New York, NY 10004 212-483-1436	Capital appreciation mainly long term with income secondary.

Fund Name *(Advisor)* Address and Telephone Number	Investment Objective and Policy
DREYFUS NUMBER NINE, INC. *(The Dreyfus Corporation)* 600 Madison Ave. New York, NY 10022 800-223-5525/212-223-0303	Long term capital growth.
DREYFUS THIRD CENTURY FUND *(The Dreyfus Corporation)* 600 Madison Ave. New York, NY 10022 800-223-5525/212-223-0303	Long term capital growth. Invests in companies with a "social conscience."
ENERGY FUND INCORPORATED *(Neuberger & Berman Management)* 522 Fifth Ave. New York, NY 10036 212-790-9800	Long-term capital appreciation; primarily invests in common stocks whose activities are related to the field of energy.
FIDELITY ASSET INVEST. TRUST *(Fidelity Group)* 82 Devonshire St. Boston, MA 02109 800-225-6190/617-523-1919	Growth: specializes in securities of companies whose market values are less than their book value.
FIDELITY CONTRAFUND INC. *(Fidelity Group)* 82 Devonshire St. Boston, MA 02109 800-225-6190/617-523-1919	Growth: seeks solid investment values among industry groups and stocks currently out of favor.
FIDELITY FUND *(Fidelity Group)* 82 Devonshire St. Boston, MA 02109 800-225-6190/617-523-1919	Growth and Income: Will invest primarily in dividend-paying common stocks and convertible securities of *well-known* companies.
FIDELITY PURITAN FUND *(Fidelity Group)* 82 Devonshire St. Boston, MA 02109 800-225-6190/617-523-1919	Growth and Income: primary emphasis on growth in income from a portfolio of common stocks, convertible and fixed-income securities.
FIDELITY TREND FUND *(Fidelity Group)* 82 Devonshire St. Boston, MA 02109 800-225-6190/617-523-1919	Growth: Seeks long-term growth by considering market, industry and company trends.

Fund Name *(Advisor)* Address and Telephone Number	Investment Objective and Policy
FINANCIAL DYNAMICS FUND *(Financial Programs, Inc.)* P.O. Box 2040 Denver, CO 80201 800-525-9831/303-779-1233	For the aggressive investor seeking capital growth through speculative investment policies.
FINANCIAL INDUSTRIAL FUND, INC. *(Financial Programs, Inc.)* P.O. Box 2040 Denver, CO 80201 800-525-9831/303-779-1233	Long-term capital growth, with income.
FINOMIC INVESTMENT FUND *(Investment Advisors Inc.)* 1100 Louisiana, 4550 First Intl. Plaza. Houston, TX 77002 713-659-2611	Capital appreciation. Primarily in common stocks of small to medium-size companies generally located in the Sun-belt.
FIRST MUTUAL FUND, INC. *(The Providence Group)* 50 South Main St. Providence, RI 02903 401-272-3800	Growth with income secondary; investments made in companies with growth characteristics and some attention given to market timing.
THE 44 WALL STREET FUND, INC. *(Forty Four Mgt. Ltd.)* 150 Broadway New York, NY 10038 800-221-7836/212-374-1146	Long-term growth, using limited number of common stocks with above average potential.
FOUNDERS GROWTH FUND, INC. *(Founders Mutual Depositor Corp.)* 1300 First Of Denver Plaza Denver, CO 80202 303-292-1820	Capital appreciation with income secondary. Purchases common stocks or convertible securities of established companies.
FOUNDERS SPECIAL FUND, INC. *(Founders Mutual Depositors.)* 1300 First Of Denver Plaza Denver, CO 80202 303-292-1820	Maximum capital appreciation through common stocks of companies relatively small in terms of assets and earnings. Also may leverage investments.
G. T. PACIFIC FUND, INC. *(G. T. Capital Management, Inc.)* 601 Montgomery St., Suite 1400 San Francisco, CA 94111 415-392-6181	Long-term growth through investment in diversified portfolio of Far Eastern Securities.

Fund Name *(Advisor)* Address and Telephone Number	Investment Objective and Policy
GENERAL SECURITIES, INC. *(Craig-Hallum, Inc.)* 133 South Seventh St. Minneapolis, MN 55402 612-332-1212	Capital appreciation and security of principal. Has flexiblity to use stocks and sometimes fixed income securities — also covered options.
GOLCONDA INVESTORS LTD. *(Golconda Management Corp.)* 11 Hanover Square. New York, NY 10005 800-431-6060/914-657-3300	Specialized; invests in bullion and internationally diversified gold mining shares.
GOLDFUND INC. *(CSA Management Ltd.)* 80 Broad Street New York, NY 10004 212-269-1227	Capital appreciation, income secondary; invests exclusively in gold bullion and gold mining stocks.
GOOD AND BAD TIMES FUND *(Growth Research and Management)* Box 29869 San Antonio, TX 78229 800-531-5777/512-696-1234	Preservation of capital and capital appreciation. Current income secondary. Invests in low debt. Financially sound, successfully managed companies.
GROWTH INDUSTRY SHARES *(William Blair & Company)* 135 S. LaSalle St. Chicago, IL 60603 312-346-4830	Appreciation of capital and growth of income through growth companies; diversification among different size companies.
GUARDIAN MUTUAL FUND, INC. *(Neuberger & Berman Management)* 522 Fifth Ave. New York, NY 10036 212-790-9800	Capital appreciation with income secondary; common stocks of seasoned companies, flexibility to shift to fixed income securities.
HARTWELL GROWTH FUND, INC. *(Hartwell Management Co., Inc.)* 50 Rockefeller Plaza New York, NY 10020 212-247-8740	Capital appreciation. Invests primarily in intermediate size growth companies.
HARTWELL LEVERAGE FUND, INC. *(Hartwell Management Co., Inc.)* 50 Rockefeller Plaza New York, NY 10020 212-247-8740	Capital appreciation. Flexible policy emphasizing appreciation potential.

Fund Name *(Advisor)* Address and Telephone Number	Investment Objective and Policy
IVY FUND, INC. *(Grantham et al.; & Furman et al.)* 201 Devonshire St. Boston, MA 02110 617-426-0636	The fund seeks to achieve long-term growth of capital through investment in equity securities.
JANUS FUND, INC. *(Janus Management Corp.)* 789 Sherman St. Denver, CO 80203 800-525-3713/303-837-1774	Growth of capital. Takes positions in a limited number of securities and may use leveraging.
JOHNSTON CAPITAL APPRECIATION *(Douglas T. Johnston & Co., Inc.)* One Boston Place Boston, MA 02106 800-343-6324/617-722-7250	Long-term capital growth with moderate risk.
LEHMAN CAPITAL FUND *(Lehman Management Co., Inc.)* 55 Water St. New York, NY 10041 212-558-2031	Capital appreciation: essentially common stocks with above average market appreciation potential.
LEXINGTON GROWTH FUND, INC. *(Lexington Mgmt. Corp.)* Box 1515, 580 Sylvan Ave. Englewood Cliffs, NJ 07632 800-526-4791/800-932-0838 (NJ only)	Capital appreciation: invests in common stocks believed to be undervalued and offering better than average growth possibilities.
LEXINGTON RESEARCH FUND, INC. *(Lexington Mgmt. Corp.)* Box 1515, 580 Sylvan Ave. Englewood Cliffs, NJ 07632 800-526-4791/800-932-0838 (NJ only)	Long-term capital appreciation; invests in common stocks of large, ably managed, well-financed companies.
LINDNER FUND, INC. *(Lindner Management Corp.)* 200 South Bemiston St. Louis, MO 63105 314-727-5305	Growth. Seeks optimum combination of low price-earnings ratio and growth.
MAIRS & POWER GROWTH FUND *(Mairs and Power, Inc.)* W-2062 1st Nat'l Bank Bldg. St. Paul, MN 55101 612-222-8478	Growth

Fund Name *(Advisor)* Address and Telephone Number	Investment Objective and Policy
MANHATTAN FUND, INC. *(Neuberger & Berman Management)* 522 Fifth Ave. New York, NY 10036 212-790-9800	Capital appreciation.
MEDICAL TECHNOLOGY FUND, INC. *(PRO Services, Inc.)* 1107 Bethlehem Pike Flourtown, PA 19031 800-523-0864/800-822-3977 (PA only)	Growth through companies engaged in products or services related to technology for medicine or health care.
MUTUAL SHARES CORP. *(Heine Securities Corp.)* 170 Broadway New York, NY 10038 212-267-4200	Capital gains. May be short term. Income secondary. Invests in common, preferred & debt securities at prices less than intrinsic value.
NATL. AVIATION & TECH. CORP. *(American Fund Advisors, Inc.)* 50 Broad St. New York, NY 10004 212-482-8100	Capital appreciation: Invests in aviation related companies and companies which use technology extensively in product development or operation.
NEUWIRTH FUND, INC. *(Wood, Struthers & Winthrop Mgt.)* 120 Broadway New York, NY 10005 800-221-7780/212-635-3551	Capital growth. Common stock of established companies with growth characteristics; also emerging growth companies.
NEWTON GROWTH FUND, INC. *(Heritage Investment Advisors, Inc.)* 733 N. Van Buren St. Milwaukee, WI 53202 414-347-1141	Long-term growth of capital, current income of lesser importance.
NICHOLAS FUND, INC. *(Nicholas Company, Inc.)* 312 East Wisconsin Ave. Milwaukee, WI 53202 414-272-6133	Growth. Concentrates in common stocks of small and medium size companies.
NORTH STAR REGIONAL FUND *(Investment Advisers, Inc.)* 600 Dain Tower Minneapolis, MN 55402 612-371-7780	Growth: common stocks primarily from seven-state upper midwest region.

Fund Name *(Advisor)* Address and Telephone Number	Investment Objective and Policy
NORTH STAR STOCK FUND, INC. *(Investment Advisers, Inc.)* 600 Dain Tower Minneapolis, MN 55402 612-371-7780	Growth with a secondary emphasis on income.
NOVA FUND, INC. *(Granahan-Everitt Investments, Inc.)* 303 Wyman Street Waltham, MA 02154 617-890-4415	Long term growth
THE ONE HUNDRED FUND, INC. *(Berger Associates, Inc.)* 899 Logan St. Denver, CO 80203 303-837-1020	Invests in successful and highly profitable corporations, with emphasis upon retained earnings.
ONE WILLIAM STREET FUND *(Lehman Management Co., Inc.)* 55 Water St. New York, NY 10041 212-558-2020	Long-term growth of capital; income secondary.
THE PARTNERS FUND, INC. *(Neuberger & Berman Management)* 522 Fifth Ave. New York, NY 10036 212-790-9800	Capital growth. Emphasis on common stocks, with a portion of assets in stocks selected for short-term gain potential.
PENN SQUARE MUTUAL FUND *(Penn Square Mgmt. Corp.)* Berkshire Towers, Box 1419 Reading, PA 19603 800-523-8440/215-376-6771	Long-term capital growth. Investments principally in common stocks of larger companies considered undervalued on a fundamental basis.
PENNSYLVANIA MUTUAL FUND, INC. *(Quest Advisory Corp.)* 127 John St. New York, NY 10038 800-221-4268/212-269-8533	Capital appreciation. Invests in common stocks generally, with special emphasis on securities of medium-sized companies.
PINE STREET FUND INC. *(Wood, Struthers & Winthrop Mgmt.)* 120 Broadway New York, NY 10005 800-221-7780/212-635-3551	Income & growth. Emphasis on stocks but also uses Gov't. agency and corporate bonds & money market instruments.

Fund Name *(Advisor)* Address and Telephone Number	Investment Objective and Policy
PLANNED INVESTMENT FUND *(F. L. Putnam & Co. Inc.)* 50 Congress St. Boston, MA 02109 617-423-3410	Long term growth of capital.
T. ROWE PRICE GROWTH STOCK *(T. Rowe Price Associates, Inc.)* 100 East Pratt St. Baltimore, MD 21202 800-638-5660/301-547-2308	Long-term capital appreciation and increased future income through investment in well-established growth companies.
T. ROWE PRICE NEW ERA FUND *(T. Rowe Price Associates, Inc.)* 100 East Pratt St. Baltimore, MD 21202 800-638-5660/301-547-2308	Long-term capital appreciation through investment primarily in companies that own or develop natural resources.
T. ROWE PRICE NEW HORIZONS FUND *(T. Rowe Price Associates, Inc.)* 100 East Pratt St. Baltimore, MD 21202 800-638-5660/301-547-2308	Long-term capital appreciation through investment in newer, smaller companies with potential to become major growth companies.
T. ROWE PRICE INTERNAT'L FUND *(T. Rowe Price Associates, Inc.)* 100 East Pratt St. Baltimore, MD 21202 800-638-5660/301-547-2308	Total return from long-term growth of capital and income through investment in foreign securities.
PRO FUND, INC. *(PRO Services, Inc.)* 1107 Bethlehem Pike Flourtown, PA 19031 800-523-0864/800-822-3977 (PA only)	Growth. Invests primarily in common stocks believed by management to have potential for capital appreciation.
THE RAINBOW FUND, INC. *(Robert Furman)* 60 Broad St. New York, NY 10004 212-964-7989	Growth of capital. A non-diversified fund primarily investing in common stocks.
RETIRE. PLAN OF AMER/EQUIT. *(Chicago Title & Trust Co.)* 111 W. Washington Street Chicago, IL 60602 800-621-1110/312-630-2540	Growth in capital through appreciation and reinvestment of income in common stocks; available only to tax sheltered retirement plans.

Fund Name *(Advisor)* Address and Telephone Number	Investment Objective and Policy
SAFECO EQUITY FUND, INC. *(Safeco Asset Management Co.)* Safeco Plaza T15 NL Seattle, WA 98185 800-426-6730	Growth & income: Invests in well known companies providing above average yields and growth prospects.
SAFECO GROWTH FUND, INC. *(Safeco Asset Management Co.)* Safeco Plaza T15 NL Seattle, WA 98185 800-426-6730	Invests in medium to small companies having good growth prospects for coming 3 to 5 yrs.
SCHUSTER FUND, INC. *(Neuberger & Berman Management)* 522 Fifth Ave. New York, NY 10036 212-790-9800	Appreciation of capital.
SCUDDER COMMON STOCK FUND *(Scudder, Stevens & Clark)* 175 Federal St. Boston, MA 02110 800-225-2470/617-482-3990	Growth. Common stocks, readily marketable securities of leading companies.
SCUDDER DEVELOPMENT FUND *(Scudder, Stevens & Clark)* 345 Park Ave. New York, NY 10022 800-225-2470/212-350-8200	Growth. Invests primarily in stocks of small or little known companies.
SCUDDER INTERNATIONAL FUND *(Scudder, Stevens & Clark)* 345 Park Ave. New York, NY 10022 800-225-2470/212-350-8200	Growth. Specializes in common stocks of non-U.S. companies and economies.
SCUDDER SPECIAL FUND, INC. *(Scudder, Stevens & Clark)* 345 Park Ave. New York, NY 10022 212-350-8200	Growth. Emphasizes common stocks of above-average risk.
SELECTED SPECIAL SHARES, INC. *(Lincoln Nat'l. Investment Mgt. Co.)* 111 W. Washington St. Chicago, IL 60602 800-621-7321/312-630-2762	Capital growth. Invests in securities which afford maximum opportunity for appreciation.

Fund Name *(Advisor)* Address and Telephone Number	Investment Objective and Policy
SHERMAN, DEAN FUND *(Sherman, Dean Mgmt. & Res.)* 120 Broadway New York, NY 10005 212-577-3850	The primary objective of the fund is capital appreciation. Income is of secondary importance.
STEINROE & FARN. CAP. OPPOR. *(Stein Roe & Farnham)* 150 S. Wacker Dr. Chicago, IL 60606 800-621-0615/312-368-7826	Long-term capital appreciation. Invests in common stocks of both seasoned and smaller companies.
STEINROE SPECIAL FUND, INC. *(Stein Roe & Farnham)* 150 S. Wacker Dr. Chicago, IL 60606 800-621-0615/312-368-7826	Maximum capital gains; invests in companies expected to benefit from special factors or trends or having unusual potential.
STEINROE & FARN. STOCK *(Stein Roe & Farnham)* 150 S. Wacker Dr. Chicago, IL 60606 800-621-0615/312-368-7826	Long-term capital appreciation. Invests substantially all assets in common stocks and other equity-type securities.
STEINROE UNIVERSE FUND, INC. *(Stein Roe & Farnham)* 150 S. Wacker Drive Chicago, IL 60606 800-621-0615/312-368-7826	Capital appreciation through investing in an unusually broad spectrum of common stocks utilizing a computerized selection process.
STRATTON GROWTH FUND *(Stratton Management Co.)* Butler & Skippack Pikes Blue Bell, PA 19422 215-542-0363	Value-oriented high yield, low P/E common stocks.
TUDOR FUND *(Tudor Management Co., Inc.)* One New York Plaza New York, NY 10004 212-422-7216	Capital appreciation. Writes covered call options.
TWENTIETH CENTURY GROWTH *(Investors Research Corporation)* P.O. Box 200 Kansas City, MO 64141 816-531-5575	Capital growth. Common stocks believed to have above-average appreciation potential.

Fund Name *(Advisor)* Address and Telephone Number	Investment Objective and Policy
TWENTIETH CENTURY SELECT *(Investors Research Corporation)* P.O. Box 200 Kansas City, MO 64141 816-531-5575	Satisfactory rate of return through dividend- paying common stocks selected for appreciation potential.
UNIFIED ACCUMULATION FUND *(Unified Management Corporation)* Guaranty Bldg. Indianapolis, IN 46204 317-634-3300/800-428-4492	Tax sheltered capital appreciation. Invests in high-yield stocks, corp. and govt. bonds. Income and capital gains accumulate tax-free.
UNIFIED GROWTH FUND, INC. *(Unified Management Corporation)* Guaranty Building Indianapolis, IN 46204 317-634-3300/800-428-4492	Capital appreciation. Medium to smaller companies with above average growth in sales and earnings. Attention to timing.
UNITED SERVICES FUND, INC. *(Growth Research and Management, Inc.)* Box 29467 San Antonio, TX 78229 800-531-5777/512-696-1234	Growth. Income. Specializes in gold shares and other precious metals.
USAA CAPITAL GROWTH FUND *(USAA Investment Mgmt. Co.)* P.O. Box 33277 San Antonio, TX 78233 800-531-8181/800-292-8181 (TX only)	Long-term growth of capital, income secondary; diversified and flexible — can take a defensive position.
VALLEY FORGE FUND, INC. *(Valley Forge Management Corp.)* P.O. Box 262 Valley Forge, PA 19481 215-688-6839	Capital appreciation through market timing. Occasionally may move into c.d.'s and/or debt securities to defend capital.
VARIABLE STOCK FUND, INC. *(Monarch Investment Mgmt. Corp.)* 1250 State St. Springfield, MA 01133 413-785-5811	Capital appreciation with income secondary, using primarily common stocks to complement ownership of fixed obligations.
VANGUARD EXPLORER FUND *(Wellington Management Company)* The Vanguard Group/Drummer's Lane Valley Forge, PA 19482 800-523-7025/800-362-0530 (PA only)	Long term capital growth by investing in small, unseasoned or embryonic companies.

Fund Name *(Advisor)* Address and Telephone Number	Investment Objective and Policy
VANGUARD INDEX TRUST *(None)* The Vanguard Group/Drummer's Lane Valley Forge, PA 19482 800-523-7025/800-362-0530 (PA only)	Seeks to provide investment results that correspond to the price and yield performance of the S & P 500 Index by owning all stocks in the S & P 500.
VANGUARD/IVEST FUND *(Wellington Management Company)* The Vanguard Group/Drummer's Lane Valley Forge, PA 19482 800-523-7025/800-362-0530 (PA only)	Seeks long-term capital growth by investing in common stocks believed to have potential for appreciation.
VANGUARD/W.L. MORGAN GROWTH *(Wellington Management Company)* The Vanguard Group/Drummer's Lane Valley Forge, PA 19482 800-523-7025/800-362-0530 (PA only)	Seeks long-term growth of capital by investing in companies believed to have above-average growth potential.
VANGUARD/WINDSOR FUND *(Wellington Management Company)* The Vanguard Group/Drummer's Lane Valley Forge, PA 19482 800-523-7025/800-362-0530 (PA only)	Long-term growth of capital and income by investing in companies with favorable prospects but currently undervalued in the market.

Appendix C: Industry Classification

Highly Cyclical: Agricultural equipment, airlines, aluminum, apparel, appliances, automobile and truck manufacturers, home building, home furnishings, iron, machinery (heavy), nonferrous metals (copper, lead, zinc), oil refining, railroads, real estate investment trusts (lenders), steel, sugar, textiles, tires and rubber, trucking.

Cyclical-Growth: Advertising, aerospace and defense, banks, broadcasting, brokerage houses, cement, chemicals, forest products, department stores, gambling, insurers (life, property, and casualty), lodging and restaurants, machine tools, mobile homes, packaging and containers, photography, precious metals, real estate investment trusts (property owners), savings and loans, semiconductors.

Relatively Stable: Auto parts, beverages, convenience stores, cosmetics, food, drugstores, grocery chains, insurance (multiline), tobacco, toys, utilities (electricity, gas, telephone).

Growth: Crime prevention and protective services, computers, consumer electronics, drugs (ethical and proprietary), fast food service, home entertainment, hospital management, oil and gas production, recreation.

High Growth: Automation (robotics, word-processing), computer software and services (computer-assisted design/computer-aided manufacturing, data processing), medical technology, instruments (process control and scientific), oilfield equipment and services, emerging technologies (genetic engineering, lasers, solar heating, synthetic fuels).

Source: Rauscher Pierce Refsnes Inc., Dallas, Texas.

Appendix D: The Language of Investing: A Glossary

The language spoken in America's investment world may sound like a strange tongue to the newcomer. Any glossary of this special language involves certain problems. Some words and phrases cannot be defined completely without going into related background material; others have nuances of meaning that even the experts may dispute. I have tried to define terms simply and easily, trimming subtle shades of meaning in the interest of brevity and readability. Many terms covered in the glossary are more fully explained in the text.

Accelerated Depreciation: writing off the cost of an asset faster than under the straight-line method, which, for example, would depreciate a $10 million asset over a 10-year period by $1 million each year.

Accounts Payable: all monies owed by the firm for materials or services purchased and due for payment at the date of the Balance Sheet.

Accounts Receivable: all monies owed to the firm for products or services and still unpaid at the date of the Balance Sheet.

Accrued Interest: interest accrued on a bond since the last interest payment was made. The buyer of the bond pays the market price plus accrued interest.

Advance-Decline Line: a charted line showing the number of stocks that have advanced compared to the number that have declined.

Amortization: periodic repayment of a debt. Includes various specific practices such as depreciation, depletion, write-off of intangibles.

Arbitrage: buying a stock in one market and simultaneously selling it in another in order to take advantage of a price difference between the two markets.

Asked Price: see Offer; also Bid and Asked.

Assets: everything that a corporation owns or that is due to it — cash, investments, materials and inventories, which are called current assets; buildings and machinery, which are known as fixed assets; and patents and goodwill, called intangible assets.

At the Market: an order to buy or sell a stock "at the market" will be automatically executed at the best price available when the order reaches the floor of the exchange (or, in the case of OTC stocks, the best price obtainable from the dealers who make a market in the issue). *See* Limit Order, Market Order.

Averaging Down: adding to one's existing holdings of a stock that has declined in order to lower one's average cost.

Balance Sheet: a condensed statement showing the nature and amount of a company's assets, liabilities, and capital on a given date. In dollar amounts, the balance sheet shows what the company owned, what it owed, and the ownership interest in the company of its stockholders.

Bankers' Acceptances: short-term obligations issued and guaranteed by banks and sold in denominations of $100,000.

Bear: someone who believes that the market will decline. A bear market is one in which stock prices are dropping.

Bearer Bond: a bond that does not have the owner's name registered on the books of the issuing company and that is payable to the holder.

Beta: a measure of a stock's volatility in relation to that of Standard & Poor's 500-stock index. *See* chapter 12.

Bid and Asked: often referred to as a quotation or a quote. The bid is the highest price anyone has offered for a security at a given time; the asked is the lowest price anyone will accept.

Big Board: a popular term for the New York Stock Exchange.

Block: a large amount of stock, usually 10,000 shares and over.

Blue Chip: the common stock of a company known nationally for the quality and wide acceptance of its products and services, and for its ability to make profits and pay dividends.

Blue Sky Laws: a popular name for laws that various states have enacted to protect the public against securities frauds. The term is believed to have originated when a judge ruled that a particular stock had about the same value as a patch of blue sky.

Board Room: a room for customers in a broker's office where the action of the market can be seen on an electronic board.

Boiler Room: a sleazy firm that uses high-pressure salesmanship to peddle, over the telephone, stocks or other investments of questionable value. A typical boiler room is simply a room lined with desks or cubicles, each with a salesman and a telephone. The salesmen call what are known in the trade as sucker lists.

Bond: basically an I.O.U. or promissory note of a corporation, usually issued in multiples of $1,000. A bond is evidence of a debt on which the issuing company promises to pay the bond-holders a specified amount of interest for a specified length of time, and to repay the loan on the expiration date. A bond-holder is a creditor of the corporation and not a part owner, as is a shareholder.

Book Value: an accounting term. The book value of a stock is determined by adding all assets (generally excluding such intangibles as goodwill), then deducting all debts and other liabilities, plus the liquidation price of any preferred issues. The sum arrived at is divided by the number of common shares outstanding, and the result is book value per common share. Book value may have little or no significant relationship to market value.

Breadth (Market): breadth has to do with the total number of stocks advancing and declining on the New York Stock Exchange. Most technical analysts use four principle breadth indexes, all derived and computed from the same data carried in the *Wall Street Journal.* The basic index is a straight advance-decline line. Two indexes are concerned with increasing and decreasing volume. The fourth is a composite breadth index.

Breakout: a term used in technical analysis to signify a decisive move upward or downward on substantial volume out of a consolidation area. For example, if a stock has been trading for a period of time in the 32–36 area, a move on volume to 37 or 31 would be termed a breakout.

Bull: one who believes that the market will rise. A bull market is one in which stock prices are advancing.

Call: see Options, also chapter 25.

Callable: a bond issue that, under specified conditions, may be redeemed wholly or in part by the issuing corporation before the maturity date. The term also applies to preferred stock.

Capital Gain or Capital Loss: profit or loss from the sale of a capital asset. A capital gain, under current federal income-tax laws, may be either short-term or long-term (one year and a day). A short-term capital gain is taxed at the reporting individual's full income-tax rate. A long-term capital gain was taxed at 40 percent of that rate in 1981. Up to $3,000 of net capital loss is deductible from the individual's taxable income during the year reported. If the capital loss is more than $3,000, as much as $3,000 is deductible annually thereafter until all of the loss has been accounted for.

Capitalization: the total amount of the stocks and bonds issued by a corporation.

Cash Flow: the reported net income of a corporation plus the amounts charged off for depreciation, depletion, amortization, and extraordinary charges to reserves, all of which are bookkeeping deductions and not paid out in actual dollars. A company's cash flow often offers a better indication of its ability to pay dividends and finance expansion from self-generated cash than the reported net-income figure.

Certificate: the actual piece of paper that is evidence of ownership of stock in a corporation. Loss of a certificate may at the least cause a great deal of inconvenience — at the worst, financial loss.

Certificate of Deposit (CD): a negotiable receipt, issued by a bank, for time deposits in the bank. CDs have maturities ranging from 1 month up to 1 year, and their minimum denomination is $100,000.

Churning: a broker who overtrades a discretionary account or encourages a customer to overtrade is guilty of churning, which is a punishable offense under the securities laws but is often difficult to prove.

Commercial Paper: short-term, unsecured promissory notes issued by major corporations in denominations of $100,000 and up.

Common Stock: securities that represent an ownership interest in a corporation.

Consolidated Balance Sheet: a balance sheet showing the financial condition of a corporation and its subsidiaries.

Convertible: a bond or preferred stock that may be exchanged by the owner for common stock of the same company, in accordance with the terms of the issue.

Coupon Bond: a bond with interest coupons attached. The coupons are clipped as they come due and are presented by the holder through a bank or broker for payment of interest.

Covering: buying a security that has previously been sold short. *See* Short Sale.

Cumulative Preferred: a stock having a provision that if one or more dividends are omitted, the omitted dividends must be paid before dividends may be paid on the company's common stock.

Current Assets: assets, including inventory and receivables, that are expected to be converted into cash within a year, plus cash on hand and readily marketable securities.

Current Liabilities: obligations that a company must meet and pay for in cash within a year.

Customers' Man: see Registered Representative.

Customers' Net Debit Balances: the net amount owed to the New York Stock Exchange by customers who have borrowed from the Exchange to help finance purchases of stocks, bonds, or commodities.

Day Order: an order to buy or sell that, if not executed, expires at the end of the trading day on which it was entered.

Dealer: an individual or firm in the securities business acting as a principal rather than as an agent. Typically, a dealer buys for his own account and sells to a customer from his own inventory. The same individual or firm may function, at different times, either as a broker or dealer.

Debenture: a promissory note backed by the general credit of a company and usually not secured by a mortgage or lien on any specific property. *See* Bond.

Depletion: the consumption of natural resources such as metals, timber, oil, and gas, which conceivably can be reduced to zero over the years. Depletion is a charge against earnings based on the amount of the asset taken out of the total reserves in the accounting period. It does not represent any cash outlay or setting aside of cash reserves; it is simply a bookkeeping entry.

Depreciation: charges against earnings to write off the cost of an asset over its estimated useful life. It is a bookkeeping entry and does not represent any cash outlay, nor are any funds earmarked for the purpose.

Dilution: actual or potential reduction of earnings per share because of stock options, warrants, and/or convertible issues outstanding.

Director: a person elected by the shareholders at the annual meeting of a company to establish company policies. The directors appoint the president, vice presidents, and all other operating officers. Directors decide, among other matters, if and when dividends shall be paid.

Discretionary Account: an account in which an investor gives the broker or someone else discretion (which may be complete or within specified limits) to buy and sell securities or commodities on his behalf.

Discretionary Order: the customer instructs the broker to use his judgment as to the price at which a security will be bought or sold. If the broker is unable to buy or sell at the price he is seeking, he cannot be held accountable for not executing the order.

Distribution: the sale of a large block of stock to a large group of investors.

Diversification: spreading investments among different companies in different fields. A company that is in many different lines of business is said to be diversified. Such companies are usually described as "conglomerates" or "multiform" companies.

Dividend: the payment designated by the board of directors to be distributed pro rata among the shares outstanding. On preferred shares, it is generally a fixed amount. On common shares, the dividend varies with the fortunes of the company and its available cash, and may be omitted if business is poor or the directors decide to withhold earnings to invest in plant and equipment. Sometimes a company that is not currently operating at a profit will pay a dividend out of past earnings. *See also* Stock Dividend.

Dividend Payout: the percentage of earnings per share paid to stockholders in dividends.

Dollar Cost Averaging: investing a fixed amount at regular intervals in a selected security. *See* chapter 19.

Dual-Purpose Fund: a closed-end investment company with two classes of stock. One class entitles shareholders to receive all of the fund's income; owners of the other class receive all of the fund's capital gains. Five dual-purpose funds are traded on the New York Stock Exchange and one trades over the counter.

Earnings Report: a statement issued by a company showing its earnings or losses over a given period.

Econometrics: the branch of economics that expresses economic theory in mathematical terms and seeks to verify it by statistical methods.

Equity: the ownership interest of common and preferred stockholders in a company. Also refers to the amount by which the value of securities in a margin account exceeds the debit balance.

Ex-dividend: a synonym for "without dividend." The buyer of a stock selling ex-dividend does not receive the recently declared dividend. Every dividend is payable on a fixed date to shareholders recorded on the company's books as of a previous date of record. For example, a dividend may be declared as payable to holders of record on a given Friday. Since 5 business days are allowed for delivery of stock in a "regular way" transaction on the New York Stock Exchange, the Exchange would declare the stock "ex-dividend" as of the opening of the market on the preceding Monday. This means that anyone who bought the stock on and after the Monday would not be entitled to that dividend.

Extra: the short form of "extra dividend." This is a dividend in the form of stock or cash in addition to the regular dividend the company has been paying.

Face Value: the value of a bond that appears on the face of the bond. Face value, or "par," is the amount the issuing company promises to pay at maturity.

Fiscal Year: a corporation's accounting year. Because of the nature of their particular business, some companies do not use the calendar year for their bookkeeping. A typical example is department stores, which find December 31 too early a date to close their books after the Christmas rush. For that reason, many stores wind up their accounting year on January 31. The fiscal year of other companies may run from July 1 through the following June 30. Most companies, though, operate on a calendar-year basis.

Fixed Charges: a company's fixed expenses — for example, bond interest, which it has agreed to pay whether or not the interest due is covered by earnings. These charges are deducted from income before earnings on equity capital are computed.

Floor: the huge trading area — about two-thirds the size of a football field — where stocks and bonds are bought and sold on the New York Stock Exchange.

Floor Broker: a member of the Stock Exchange who executes orders on the floor of the Exchange to buy or sell listed securities.

Formula Investing: a method of investing under which purchases and sales are made automatically, in accordance with a hard-and-fast formula. One formula calls for the shifting of funds from common stocks to money-market securities when the market has risen a predetermined percentage, and the switching of funds into common stocks when the market drops a predetermined percentage.

Funded Debt: usually interest-bearing bonds of a company. The term could include long-term bank loans, but not short-term loans.

Gilt-edged: a high-grade bond issued by a company that has demonstrated its ability to earn a comfortable profit over a period of years and pay its bond-holders their interest without interruption is called gilt-edged.

Glamour Stocks: the stocks of companies whose prospects investors consider particularly exciting. Such stocks tend to sell at the highest prevailing P/E ratios.

Good till Canceled Order (GTC), or Open Order: an order to buy or sell that remains in effect until it is either executed or canceled.

Head-and-Shoulders: a term used by technical analysts to describe a chart pattern (resembling a human head and shoulders) that is taken as signaling the reversal of a trend.

Holding Company: a corporation that owns the securities of other companies, usually with voting control.

Hypothecation: the pledging of securities as collateral for a loan.

Indenture: a written agreement under which debentures are issued, setting forth maturity date, interest rate, security, and other terms.

Index: a statistical yardstick expressed in terms of a base year or years. For instance, Standard & Poor's 500-stock index is based on 1941–1943 as 10. An index is not an average, but the two terms are popularly treated as synonymous.

Investment Banker: also known as an underwriter. He is the middleman between the corporation issuing new securities and the public. The usual practice is for one or more investment bankers to buy outright from a corporation a new issue of stocks or bonds. The group forms a syndicate to sell the securities to individuals and institutions. Investment bankers also distribute very large blocks of stocks or bonds — perhaps held by an estate.

Investment Counsel: a professional money manager who handles accounts for institutions or individuals on a fee basis.

Investment Trust: the two principal types are closed-end and open-end mutual funds. Shares in closed-end investment trusts, most of which are listed on the New York Stock Exchange, are bought and sold like other shares. The capitalization of these companies remains the same. Open-end funds issue new shares to investors and stand ready to buy back their old shares at their net asset value; they are not listed on an exchange. These funds are called open-end because their capitalization is not fixed.

Keogh Plan and IRA: tax-sheltered retirement plans. Keogh allows self-employed persons to defer taxation on up to 15 percent of their annual income (but not more than $15,000 a year) by contributing to a tax-sheltered pension fund for themselves and their employees. An employed person who *is* covered by a company retirement plan may contribute up to $2,000 each year to a tax-deferred Individual Retirement Account.

Leverage: the effect on the per-share earnings of the common stock of a company when large sums must be paid for bond interest or preferred stock dividends, or both, before the common stock is entitled to share in earnings. Leverage is advantageous for the common stock holder when earnings are good but damaging when earnings decline. *See* chapter 15.

Liabilities: everything a company owes. Current liabilities include wages and salaries payable, declared dividends payable, and accrued taxes. Fixed or long-term liabilities consist of bonds, bank loans, lease commitments, and certain pension obligations.

Limit Order: an order to buy stock at not more than a specified price or to sell a stock at not less than a specified price.

Liquidation: the process of converting securities into cash. Also, the dissolution of a company.

Liquidity: the ability of the market in a particular security to absorb a reasonable amount of buying or selling without sharp price changes. Liquidity is the hallmark of a good market.

Listed Stock: a stock that is traded on a securities exchange. To qualify for listing, companies have to meet certain requirements in regard to market value, net income, number of shares publicly held, and number of shareholders.

Load and No-Load: a load is the portion of the offering price of shares in open-end mutual funds that covers sales commissions; it is typically 8½ percent. There is usually no charge when shares are redeemed. No-load funds are those whose shares are sold directly to investors at their net asset value with no commission added.

Long: signifies ownership of securities. "I am long 100 Mobil" means that the speaker owns 100 shares.

Management: the board of directors, elected by the stockholders, and the officers of the corporation, appointed by the board of directors.

Manipulation: an illegal operation. Buying or selling a security in order to create a false or misleading appearance of active trading or for the purpose of raising or depressing the price to induce purchase or sale by others.

Margin: the amount put up by a customer when he borrows from his broker to buy a security. The margin requirement, which is set by the Federal Reserve Board, has, over the past 20 years, ranged from 40 percent of the purchase price all the way to 100 percent.

Margin Account: an account that permits the customer to use a brokerage firm's credit to buy securities. To open a margin account the customer must sign a margin agreement, which authorizes his brokerage house to lend to itself or to other brokers any securities carried in the account.

Margin Call: brokerage firms issue a margin call when a customer's equity in a margin account declines below a minimum standard set by the firm or the New York Stock Exchange. If an investor cannot put up the amount required in cash (or securities whose marginable value equals that amount), the brokerage firm sells stock in his account. A steep decline in stock prices can cause an avalanche of margin calls, and the resulting forced liquidations drive prices down still farther.

Market Order: an order to buy or sell a stated amount of a security at the best price obtainable when the order reaches the floor of the exchange.

Market Price: the last reported price at which a stock or bond sold.

Maturity: the date on which a bond comes due for redemption.

Mortgage Bond: a bond secured by a mortgage on property.

Municipal Bond: a bond issued by a state or political subdivision, such as a county, city, town, or village. The term also designates bonds issued by state agencies or authorities. In general, interest paid on municipal bonds is exempt from federal income taxes.

NASD: the National Association of Securities Dealers, Inc., an association of brokers and dealers in the over-the-counter securities business. One of the NASD's functions is to "administer and enforce rules of fair practice and to prevent fraudulent and manipulative acts."

NASDAQ: the NASD's automated quotation system, which provides quotes and other data on about 3,400 over-the-counter stocks.

Negotiable: refers to a security the title to which is transferable by delivery.

Net Asset Value: an investment trust (mutual fund) computes its assets daily by totaling the market value of all its security holdings. After all liabilities have been deducted, the balance is divided by the number of shares outstanding; the resulting figure is the net asset value per share.

Net Change: the change in the price of a security from the closing price on one day to the closing price on the following trading day. In the case of a stock that is entitled to a dividend one day but is traded "ex-dividend" the next, the dividend is considered in computing the change. The same applies to stock splits. A stock selling at $100 before a 2-for-1 split and closing the next day at $50 would be considered unchanged. The net change is ordinarily the last figure in a newspaper stock table.

New Issue: a stock or bond sold by a corporation for the first time.

Odd Lot: an amount of stock less than the normal 100-share unit of trading.

Offer: the price at which a security is offered for sale; also referred to as the asked price.

Open Order: see Good till Canceled.

Options: contracts that give the holder the right to buy (in the case of a "call") or sell (in the case of a "put") a specified number of shares of a particular stock within a specified time at a specified price. *See* chapter 25.

Overbought: when a stock or the market has advanced vigorously for some time on heavy trading volume and without any appreciable setbacks, it is often said to be overbought. The term reflects the opinion that investors no longer have the buying power required to sustain a further advance and that prices will go down, at least temporarily. "Oversold" means that a wave of selling has probably run its course and that prices are due for at least a temporary rebound.

Over-the-Counter: the market where securities not listed on the regular exchanges are traded. *See* chapter 1.

Paper Profit or Loss: an unrealized profit or loss on a security that one is still holding.

Penny Stocks: low-priced issues, nearly always highly speculative ones, that are selling at less than $1 a share.

Pink Sheets: the prices of thousands of small stocks traded over the counter are not published in newspapers. But bid and asked prices for all OTC stocks can be found in the Pink Sheets (so-called because of their color), a service to which brokerage houses subscribe. The service also gives the names of the market-makers for each stock — the firms that stand ready to buy the stock from investors or sell it to them from their own inventory. An OTC market-maker sometimes performs functions somewhat similar to those of a Specialist on a regular exchange.

Point: in the case of shares of stock, a point means $1; in the case of bonds it means $10, since a bond is quoted as a percentage of $1,000. A bond that rises 3 points gains 3 percent of $1,000, or $30, in value.

Point-and-Figure: one of the two main types of charts used by technical analysts, the other being the "bar" chart.

Portfolio: holdings of securities by an individual or institution.

Preferred Stock: a class of stock that has priorities over common stock, both in regard to dividends and to claims on the company's assets if it goes into bankruptcy. Preferred stockholders must receive specified dividends before any dividends may be paid on the common.

Premium: the amount by which a preferred stock or bond is selling above its par value. In the case of a new stock or bond issue, the premium is the amount by which the market price rises over the original selling price. When the shares of a closed-end mutual fund are selling above their net asset value, they are said to be selling at a premium.

Price/Earnings Ratio: the current market price of a share of stock divided by the company's earnings per share for a 12-month period. *See* chapter 4.

Prime Rate: the rate of interest that commercial banks charge their most creditworthy customers for short-term loans.

Principal: the investor for whom a broker executes an order, or a dealer buying or selling for his own account. The term *principal* may also refer to a person's capital or to the face value of a bond.

Profit-Taking: selling to realize a profit; the process of converting paper profits into cash.

Prospectus: a circular, required by the Securities Act of 1933, that describes securities that are being offered for sale to the public.

Proxy: written authorization given by a shareholder to someone else to represent him and vote his shares at a shareholders' meeting.

Proxy Statement: a circular containing information that, under SEC regulations, must be given to stockholders when their proxies are being solicited.

Put: see options, also chapter 25.

Quotation, Quote: the highest bid to buy, and the lowest offer to sell, a security in a given market at a given time.

Rally: a brisk rise following a decline in the market or in an individual stock.

Red Herring: an advance copy of the prospectus that will be filed with the SEC by a company intending to go public or issue new securities. *See* chapter 26.

Registered Bond: a bond that is registered on the books of the issuing company in the name of the owner. It can be transferred only when endorsed by the registered owner. *See* Bearer Bond.

Registered Representative: a stockbroker, also known as an account executive. In a New York Stock Exchange member firm, a registered representative is a full-time employee who has met the requirements of the Exchange as to background and knowledge of the securities business.

Registered Trader: a member of the New York Stock Exchange who trades in stocks on the floor for his own account.

Registration: before a public offering may be made of new securities by a company, or of outstanding securities by controlling stockholders — through the mails or in interstate commerce — the securities must be registered under the Securities Act of 1933. A registration statement filed with the SEC by the issuer must disclose information relating to the company's business, sales, and earnings (or losses), financial condition, management, and the purpose of the public offering. Before a security can be traded on a national securities exchange, it must be registered under the Securities Exchange Act of 1934. The application for registration must be filed with the Exchange and the SEC by the company issuing the securities.

Regular Way Delivery: unless otherwise specified, securities (other than Government Bonds) must be delivered to the buying broker by the selling broker, and payment made to the selling broker by the buying broker, on the fifth business day after the transaction. Regular way delivery for Government Bonds is the business day following the transaction.

Regulation T: the federal regulation governing the amount of margin credit that may be advanced by brokers and dealers to customers for the purchase of securities.

Round Lot: a unit of trading or a multiple thereof. The unit of trading is generally 100 shares for stocks and $1,000 par value for bonds.

Rule of 72: a simple formula for determining approximately how long it will take for money to double at a fixed rate of interest that is reinvested and compounded; just divide the number 72 by the rate of interest. For example, if the interest rate is 8 percent compounded annually, your money will double in 9 years.

Seat: a figure of speech for a membership in a securities or commodities exchange.

SEC: the Securities and Exchange Commission, established by Congress to regulate the securities industry and protect the investing public's interests. The SEC administers the Securities Act of 1933, the Securities Exchange Act of 1934, the Trust Indenture Act, the Investment Company Act, the Investment Advisers Act, and the Public Utility Holding Company Act.

Secondary Distribution: a sale of a large block of previously issued stock at a fixed price by a securities firm or group of firms. A "secondary"—often a sale by a large shareholder—must be registered with the SEC.

Short Sale: a short sale is a sale of borrowed stock—the borrowing is done by your broker—made in the expectation that the stock's price will go down. Eventually, the short seller has to buy the stock and return it to its owner, an action known as covering his short. If he buys it at a price lower than the sale price, he makes a profit; if the stock rises and he buys it at a higher price, he suffers a loss. Short sales are made in a margin account, and a short sale is subject to the same margin requirements as a purchase; if the margin requirement is 50 percent and you sell short $6,000 worth of stock, you have to put up $3,000. The proceeds of the sale—$6,000—are credited to your margin account, but you cannot draw on them unless the price of the stock drops, causing your equity in the account to rise. A short sale can be made only on an "up-tick" or "zero-plus" tick. An up-tick means that the stock has traded at a price higher than the previous transaction. A zero-plus tick describes a transaction made at the same price as the preceding trade or trades but higher than the most recent different price at which the stock changed hands. Short selling is basically a speculative tactic and a very risky one if the stock is volatile. When you buy a stock at $15, the worst possibility is a drop to zero, which hardly ever happens. But if you sell a $15 stock short and you have to cover at $40, you lose $25; your liability when you go short is unlimited.

Sinking Fund: money regularly set aside by a company to redeem its bonds or preferred stock from time to time, as specified in the indenture or charter.

Specialist: a member of the New York Stock Exchange who has two functions. One is to maintain an orderly market, insofar as is reasonably practicable, in the stocks in which he is registered as a Specialist. To maintain an orderly market, the Specialist engages in "stabilizing" transactions, which bridge temporary gaps between supply and demand; he buys for his own account when supply exceeds demand, and he sells short when demand is appreciably greater than supply. The Specialist's second function is to act as a brokers' broker. When a commission broker on the Exchange floor receives a limit order — an order, say, to buy at $58 a stock then selling at $60 — he cannot wait at the particular post where the stock is traded until the price reaches the specified level. So he leaves the order with the Specialist, who enters it in his "book" and will execute it in the market if and when the stock declines to the specified price. There are about 350 Specialists on the New York Stock Exchange, and there are Specialists on the other stock exchanges.

Split: the division of the outstanding shares of a corporation into a larger number of shares. A 3-for-1 split by a company with 1 million shares outstanding results in 3 million shares outstanding; each holder of 100 shares before the split winds up with 300 shares. But his proportionate equity in the company remains exactly the same, and the split in itself doesn't change the market value of his investment.

Stock Ahead: sometimes an investor who has entered an order to buy or sell a stock at a certain price will see transactions at that price reported on the electronic ticker while his own order has not been executed. His broker will explain that there was "stock ahead," which means that other buy and sell orders at the same price reached the Specialist ahead of his and had priority.

Stock Clearing Corporation: a subsidiary of the New York Stock Exchange, which acts as a central agency for security deliveries and money payments between member firms of the Exchange.

Stock Dividend: a dividend paid in shares of stock rather than in cash.

Stop Order: an order to buy or sell a stock when it reaches a specified price. A stop order to buy becomes a market order when a transaction in the security, which has been trading at a lower price, occurs at or above the stock price; short sellers often use such orders to protect themselves against potentially large losses. A stop order to sell becomes a market order when a transaction in the security, which has been trading at a higher price, takes place at or below the stop price. Such orders are used to protect a paper profit or to limit losses. But since any stop order becomes an "at-the-market" order when the stop price is reached, a stop sell order may be executed at a lower price, and a stop buy order at a higher price.

Street Name: securities held in the name of a brokerage firm instead of the customer's name are said to be carried in "street name." This procedure is mandatory when the securities have been bought on margin. An investor may keep his securities at a brokerage house in his own name, but if he's an active trader there are advantages in having the securities registered in street name.

Syndicate: a group of investment bankers who together underwrite and distribute a new issue of securities or a large block of an outstanding issue.

Tax Selling: securities sales made, usually late in the year, to realize gains or losses for income-tax purposes.

Thin Market: the term — which generally applies to an individual stock but can refer to the market in general — means that there are comparatively few bids to buy, or offers to sell, or both. In a thin market, relatively small changes in supply and demand can cause sharp price changes. A thin market is the opposite of a liquid market.

Ticker: a machine that reports the prices and the volume of security transactions. The action of the ticker is usually displayed on an electronic board in brokerage house board rooms.

Topping Out: this term can be applied to the general market, to a group of stocks, or to an individual issue. It signifies that an uptrend is, or appears to be, coming to an end. The opposite term is Bottoming Out.

Trader: one who buys and sells for his own account for short-term profit.

Trading Crowd: members of a stock exchange assembled at a trading post to execute buy and sell orders.

Trading Post: one of 14 horseshoe-shaped trading locations on the floor of the New York Stock Exchange at which stocks assigned to that location are bought and sold. About 75 stocks are traded at each post.

Transfer Agent: a transfer agent — normally a bank — keeps a record of the name of each registered shareowner, his or her address, and the number of shares owned, and sees to it that certificates presented to his office for transfer are properly canceled and new certificates issued in the name of the transferee.

Transfer Tax: a tax imposed by New York State on transactions that occur on exchanges or between dealers within the state. The tax is paid by the seller. The current tax ranges from 1¼ to 5 cents a share, depending on the selling price of the stock. There is no tax on transfers of bonds.

Treasury Stock: stock issued by a company but later reacquired. It may be held in the company's treasury indefinitely, reissued to the public, or retired. Treasury stock receives no dividends and has no vote while held by the company.

Underwriter: see Investment Banker.

Warrant: a certificate giving the holder the right to purchase a security at a stipulated price within a specified time limit or perpetually. Sometimes warrants are included in a securities offering as an inducement to buy.

When Issued: a short form of "when, as, and if issued." For example, after a stock split has been announced, trading on the split stock usually begins on a "when issued" basis before the split has occurred. All "when issued" transactions are on an "if" basis; they are settled if and when the actual security is issued and the exchange on which the stock is traded or the NASD rules that the transactions are to be settled.

Wire House: a national brokerage firm with a communications network linking its branch offices throughout the country. *See* chapter 13

Yield: also known as Return. The annual dividends or interest paid by a company divided by the current price of the stock or bond, or, if you already own the security, by the price you originally paid.

Index